I'LL MAKE ME A WORLD

ALSO BY JARVIS R. GIVENS

American Grammar: Race, Education, and the Building of a Nation
School Clothes: A Collective Memoir of Black Student Witness
Fugitive Pedagogy: Carter G. Woodson and the Art of Black Teaching

I'LL MAKE ME A WORLD

The 100-Year Journey of Black History Month

JARVIS R. GIVENS

An Imprint of HarperCollins*Publishers*

Without limiting the exclusive rights of any author, contributor or the publisher of this publication, any unauthorized use of this publication to train generative artificial intelligence (AI) technologies is expressly prohibited. HarperCollins also exercise their rights under Article 4(3) of the Digital Single Market Directive 2019/790 and expressly reserve this publication from the text and data mining exception.

I'LL MAKE ME A WORLD. Copyright © 2026 by Jarvis R. Givens. All rights reserved. Printed in the United States of America. No part of this book may be used or reproduced in any manner whatsoever without written permission except in the case of brief quotations embodied in critical articles and reviews. For information, address HarperCollins Publishers, 195 Broadway, New York, NY 10007. In Europe, HarperCollins Publishers, Macken House, 39/40 Mayor Street Upper, Dublin 1, D01 C9W8, Ireland.

HarperCollins books may be purchased for educational, business, or sales promotional use. For information, please email the Special Markets Department at SPsales@harpercollins.com.

FIRST EDITION

Designed by Bonni Leon-Berman

Library of Congress Cataloging-in-Publication Data

Names: Givens, Jarvis R., author
Title: I'll make me a world : the 100-year journey of Black History Month / Jarvis R. Givens.
Other titles: I will make me a world
Description: First edition. | New York, NY : Harper, [2026] | Includes bibliographical references. |
Identifiers: LCCN 2025033902 (print) | LCCN 2025033903 (ebook) | ISBN 9780063478824 hardcover | ISBN 9780063478848 ebook
Subjects: LCSH: African American History Month—History | African Americans—History
Classification: LCC E185 .G535 2026 (print) | LCC E185 (ebook)
LC record available at https://lccn.loc.gov/2025033902
LC ebook record available at https://lccn.loc.gov/2025033903

26 27 28 29 30 LBC 6 5 4 3 2

To the captives who refused to forget, creating a tradition of black memory work that dispels lies, cultivates dreams, and inspires action toward a more liberated future

CONTENTS

Introduction: For My People   1

PART I: The Creation   29

PART II: The Negro Digs Up His Past   69

PART III: When Truth Gets a Hearing   117

PART IV: Where Do We Go from Here?   171

Acknowledgments   219

Notes   221

Index   233

I'LL MAKE ME A WORLD

INTRODUCTION

FOR MY PEOPLE

Remembering the "Black" in Black History Month

For the cramped bewildered years we went to school to learn
to know the reasons why and the answers to and the
people who and the places where and the days when, in
memory of the bitter hours when we discovered we
were black and poor and small and different and nobody
cared and nobody wondered and nobody understood;

—Margaret Walker, "For My People" (1937)

AFRICAN AMERICANS HAVE ALWAYS HAD something to say about the past. Even during the time of slavery, they wrote and published accounts of their individual lives and at times produced historical accounts of their race in books, newspapers, and other forms of print culture. Some created reading rooms and literary societies during the antebellum years where they engaged with texts about the black past, with some men and women collecting historical materials to be displayed and studied in the parlors of their homes, doing so at a time when no research center or library existed that recognized what is now widely understood to be "black history" as a legitimate area of scholarship. However, even in the absence of widely accessible written texts by black people, there was an enduring tradition in African American communities of passing down stories orally, through rituals, and through distinct ways of being, from one generation to another, where historical perspectives emerged from the terrain of black consciousness; where they continued to be "carved on the fleshly tablets" of black people, as explained by the African American historian George Washington Williams in 1881.[1] Simply put, African Americans, like all people, have concerned ourselves with history by studying the events and people that have influenced the development of the world we live in; and as a persecuted group, we have paid special attention to those that contributed to our oppression while also remembering those who sacrificed to advance our liberatory struggles.

The year 2026 marks the one hundredth anniversary of Negro History Week, which was established in February 1926 by famed educator and historian Carter G. Woodson, then expanded to Black History Month in 1976. This milestone presents an opportunity to reflect on the black historical tradition, a critically important task given the current political conflicts pertaining to what can and cannot be taught about race and history in American schools and colleges or engaged in public spaces. Such critical reflection is the purpose of *I'll Make Me a World*, which commemorates the one-hundred-year journey of Black History Month by deeply engaging the tradition that informed its creation.

To thoughtfully engage this legacy, I will employ the language of "black memory work" and "black memory workers" as capacious terms borrowed from black women archivists to describe the enterprise of recovering, preserving, and bearing witness to black history.[2] I do so because any sincere appreciation of this tradition demands recognizing a diverse cast of characters. It requires recognizing professionals engaging in historical work as their primary occupation, such as academics, archivists, museum curators, and schoolteachers, while also acknowledging a collective of black memory workers that includes the likes of community storytellers, youth activists, preachers, filmmakers, political organizers, poets, and musicians, as well as family members who preserve old photographs marked by handwritten descriptions that can be passed down to a nephew generations later.[3] Black memory work has been sustained by many hands. It can also be traced to many places: formal archives as well as less formal collections containing ephemera paperclipped together in old suitcases. This tradition is concerned less with rigid boundaries drawn around the broader historical enterprise and more with where we can look to find the most truthful and expansive visions of black life, especially histories of everyday black people, their social worlds, and their beliefs.

This book is particularly concerned with a tradition of memory work among African Americans that grew out of the perspectives of enslaved people who recognized that there were things that could be known from their social location, from a black perspective, that could not be known from any other perspective in a world built on their subjugation. I think it is important to make this clear. Black history is not just another history of a particular ethnic or racial group to be wedged into dominant narratives from which black people were previously excluded; its contributions are not limited to making such scripts about the past more multicultural or multiracial in form. For this reason, I usually reject (at least in part) proclamations that "black history is American history," insisting instead that the former is both part of and apart from the latter. For indeed, the enslaved people who were the early shapers of the black historical tradition were categorically defined as quintessentially ahistorical by those in power, as a people absent history and culture; and early black memory workers came to recognize how such antiblack historical myths were used to justify their status as a people who could be property. Thus, they recognized the problem and promise of black memory work to be a project of historical knowledge production that was distinct in kind.

Black history therefore emerged as a criticism of racial chattel slavery and the formation of its afterlives in the modern world. What's more, black history, from its inception, even as it developed in an American context, was always informed by an international disposition or what we might think of as an African diasporic consciousness for at least two primary reasons. First, African Americans were forced to interrogate their relationship to Africa as immediate descendants of people who were natives to the continent, having recognized that genealogical fact was partly the basis of their distinct experience of racialization as black people. Second, African Americans recognized their struggle against slavery to be connected with black struggles against slavery and antiblack colonialism elsewhere in the world. The critical importance of the Haitian Revolution in early black historical narratives by African Americans, for instance, offers striking evidence of this.[4] Therefore, to frame black history as American history elides such conceptual distinctions that conditioned the origins of black memory work in the United States, just as it did elsewhere in the diaspora.

Black history, I argue, emerged as a critical history. Its task was, and is, at least threefold: to correct racist distortions that proliferate about black people in public memory and historical scholarship; to describe the facts, dates, and figures of the black past in the most compelling and rigorous ways possible; and to leverage this knowledge in the pursuit of racial justice, thus rendering a usable history that can inform action. Intellectuals in the black historical tradition have worked to recover and repair narratives about the vast array of black experiences that were long deemed unworthy of treatment within the mainstream historical enterprise in order to delegitimize the myths used to justify black oppression; and by advancing historical knowledge about the lives and culture of African-descended people grounded by black perspectives, these intellectuals engaged in black memory work. While this tradition evolved in form and style over the years—from the slavery era through the dramatic expansion of "Negro history" and "black history" through the twentieth century and beyond—the politics underlying this body of critical history has persisted.

Black history should not be conflated with just any and all historical narratives about African-descended people, as there is a long lineage of historical scholarship about black communities written primarily from nonblack perspectives that are at odds with the historical tradition derived from black memory workers. For indeed, early white scholars had much to say about black people even when they showed little concern for what black people had to say about their own lives. Yet, authentic black histories are those that account for black people as historical subjects, not merely objects in the social context of white worlds, and such narratives are written from a vantage point that takes seriously black people's interpretations of events and social realities while also using historical sources that reflect black lives and voices as the basis for constructing narratives about the past.[5] And when such authentic accounts of black life are confronted, a massive amount of historical detail emerges that disrupts the perceived coherence and truthfulness of the stories told and retold about the United States and the Western world. Black history, as critical history, names the realities of power and social hierarchies that plague the human condition in the most honest of ways, exposing those who have abused power to extract value from vulnerable populations. These histories provide a more expansive account of human life, one that presumes that black people were always present, alive, and political actors throughout the time of American history and well before.

Recognizing the political significance of such historical recovery and preservation, leaders in the black historical tradition sought to empower African Americans to collectively participate in black memory work in the hope of adding to and rounding out the historical record. However, those scholars also did so because they understood black interpretations of history to be an essential part of liberatory education; and such liberatory education they understood to be a foundational pillar of the black freedom movement. As I will show throughout this book, Black History Month grew out of this pedagogical mission grounded in liberatory struggle.

Black historical knowledge has long informed the intellectual foundation of black resistance, where knowledge about the black past has been used to achieve justice in the present and future. In raising this point, I am reminded of a story from 1807 that underscores such political uses of black history, where one enslaved community intentionally taught newly arrived captives about previous rebellions against white masters as a form of political education. The man who claimed those people as his property learned of their "Improper Communication," as he referred to their passing on of accurate historical knowledge, specifically detailing how "all new negroes know of the insurrection of 40 years ago." The enslaver insisted that something was afoot, that the enslaved people seemed to be using historical knowledge about past rebellions to cultivate the political consciousness of those who had recently arrived as survivors of the middle passage. Indeed, he asked, "for what [other] reason would they tell these New Negroes who have not been four months on the island of what happened before any of the negroes sent there were born?" This story is from St. Mary's Parish, Jamaica, but it is a story that can be found across the Americas. What's more, not only does it reflect how the teaching of black historical knowledge was used as a pedagogical practice for cultivating black consciousness, it also exposes practical concerns among powerful white elites who sought to police that consciousness and suppress the freedom struggle waged by enslaved African people.[6]

The social aim of black memory work—dare I say its politics—is to correct knowledge in circulation about the past by attending to more honest accounts of black life in the hope of displacing racist ideas premised on historical myths that justify and even motivate racial oppression. It aims to offer such corrections while also providing usable histories that inspire black people to see the full range of their humanity and hopefully to help others see it in the process. In this way, black people created a historical tradition for themselves—that is, for black people—though they also hoped to impact the historical consciousness of other members of the social world who were not racialized as black. They hoped that scholars and members of society who are not black-identified people would also study and help preserve and circulate critical knowledge about the black past in service of transforming historical knowledge in the broader public and for the greater good of humanity. These aims are complementary, though not reducible to each other.

Black history emerged as a rejection of foundational historical claims propping up a world structured through antiblackness, thus calling for the transformation of historical knowledge altogether. This heroic tradition of historical truth telling is one that leaned into discomforting facts of the past, because the enslaved and their progeny recognized that such details demanded witness, lest acts of wanton violence and barbarism that threaten human life be allowed to proliferate in the shadows of today and tomorrow. Furthermore, bearing witness to the past was critical, black memory workers insisted, because it helped guide contemporary battles against the forces of evil and greed within a broader moral war among the human species that demands urgent attention—one in which humanity must face the past in order to make decisions about what is right and wrong, what is good and bad, and what vision of justice is worth striving for. Black people look to the past as a usable resource, having recognized that so much justice and truth continued to be withheld from those in need of it most.

Importantly, black perspectives about the past have not aimed solely to combat the master narrative constructed by mainstream white historians, because black memory work is not merely about striking back, not just a response to white hostility and naysayers. These histories are also decidedly forward looking, aiming to equip the generations to come with lessons about what it means to live meaningful lives and tools to create a brighter future. This latter work is possible only if we diligently acknowledge the good in black history, the things worthy of holding on to, and when we remember courageous actions worthy of study and emulation; it is possible only when we appreciate and study life-giving creations such as music, art, and social relations that merit being remembered and sustained because of the positive work they do in the world. Black history, as critical history, is always about the beautiful even as it documents the terrible, even as it analyzes an archival transcript replete with unspeakable acts of violence.

Black History Month is a national observance in the United States that extends from this longer and more expansive tradition of black memory work. Over the span of the last hundred years, this tradition has seen many twists and turns: many wars in the international arena, many social movements and technological developments, many shifts in the political-economic character of the nation and global marketplace, and indeed many shifts in the racial regime that colored such social developments. Across these historical transformations, black people have experienced many gains and also many backward steps. Freedoms have been won, and they have also been taken away. All the while, knowledge about the past has been one of the most important resources for sustaining black life and inspiring meaningful political struggle. Knowledge of the past has also served as a necessary reminder of the beauty in black life despite the external realities of anti-blackness. For indeed, authentic accounts of the black past have described the tension between such realities without compromising their honesty about one or the other. They remind us, as African American studies scholar Imani Perry has written, that "Joy is not found in the absence of pain and suffering. It exists through it." Historical accounts by African American memory workers like Perry have clarified that while "racism is terrible, blackness is not."[7]

Yet the "black" in Black History Month is often stripped of its political significance. The same can be said of contemporary teaching about the black past in schools and public memory, which is often done in extremely sanitized and reductionist fashion. By this I mean that public engagement with the heritage of African-descended people has drifted far away from resembling authentic black history, leading many black memory workers to say that the tradition has lost its criticality. These are legitimate concerns, and they are not new. African American historians raised similar concerns in the 1970s, just as the weeklong observance of black history was being expanded to a month. Their deliberations leading up to 1976, as what was originally Negro History Week became Black History Month, are revelatory for present-day assessments of the state of our national observance of black heritage.

IN OCTOBER 1975, members of the Association for the Study of Afro-American Life and History (ASALH), comprising professors, archivists, educators, and community members concerned with the black past, gathered at the Hyatt Regency Hotel in Atlanta, Georgia. At that annual meeting of ASALH (pronounced A-*sah*-luh), many historic milestones were the topic of conversation: The organization had been founded sixty years prior, on September 9, 1915, fifty years after black emancipation; the founder of ASALH and Negro History Week, Carter G. Woodson, had been born on December 19, 1875, one hundred years prior, during the Reconstruction period, as the child of formerly enslaved people; and as their members looked to the year ahead—1976—they anticipated extensive celebrations across the country for the two hundredth anniversary of American independence.

Speaking to the attendees, J. Rupert Picott, ASALH executive director and professor of history at Virginia State University, said that the organization planned to capitalize on that convergence of events in black history and the nation's bicentennial. He said that given the national importance of the year 1976, combined with Woodson's one hundredth birthday and the fiftieth anniversary of Negro History Week, the entire month of February 1976 would be devoted to black history under the theme "America for all Americans." The theme selected for the first Black History Month was intentionally subversive, suggesting that America had not lived up to its potential of social equality for all despite the multiracial democracy it represented itself to be.[8]

Black memory workers prepared themselves for the stories of American exceptionalism that were likely to be told during the nation's bicentennial. The country's leaders and prominent white historians would shout from the mountaintops about how the United States had become the greatest nation in the world, a place where freedom carried the most meaning and where democracy was at its best. America was the exception in a world ruled by tyrants and antiquated political systems that stunted human civilization, they would say. Those headlines would dominate the nation's celebrations of its past, thus frustrating the historical consciousness of black Americans, a population who traced their heritage back to the more than 500,000 Africans enslaved in the American colonies during the Revolution, a community that continued to experience aggressive neglect by the US government as the political victories black people had gained in the 1960s were being rolled back as a result of white backlash and as policing and prisons continued to disproportionately target African Americans in a rapidly growing fashion.

As ASALH staff member Thelma D. Perry explained, "we have lived almost a generation since" the victories of the Civil Rights Movement.[9] Reflecting on the various manifestations of white backlash, Perry declared, "It would serve no useful purpose to rehash the assassinations, the riots and injustices of intervening years. The recent incidents are impressive enough to warrant an understanding that black people have now no other alternative than to seek power." She continued, "The pictures that intrude are like a kaleidoscope—Medgar Evers, murdered children in a Birmingham Sunday School, murdered college students in Orangeburg, South Carolina, murdered whites in Mississippi and elsewhere because they dared to engage themselves in the freedom struggle, Fred Hampton killed in bed," and the list went on. As a historian of African American education, Perry was also intimately aware of the chaotic struggles around school desegregation in the United States as it was rolled out in the most inequitable fashion, where black students entered hostile territory in formerly all-white schools, and as massive numbers of black teachers and principals around the country were fired. Picott agreed with Perry's assessment of the backward steps occurring within the nation as they pertained to matters of racial justice, and he particularly noted the undermining of black education. He noted that at the time of *Brown v. Board of Education* in 1954, black school principals could be found in large numbers across the southern states, yet in the wake of desegregation efforts, many had been unfairly fired or demoted. He cited the number of black high school principals in the South as decreasing, between 1964 and 1973, from more than two thousand to fewer than two hundred.[10]

As the nation's bicentennial approached, the Black Power era gained full momentum. The transition from Negro History Week to Black History Month was not only about the nation's two centuries of independence; it also coincided with the pendulum swing in black consciousness as African Americans became disillusioned with the United States' ability to fully recognize them as equal citizens deserving of the same dignity and respect as the nation's other constituencies. The nation's bicentennial became an important moment to express a black perspective on the nation's history in an even more pronounced fashion, and the half-century milestone since the inaugural Negro History Week celebration made it the perfect occasion to do so. What's more, ASALH leaders were aware that some African Americans around the country had already, in the preceding years, initiated an expansion of the weeklong celebration to a full month. Early examples can be found among Chicagoans and communities in Virginia, as well as black students on several university campuses. For instance, amid the black student movement that led to the establishment of Black Studies departments around the country, black student organizers at Kent State University organized Black History Month celebrations beginning in 1969.

Seizing the historical moment, Picott and other ASALH leaders strategized about ways to force the general public to be more accountable to the black past as the country prepared for its bicentennial celebrations. To do so, Picott helped draft a proclamation announcing National Black History Month. He, alongside other ASALH leaders, including his Alpha Phi Alpha fraternity brothers Edgar Allan Toppin and Benjamin Quarles, president and vice president of the association, respectively, hoped that the proclamation would be adopted by the US president. Therefore, they sent the proclamation to President Gerald Ford's administrative team, and it was that action that began the process of formally declaring what has now become the nation's annual observance of black heritage for the entire month of February.

President Ford, however, did not issue a presidential proclamation. Such an action, according to custom, could be done only with congressional support. What he offered instead was a presidential message. (A presidential proclamation of Black History Month would be issued by President Ronald Reagan only in 1986.) This distinction is important because a proclamation carries more weight and is akin to an executive order, whereas a presidential message is generally a public gesture or endorsement that demands no formal action on the part of public agencies.[11]

ASALH's draft proclamation and letter to the Ford administration prompted John C. Calhoun, an African American man serving as the special assistant to the president on minority affairs, to urge presidential action. On January 9, 1976, he wrote the White House assistant general counsel a memo that included the proclamation drafted by Picott and his colleagues, as well as a note that read, "Request a Presidential proclamation proclaiming the month of February National Black History Month." He asked that his colleague expedite the process. As he saw it, it was an opportunity for President Ford to demonstrate his commitment to African Americans and, by doing so, hopefully gain him more support among black voters in the upcoming presidential election. Accepting the recommendation of the White House assistant general counsel, President Ford issued a presidential "message," and his endorsement was, at best, a moment of interest convergence at a time when the aims of an African American interest group converged with the political needs of a white presidential candidate hoping to increase his favor among a particular voting bloc. The president's action seemingly had less to do with the real substance of black history itself, as it failed to honestly confront the historical violations committed against black communities, past or present. In fact, the president's half-hearted commitment to commemorating the black past is best represented in an egregious historical inaccuracy in his message issued on February 4, 1976, in which he confused the date of ASALH's founding with the birthday of Carter G. Woodson:

THE WHITE HOUSE
WASHINGTON
NATIONAL BLACK HISTORY MONTH
FEBRUARY 1976

In the Bicentennial year of our Independence, we can review with admiration the impressive contributions of black Americans to our national life and culture.

One hundred years ago, to help highlight these achievements, Dr. Carter G. Woodson founded the Association for the Study of Afro-American Life and History. We are grateful to him today for his initiative, and we are richer for the work of his organization.

Freedom and the recognition of individual rights are what our Revolution was all about. They were ideals that inspired our fight for Independence: ideals that we have been striving to live up to ever since. Yet it took many years before ideals became a reality for black citizens.

The last quarter-century has finally witnessed significant strides in the full integration of black people into every area of national life. In celebrating Black History Month, we can take satisfaction from this recent progress in the realization of the ideals envisioned by our Founding Fathers. But, even more than this, we can seize the opportunity to honor the too-often neglected accomplishments of black Americans in every area of endeavor throughout our history.

I urge my fellow citizens to join me in tribute to Black History Month and the message of courage and perseverance it brings to all of us.

Gerald R. Ford[12]

Though ASALH's draft proclamation named Woodson's birthday as December 19, 1875, it seems that those involved in drafting the president's message confused it with the year he had founded the association in 1915.

In hindsight, the incorrect date is less important, though it certainly anticipates the kind of minimal engagement with the black past that would follow as observances of black heritage were scaled up across the nation, particularly by corporations and those motivated to exploit black consumers. More important is what was not included in President Ford's message. Though it acknowledged that black Americans had made "impressive contributions" to the United States, there was no mention of their suffering. While African Americans in 1976 were publicly criticizing the abandonment of civil rights gains made in the recent past, the president's message acknowledged only the significant strides made toward "the full integration of black people into every area of national life." It projected to the world a model of Black History Month that could be a source of "courage and perseverance" for "all of us." It was a version of black history that could be all the good things, all the positive achievements, absent any details that might prompt critical self-reflection by the nation as a whole or its individual citizens. Such a sanitized and whitewashed version of black history would be so tailored and depoliticized that it was unrecognizable by most black people living in the reality described by Thelma Perry or documented in the many books and academic articles published by scholars such as Picott, Toppin, and Quarles, as well as the many African American scholars who were expanding the tradition of black memory work in the 1970s, especially with the pioneering work in black women's history launched during the same decade leading to the founding of the Association of Black Women Historians in 1979.

To be clear, African Americans certainly would not have expected President Ford to issue a radical interpretation of history informed by the full weight of critical black historical scholarship. However, they likely expected him to get basic dates right in his message to the American people. Furthermore, some gesture to the need for more political work that addressed past and present harms experienced by African Americans would have been welcomed.

THE WRITING WAS on the wall, some might say. With the scaling up of Negro History Week to Black History Month in 1976, threats to the tradition were bound to occur, and increased corporate interest in the celebration was likely inevitable. A tradition that had grown out of the labors of black memory workers, wherein a designated time of year was set aside for massive, coordinated outreach to tell the truth about black heritage in the face of persistent myths, would ironically become a shiny opportunity for capitalist exploitation. However, that was a trend reflected in many avenues of black cultural expression by the 1970s, to be clear. Indeed, scholars have documented how corporate elites found ways to exploit nearly all forms of black power politics, from the celebration of black history to demands for local political influence, as opportunities to advance capitalist expansion.[13] It is interesting to note that critiques about Black History Month becoming a watered-down, capitalist-driven annual observance like most other American holidays go back to the time the transition occurred in the 1970s, and they proliferated over the decades that followed.

In 1997, the late historian John Hope Franklin expressed his discontent, arguing that "the expansion of the 'week' into a 'month' does not necessarily mean that we're moving towards the Woodson ideal" of approaching a time when black history is so thoroughly engaged in schools and public memory that there will eventually be no need for a separate observance. Instead, he insisted, "The commercialization of the 'month' provides the hucksters with a longer period in which to sell their trinkets and souvenirs, corporations a greater opportunity to display their special brand of 'civic awareness,' and lecturers the golden chance to show off their knowledge of black history."[14]

Franklin's comments were shared in a published forum organized by *The Journal of Blacks in Higher Education*, in which the editors posed the question: Does Black History Month still serve a useful purpose? The editors presented the inquiry to several African American historians, while also declaring that they were skeptical about the value of Black History Month. They explained, "Critics of Black History Month say that singling out African Americans for special attention in February reinforces white beliefs that black history is not worthy of general recognition. Furthermore, many African Americans object to the fact that Black History Month has been usurped by large corporations such as Philip Morris, Anheuser-Busch, and Coca-Cola, companies that make token efforts to promote an awareness of black history in an effort to further their marketing efforts in the black community." They insisted that even the book-publishing industry exploited the month, only to then ignore black authors for the rest of the year: "Major book publishers bunch their releases on African-American topics into February in order to win Black History Month attention for their titles. In February many magazines and newspapers publish special review sections dedicated to black titles." Some bookstores also followed the trend, the editors noted, pushing black books in February before removing the books from their shelves come March, then proceeding with "an 11-month period when black-related titles are nowhere to be found."[15]

As argued by Franklin, such concerns about commercialization already existed before the week was extended to a month, and it was a phenomenon that applied to the exploitation of black heritage for commercial enterprises more generally. Black memory workers were deeply aware of that threat to their work in the 1970s. Anticipating Franklin's comments by a little more than two decades, the senior editor of *Ebony* magazine, Lerone Bennett, Jr., offered language encapsulating the conundrum just months before the first National Black History Month. He criticized the way black heritage was being popularized for commercial purposes by corporations with no political commitments to black people while black communities continued to suffer and the politics of black history were being watered down and its original aims negated. Speaking to members of ASALH in October 1975, Bennett declared, "There are images and echoes of black heritage almost everywhere today. There are sights and sounds on TV. There are lesson plans in the schools and courses in colleges. Never before have we been so popular. They have even heard of us on Madison Avenue. Black heritage sells soap, whiskey, and detergent. It sells everything, in fact, except the meaning of black heritage and the humanity of black people. Which is precisely the point. Never before have so many talked so much about black heritage in so many places with so little understanding."[16]

The months ahead revealed his words to be true, as did past corporate trends. The acceptance and appropriation of black heritage by commercial enterprises had its own history and was a source of mixed emotions on the part of African American people. The trend originated in corporations desiring to exploit black consumers; however, black consumer protests—from boycotts of public transportation to political demonstrations at lunch counters and department stores—forced "white business owners, advertisers, and consumers to recognize and value African Americans in the consumer sphere." Such protests caused businesses to abandon some of the discriminatory practices that had caused much harm in previous decades. As the historian Traci Parker noted, the department store, similar to public transportation and the lunch counter, became "a training ground for black consumer protest in the twentieth century," particularly in early civil rights struggles, that could be traced back as far as the "Don't Buy Where You Can't Work" campaigns waged by black labor organizers in the 1930s. It is within this context that one must interpret even early Negro History Week observances in department stores, such as the examples that can be traced back to the 1950s in places such as Washington, DC, Chicago, and parts of California. Thus, the expansion from week to month provided an opportunity to accelerate such corporate practices while also providing a longer duration for black memory workers to organize and stimulate momentum for educational work regarding the black past throughout the year. It is important to note that it was never one or the other; both things were true.[17]

Bennett's concern with superficial engagement with black heritage by the American public stemmed from his personal connections to the tradition, as someone who had been inspired by critical interpretations of black history while growing up in Clarksdale, Mississippi. Indeed, his understanding of black heritage emerged from his early exposure to Negro History Week and the knowledge he gained as a student attending segregated schools in the 1940s and '50s. According to Bennett, his early interest in black life and culture had been stimulated by his African American teachers and local black newspapers. To emphasize this point, he recalled reading a speech by Abraham Lincoln in which the president had expressed the views that blacks should not have the right to vote, marry whites, or be treated as equals. That speech caused him to question the idea of Lincoln as "the great emancipator." Aware that such a perspective on Lincoln was unorthodox thinking, even among black Americans at the time, he recalled that it had been an African American teacher who encouraged his emerging criticism of the master narrative. He also recalled stories about Frederick Douglass, Harriet Tubman, and Sojourner Truth being told frequently in his school. And they were more than just names to be memorized; they were folk heroes providing moral lessons for black students' lives. The ideas and stories of those fugitive slaves carried ideas that inspired students like Bennett as black political subjects and budding intellectuals. For these reasons, he credited his teachers at Lanier High School as having set him on his way to publish his first book, *Before the Mayflower: A History of Black America*, in 1962. As he proclaimed, "I was prepared to do it."[18]

It is worth noting that all five of the African American historians responding to the query of *The Journal of Blacks in Higher Education* in 1997 shared a similar trajectory as Bennett. They were all scholars who engaged in black memory work, having first been inspired by education within their own communities, particularly by black teachers or librarians, while growing up in the Jim Crow era. Furthermore, even as these historians critiqued the corporatization of Black History Month, they all insisted that as long as the black past continued to be sidelined in the American mainstream, there was a need to sustain the commemorative practice as a tool of public accountability and a mechanism for cultivating momentum to maintain the ongoing work of digging up, preserving, and studying black life and culture throughout the year.

Speaking from intimate perspectives about the continued undermining of black history in the broader historical enterprise, those scholars insisted that Black History Month did need tinkering with, but it should not be abandoned by any means. Their criticisms were levied in the spirit of strengthening the tradition, not ending it; as experts on the subject of black history, they had no question about the merits of the national observance. What's more, Allen Ballard argued in response to *JBHE*'s query, insisting that despite its limitations, much good still results from Black History Month observances. Outside the noise of predatory corporate activities, there were people on the ground still striving to honor the tradition as best they could. At minimum, he explained, "There must be thousands of essay-writing contests going on all across the country in schools—black and white—about black history. Something good must be happening as a result of this." He continued, "Some teachers might be incapable of doing this, and others simply might not want to do so—but at least the existence of the celebratory month stirs some kind of thought about black history amongst them."[19] Despite its limitations, the scholars felt, there was no need to cede ground, given the continued resistance to fully recognizing black history and culture in the nation's schools, colleges, and sites of public history in a more thorough manner.

•

ONE HUNDRED YEARS since the inaugural Negro History Week celebration and fifty years since its official expansion to Black History Month, there is much to be discussed about the past, present, and future of black history and the work needed to sustain the tradition of black memory work. As we enter the second quarter of the twenty-first century, and indeed as we approach the semiquincentennial of the United States in 2026, African Americans find themselves in a similar moment of disillusionment with the nation, especially when it comes to matters of historical memory and an honest reckoning with the past. These anniversaries come at a time when President Donald Trump and other Republican elected officials have criminalized the teaching of critical aspects of black history and as information about black history is being removed from federal buildings, government websites, and even museums created for the sole purpose of memorializing African American history and culture. Such actions are occurring in the wake of a virulent backlash to historical interpretations presented in *The 1619 Project*, which has now been recognized as an inflection point. This special issue of *The New York Times Magazine* edited by Pulitzer Prize–winning journalist Nikole Hannah-Jones in 2019, and the subsequent anthology by the same name, would be banned in schools across various states as early as 2021, and this trend has persisted. Books about black history are being banned, and misinformation about the past abounds. For instance, after criminalizing the teaching of Advanced Placement African American studies, the state of Florida would revise its teaching standards for African American history to reflect some of the most antiquated conservative interpretations of history, even on the subject of slavery. According to a document produced in May 2023 by the state's African American History Standards working group, instruction about the history of slavery should include "how slaves developed skills which, in some instances, could be applied for their personal benefit." Such flat, sloppy interpretations of the black past fail to account for the lived experiences of black people. Even when they purport to be about African Americans, they are not authentic historical accounts of black life but instead bad-faith narratives of the past.[20]

Yet while the current hostility toward black history is disturbing, I would insist that it is not the only cause for concern. Somewhere along the way from 1926 to now, the original intent of Black History Month got lost, even among strong supporters of black history. It is common to hear people implicitly criticize the commemorative holiday by asserting that "black history is American history," that "black history should not be confined to a month," and that "black history should be celebrated 365 days a year." Others raise concerns about the selection of February; flippant complaints about Black History Month occurring during the shortest month of the year are not unusual. I've always found such criticisms concerning, and not because I don't also believe that black history is an integral part of human history and critical to the story of our nation's development, because it absolutely is. Black American history is integral to the broader story of US history, and it should be studied comprehensively throughout the year. It is impossible to tell the history of this country without the history of black people. However, we also know that for so long—centuries, even—black people were forced to operate as a nation within a nation as they organized and fought for black freedom within the context of American freedom—the latter for so long having been constructed through the denial of the former. Thus, the black past is a distinct history in the American context, and we must name and remember it as such. Failing to do so would be to dishonor the freedom workers whose labors made possible many of the privileges enjoyed by historically marginalized groups today. When commentators make the previous critiques, much of the nuance about black people's relationship to the national context can easily be glossed over and flattened.

More important, I take issue with such misguided criticism because it participates in the erasure of black agency as well as the intentions of people such as Carter G. Woodson and the thousands of educators and activists working before and alongside him, who fought and organized for the teaching, studying, and commemoration of black history. These intellectuals certainly did not believe that the study of black life and culture should happen for only a single week or a single month. In fact, they made it clear that such periods of commemoration were to be moments for concentrated focus and reflection on lessons learned during the entire year. What's more, the suggestion that "we got the shortest month" implies that Black History Month was given to us in the first place, when nothing could be farther from the truth. This tradition was created through determined organizing and study by ordinary black people in partnership with committed black scholars.

It seems to me that the heroic tradition of black history as it was developed and sustained by black memory workers is one that is desperately needed in this moment. I call this tradition "heroic" because it emerged from enslaved people who, even in the face of powerful hegemonic narratives about the past, chose to think otherwise and in doing so established a tradition of memory work committed to the truths about black life even when such knowledge was forbidden by those in political power and castigated by white scholars.[21] I think there is much to be learned from this tradition that paved the way for Black History Month.

While this book marks the centenary of the nation's observance of black history in February, I want to be clear that it is not a retelling of events chronicling the development from Negro History Week through Black History Month, though some of those details will appear. Instead, it focuses on the importance of black memory work(ers) in chronicling and facilitating black history, it traces stories and historical analyses that enable us, in the contemporary moment, to wrestle with what is at stake in preserving the traditions that led to the commemorative holiday, and it explores why critical study of those traditions and the politics that informed them are useful for us in the present. Furthermore, as implied by the title of this introduction, borrowed from the poet Margaret Walker, I am concerned mostly with reflecting on the traditions of black memory work for the benefits it offers to black people; and I will express this concern openly in the pages of this book, even as I speak to the value that knowing the truths about black life offers to all of humanity.

This book's title, *I'll Make Me a World*, is taken from the first stanza of "The Creation," a 1927 poem by the educator, writer, and civil rights activist James Weldon Johnson, the author of "Lift Every Voice and Sing," which he wrote in 1900, after which it gradually became known as the black national anthem. Johnson's song and poem were sung in segregated schools and recited by black youths, not only during the commemorative celebrations in February but as recurring rituals in the everyday. I draw inspiration from his poem about God creating the world in six days, because its themes of agency, imagination, and building reflect important elements in the story of Black History Month's origins; these themes are reflected in the content of historical narratives from the black past, and they are also expressed through the actions of the African Americans who created and sustained the tradition of black memory work: the narrators, the archivists, the artists, and the memorializers. Indeed, the struggle to construct more expansive and honest narratives about the black past has always been an essential part of black people's work to envision and shape a new world not predicated on their suffering.

The pages ahead consist of four essays, each drawing from the historical record and also from my personal experiences studying, researching, and writing about black history, as well as my encounters with other people along the way—my grade school teachers, my family, intellectual collaborators, and young people in American schools. The first fifty years of this tradition feature prominently in the text, as the earlier years of Negro History Week (which gradually became Black History Week) provide the foundational framework and principles on which the next fifty years would rest. I also find these earlier examples of black history observances to be less riddled with distractions, thus allowing for more engagement with the core politics of black history and its uses by African Americans in service of their broader political struggles. Inspired by and titled after important texts in black history, these essays engage the content of those historical writings while placing them into a conversation with the personal and historical stories that unfold.

While many themes will emerge over the course of these essays—many historical events and lines of historical argumentation and reflection—there is perhaps one theme that is paramount. Threaded throughout these stories is an argument that one of the most critical things we can do to evolve the tradition is to be more explicit about the dynamics of power that continue to structure the production of history at every level; to clarify how memory work and black history itself are political, particularly when we understand who has the power to make decisions about historical preservation, which historical projects are funded, and what kinds of historical books are published and taught in schools. This lesson, about history and power, is fundamental to the story of black memory workers and the truths they have struggled to preserve. To expose this reality, I explore details about political actors and events in history as well as the black memory workers who narrate and preserve those memories about that past. I attend to distinct features in the memories black people carried with them over the generations, while also unveiling the labor carried forward by so many of them to preserve, study, and interpret those memories for the truth they reveal about black history and cultures, as well as the social world as black people encountered it.

PART I

THE CREATION

Black History Month and Its Many Beginnings

And God stepped out on space,
And he looked around and said:
I'm lonely—
I'll make me a world.

—JAMES WELDON JOHNSON, "THE CREATION" (1927)

MY FIRST TEACHER OF BLACK history was Miss Myron Ruth Butterfield, my preschool teacher during the 1992–1993 academic year at a small parochial school in Compton, California. Miss Butterfield was a dark-skinned woman from a town just outside Grenada, Mississippi, born in 1939 into a family of tenant farmers. I remember that her hair was always pulled back into a bun, and she wore a shiny gold wristwatch that I studied, as it often caught my attention. As a preschool student I could not tell time, but I was marked by time nonetheless; marked by social relations and events of the past even before my name had ever been spoken. That was part of my first lesson in black history, though it would take years for me to fully grasp its meaning.

My first Black History Month program occurred under Miss Butterfield's tutelage, and it was a formative experience in my early development. She prepared me and my classmates, all between three and five years old, to recite excerpts from Dr. Martin Luther King, Jr.'s "mountaintop" speech for our school's public program. Nearly four years old at the time, I had begun recognizing words by sight, could write my name, and could identify numbers; however, I was far from a fluent reader. It was Miss Butterfield who prepared me with the confidence and public speaking abilities to execute the tall task placed before me. For us preschoolers, our mountaintop consisted of conquering our individual fears, remembering the string of words she taught us, and speaking before hundreds of people—older schoolmates, teachers, families, and members of the local community. Miss Butterfield taught us our lines, we rehearsed, and we experienced a collective triumph that February evening.

Our school's Black History Month program was the biggest event of the year, and I realize now that our preparation had begun long before the month of February. From the beginning of September, we had participated in morning devotion, during which we recited poems by black authors, said the Pledge of Allegiance, and sang various songs, including "Lift Every Voice and Sing," colloquially known as the black national anthem. Those practices had been lined out for us preschoolers by Miss Butterfield, and they became a standard part of our socialization into the academic culture at St. Timothy's Episcopal Day School, a pre-K through eighth grade school where few of the teachers and students were Episcopalian, though all were black—mostly African American but also Afro-Panamanian, Kenyan, and Ugandan. I remember that Miss Butterfield enthusiastically performed those songs and recitations for us new students, making sure we could see her expressions and hear the cadences. She then broke the texts down into manageable lines. She would say or sing one line; then we would repeat her words. We learned the words and the rhythm in chunks before putting them all together. Sometimes Miss Butterfield called a student forward to perform what they had just learned. She then told us what we had done well and what needed correcting. It became a friendly competition as we watched and listened to one another recite lines and as we sang our songs or uttered our words in unison. Every morning was an opportunity to try again. Our parents were instructed to practice with us at home, and we were tested the next morning. "Jarvis!" Miss Butterfield would say. "Let me hear my favorite poem." That was my cue to begin reciting. We were taught to begin with the title followed by the author's name: "'Dreams' by Langston Hughes," I would say before starting the poem. "Hold fast to dreams / For if dreams die . . ." Sometimes she'd stop a student in midsentence, then quickly ask another student to pick up where the previous speaker had left off. "Jentri, what's next?" she might ask. The same strategy was applied to our learning of Dr. King's "mountaintop" speech.

Miss Butterfield's pedagogy was itself a historical artifact. It was the same way she had learned songs and speeches as a student in Jim Crow schools in Mississippi. What's more, her method of teaching us those black texts carried deep meaning in the African American oral tradition, though I've only recently come to appreciate this fact. When I reflect on Miss Butterfield initiating us students into the black past, I think of a beautiful essay entitled "Sister, Can You Line It Out?: Zora Neale Hurston and the Sound of Angular Black Womanhood," wherein the scholar Daphne Brooks wrote about Zora Neale Hurston's ethnographic studies of black sound during the Black Renaissance era. During the 1920s and '30s, Hurston traveled around the South studying black culture(s) in rural communities, learning their songs, folktales, and sayings while documenting how those performances interacted with the material realities of the people's lives as exploited workers. Men working on the railroads sang their songs over and over for Hurston, "lining out" every few words, as she learned each part well enough to sing it back to them and gain their approval.

In transforming herself into a human tape recorder, Hurston became a culture keeper, an embodied archive. As Brooks later explained, "In the tradition of African American hymn singing, 'lining out' is crucial to the performance as it entails the act of leading and clearing a path for others. In antebellum culture, these hymns were often 'intoned a line at a time—by someone who could read the text, and were then taken up by the congregation.'"[1] The practice of lining out songs, scriptures, and stories was a practice of communal literacy and knowledge sharing, and it is a beautiful part of black history that I took part in every day of my childhood in Miss Butterfield's classroom. I never knew this ritual to be anything other than our way of doing things. It was how one learned the poems, songs, and speeches Miss Butterfield insisted we needed to know. Yet in using our bodies as instruments that way, we engaged in a process of embodied learning that went far beyond the spoken word or songs we sang. Miss Butterfield was our line leader, and we became the chorus.

In 2019, I sat down to talk with Miss Butterfield. We met at her home in Compton, California, less than a five-minute drive from my childhood home, where my family still resides. During our conversation, she shared more insights about that Black History Month program in 1993 along with details of her own education in the Mississippi Delta. Learning about her journey helped me understand my first lesson in black history with a new level of clarity. It provided critical context for situating her pedagogy, as she made explicit the political commitments that had shaped her passion for introducing her students to the black past. Not only did she teach us those lessons because her teachers had done the same for her and she remembered being inspired by them, she also did it because we needed to know that "there were black people who did things" and she hoped we might grow to understand that there was still much more to be done.

Miss Butterfield brought up our Black History Month program before I could even ask. She explained, "I love all my kids [her former students]. I didn't make no difference, but you and Louis [one of my classmates]—I would teach on Black History Week, and you'd be Martin Luther King, and y'all was better than the big kids. Everybody said it!" I smiled as I could see her eagerness to discuss the topic; while the program was a proud moment for us as her students, it was equally a source of pride for her as our teacher.

Miss Butterfield's reference to Black History Week, as opposed to Black History Month, was more than a slippage of terms. She conflated what she recalled as the weeklong celebration of her youth with the monthlong celebrations that began in the 1970s, a convergence of decades of memories that tracked the evolution of the commemorative holiday. The famed historian Carter G. Woodson, once a schoolteacher himself, founded Negro History Week in 1926 before it was nationally extended to Black History Month in 1976. I made a mental note of that during our conversation because it implies the continuum of a tradition that was present in the story Miss Butterfield told, even as it goes unnamed. I also smile at the slip in her language because it is a common occurrence when discussing Black History Month with African American elders. Having first been initiated into the black past prior to 1976, they are often prompted to think of the Negro History Week celebrations of their youth. I appreciate such moments, because in these instances I witness a merging of many times and many spaces of black history. I am reminded of the tradition and of its evolution. I am reminded, at once, of change over time and yet "the changing same."

Miss Butterfield's excitement over the memory of our 1993 program brought us both to laughter. However, we tried not to be too loud out of respect for her husband, who was bedridden and resting in the next room. I assured Miss Butterfield that the memory loomed large in my own recollections. My family never let me live it down. When she asked, "Jarvis, do you remember that?" I replied, "Yeah, I do. And I remember my grandma smiling and asking, 'Who put you on that stage saying that Martin Luther King speech?'" Miss Butterfield continued laughing and gleaming with pride.

It wasn't just the words of Dr. King's speech that impressed the families of Miss Butterfield's students. Speaking of my own family, they were impressed by the qualities she seemed to bring out of children, even at such early ages. They appreciated the content of our Black History Month program, which centered on important political and cultural aspects of black life, and they also appreciated the formal manner in which we presented the information we learned. Our families celebrated the confidence we displayed as young children doing things we had never known we could do. They experienced our presentations as evidence of our socio-emotional well-being as black children. The content and form of our performances were all important, as well as our self-comportment and disposition. Those things had much to do with one another. There was a seriousness about who we were and what we were learning, and it expressed a distinct kind of rigor that was communally valued both by our educators and by the black families in the auditorium.

•

"SAY IT USING your outside voices," Miss Butterfield would stress. There was a way the words were supposed to be spoken, she emphasized. We were to convey something that went beyond what was uttered; she was also communicating to us her memory of a feeling associated with the words. At four years old, we had no full understanding of what the words meant, but we worked to convey the feeling Miss Butterfield radiated as she lined out our speeches and our songs. In retrospect, I recall how her emphasis on phonetics and pronunciation aligned with traditions in black formalism, or black ways of saying that are most associated with black churches, indeed speech acts that were integral parts of an African American political tradition. For indeed, just as African Americans have a vernacular tradition, they have also established their own values and modes of expression when it comes to matters that are serious and at times consecrated.

There were about twenty preschoolers in our class. Our first big test was to perform what we had learned in front of the larger school during a dress rehearsal a few days before the main event. All the grade levels came together to form an audience, and the other teachers weighed in on how each class might improve. When the big night came, all of us students came together wearing our best clothes, lining up onstage in the Compton Unified School District's auditorium on Tamarind Avenue. Miss Butterfield prepared us for the space before we arrived there. During our rehearsals, she emphasized that I was to point into the distance as I stretched the middle part of the word "been" when reciting the line "Because I've beeeeeen to the mountaintop." In similar fashion, I was to look into the distance while holding my hand above my eyes when declaring "I've seeeeeeen the promised land." The word "longevity" was a challenge at first; however, by the day of our program I grew comfortable with its pronunciation. In the days leading up to the event, she would ask, "Jarvis, what's that big word you're going to say?" And I'd say the word—"lon-*jeh*-vity"—while struggling not to get tongue tied.

When the time came, I stepped forward, wearing black slacks and a white shirt, and said my part as I had practiced it, trying to hit all my rehearsed pauses and making sure to emphasize specific words the way Miss Butterfield had coached me. We could all feel her eyes on us as she stooped at the side of the stage in the wings; however, we avoided looking at her because she had prepared us to look ahead at the people in the crowd. When we occasionally glanced at her, Miss Butterfield pointed to the audience, redirecting our attention. I was the last student to recite in that segment of our program.

"We've got some difficult days ahead," I began, speaking slowly. "But it doesn't matter with me now. Because I've beeeeen to the mountaintop. And I don't mind. Like anybody, I would like to live a loooong life. Longevity has its place. But I'm not concerned about that now. I just want to do God's will. And He's allowed me to go up to the mountain. And I've looked over. And I've seeeeen the promised land. I may not get there with you. But I want you to know tonight, that we, as a people, will get to the promised land." As we progressed through our speeches, the crowd of people was shouting back at me and my classmates. It was as though they, too, had rehearsed the part they were to play in our program. They were smiling and taking pictures, cheering, and standing. It was all slightly confusing. I did not understand why those words caused such a stir. But I remembered the feeling; I knew we were doing a good thing.

Other details from that evening's program have faded from my memory. However, the feelings of pride and purpose I experienced stuck with me. As I progressed through elementary and middle school, I witnessed other students in Miss Butterfield's class recite similar excerpts from King's speeches, perform skits about Mary McLeod Bethune, or dress up as Billie Holiday and sing "God Bless the Child." Miss Butterfield continued her rituals of starting students on their way, teaching them to embody the struggle and courage of those that came before us, and working carefully to cultivate some feeling in us about who we were and of our inheritance as black children. I know now that in addition to the words we committed to memory, there was also knowledge in the feeling she sought to pass on. That, too, was part of the teaching of black history. It was part of my becoming a black political subject, a child who was connected to a particular set of people, places, and social arrangements that had preceded me. It was her way of teaching us that we were part of a heritage that could be traced back and used as equipment for living and learning in the present.

While many families, like my own, will always remember the day when their small children collectively became Martin Luther King, Jr., all I see and hear when I remember the story is Miss Butterfield. I remember her careful labor. I hear the repetition of our rehearsals. I recall how we explored our voices and found confidence in the cadence of King's speech. Our final performance only solidified the lessons we had already learned through our preparation, a protocol that had begun before the month of February, though that was when we were to put those lessons on display for all to see. That February evening in 1993 was but one iteration of the many beginnings of Black History Month. It's the story of its origin in my own life; however, the story of this commemorative holiday has many starting points that stretch far and wide in the African American tradition.

•

BLACK HISTORY MONTH is a beautiful creation that was dreamed up, pieced together, and sustained by a narratively condemned people. African Americans recognized how racist storylines based on whitewashed conceptions of history were used to justify their oppression. They detected how choices were made about what should be remembered and what should be forgotten, what should be prominently displayed and what should be tucked away or even sculpted out. Having studied that power-laden process of history's production, they created a tradition of truth telling grounded in black memory work that included both their own lived realities and those of their predecessors. Through sustained practices of historical preservation and study, African Americans worked to generate more reliable and truthful knowledge about the black past as a resource for imagining more just and liberated futures. It is this intellectual tradition that paved the way for the hundred-year journey of Black History Month in the United States.

In marking the centennial anniversary since the first Negro History Week celebration, we should all revisit our individual connections to black history—and by "we," I am referring first to black people and then to the nation's citizens as a whole, given that this milestone is significant for both, even if for distinct reasons. Indeed, we all have our own memories and first encounters with this tradition. What's more, now is an important time to critically reflect on the political stakes of this century-old tradition of sustained storytelling about the black past, to remind ourselves of the role it can and should play in relationship to ongoing justice-oriented struggles. The urgency of such critical reflection is likely evident to most readers, as we experience an era, during the second administration of President Donald Trump, in which attacks on African American history have reached new heights. Yet even as I note this uptick in America's culture wars, when book bans abound and academic freedom continues to be attacked across the educational sector, I must also recognize that critical knowledge about the black past has never ceased to be viewed with suspicion, even in more recent times. It has always been surveilled; and even when black history is "tolerated" or "included," it is often watered down and sanitized in mainstream school curricula and public memory.[2] It is true that African American and African diaspora history became recognized in the US academy as legitimate fields of study during the second half of the twentieth century and that such knowledge about the past became accessible to the American public in unprecedented ways. However, such historical knowledge has never been fully embraced for the larger correctives it offers for transforming national narratives or public historical memory about our modern world, which has been structured by slavery and its afterlives. Prior to the current administration, black history continued to be contained, thinly tolerated, and at times explicitly marginalized. The current backlash is in many ways a dramatic resurgence of well-documented and -sustained efforts to silence liberatory histories that value and take seriously the experiences of the oppressed. Even during the most "inclusive" phases of US history, such marginalization of black history persisted.

At the same time, I don't want to minimize the current organized attacks on black history. The reality is that these attacks sound and feel eerily similar to the dominant rhetoric of the period when the movement to popularize black history began in the early twentieth century. When I think of the accusation by Florida Governor Ron DeSantis in 2023 that the College Board's

AP African American Studies course "lacks educational value," I cannot help but recall Carter G. Woodson's recollections on disparaging comments made by scholars at Harvard and the University of Chicago, where his professors explicitly told him that black people had no history and culture, at least none worthy of respect and study—sentiments those same professors expressed when writing about black people in their scholarly works and personal correspondence. While that was the context in which Woodson founded Negro History Week, current executive orders and assertions that the study of black life and history "lacks educational value" help clarify why Black History Month continues to be important as a means of public accountability, a medium through which we might refuse to allow black history to be pushed into the shadows, and a platform to insist that the American public have recurring encounters with the truth about black struggles and black survival as a means of cultivating our collective sense of civic responsibility. Despite the exploitation of the commemorative holiday by corporations for capitalist gains, it can still be reclaimed as an important organizing tool and an opportunity for coordinated community education campaigns, and when used appropriately, Black History Month can facilitate the momentum of the continued struggle to dig up, preserve, and study the black past as a source for inspiring present and future generations to justice-oriented action year-round.

While taken for granted by many today, it wasn't so long ago that leading academic scholars considered black history to be a contradiction in terms. They insisted that "black" and "history" were antithetical. According to influential white historians and philosophers of history, such as the nineteenth-century German philosopher Georg W. F. Hegel, whose writings had a tremendous influence on modern Western thought, and therefore the shaping of the US political sphere, Africa and its people were "known" to be without history and culture. In his influential 1837 book *Lectures on the Philosophy of History*, he declared, "What we properly understand by Africa, is the Unhistorical, Undeveloped Spirit, still involved in the conditions of mere nature, and which had to be presented here only as on the threshold of the World's History." For Hegel and his contemporaries, blackness as a racial category, as well as the people marked by it, represented the absence of history and a lack of cultural achievement.

Leading scholars in the American academy reinforced and elaborated on Hegel's ideas. In the words of a North Carolina university president in 1901, "The Negro is a child race" and therefore "must aim at white civilization, and must reach it through the support, guidance, and control of the white people among whom he lives."[3] Such words had real-life implications. They informed ideologies that shaped social policy; they influenced the actions of government officials on matters ranging from housing and policing to public health and especially education. To be clear, such concerns are not merely matters of the past; contemporary scholars who analyze social studies and history curricula across states consistently document the underrepresentation of black and other ethnic histories in chronicles of the human past. Educators such as Woodson interpreted this silence to be directly related to the structural and interpersonal forms of oppression that black people experience in the social world. When reflecting on the first Negro History Week celebration and the antiblack violence it was meant to disrupt, Woodson explained, "We call this race prejudice, and it may be thus properly named; but it is not something inherent in human nature. It is merely the logical result of tradition, the inevitable outcome of thorough instruction to the effect that the Negro has never contributed anything to the progress of mankind. The doctrine has been thoroughly drilled into the whites and the Negroes have learned well the lesson themselves; for many of them look upon other races as superior and accept the status of recognized inferiority."[4] The sheer volume of Eurocentric history and literature in schools in comparison to the low and shallow depictions of others is about more than a failure to include everything about everyone. Such imbalanced portrayals of the past and present cultures of the world communicate strong messages—explicitly and implicitly—about what is and is not valued, what is and is not worth knowing.

While mainstream white scholars argued throughout a large portion of the twentieth century that black people had no worthwhile history, there were also those who actively suppressed knowledge that would expose such myths. In my previous work *Fugitive Pedagogy: Carter G. Woodson and the Art of Black Teaching*, I documented how black educators were targeted for teaching historical knowledge that refuted conventional antiblack storylines. Indeed, it is this tradition of ordinary African American educators teaching against the grain and organizing in local communities to study and rethink knowledge about the black past that led to the establishment of Black History Month. African Americans and their allies recognized that coordinated strategies to sustain and raise awareness about black history were essential, creating a movement around the study of black life and culture in the face of widespread curricular violence in American education. Now, as we witness the spreading of old forms of epistemic injustice through book bans, "antiwoke" legislation, and bad-faith claims meant to undermine entire bodies of scholarship such as African American studies, there is much to be learned from the tradition that gifted us Black History Month. However, to truly appreciate this tradition requires that we look beyond the emergence of Negro History Week in 1926, turning instead to key developments in black intellectual life that had begun at least a century prior.

To fully appreciate the legacy of black history and Black History

Month requires that we pay careful attention to how it emerged. This includes attending to the opposition it faced as well as the strategies employed by African American communities to preserve it. These are the stories I seek to tell in the pages that follow.

•

BLACK HISTORY MONTH is a beautiful creation with many beginnings. As previously explained, it is most directly traced to February 1926, when the inaugural celebration of Negro History Week occurred under the direction of Carter G. Woodson. Dr. Woodson, a child of formerly enslaved people and the second black person to receive a PhD in history from Harvard in 1912, initiated Negro History Week through the Association for the Study of Negro Life and History, which he founded in 1915 while working as a public school teacher in Washington, DC. He created the weeklong celebration with explicitly political aims, its objective being to popularize the study and public commemoration of black life and culture as a counterweight against the antiblack narratives used to justify the violent mistreatment and second-class citizenship of black people in US society and around the globe.

Negro History Week quickly spread through African American community institutions; its expansion was grassroots in nature, the result of intentional, sustained organizing by ordinary community members, especially educators, in addition to wide coverage in the black newspapers that connected African Americans across the country. Most notable was the commemorative holiday's immediate growth in black segregated schools, teacher networks, historically black colleges, and churches. When describing the first year's celebration, Woodson recalled that "Many ministers opened their churches for these [Negro History Week] exercises.... Others, like most of the heads of schools, worked out well-prepared programs in a way peculiar to their special needs and held exercises every day during the week. In some cases, programs were rendered certain evenings to reach persons who were so circumstanced as not to be able to attend during the day." Reflecting on the first celebration, he noted, "The observance of Negro History Week proved to be one of the most fortunate steps ever taken by the Association [for the Study of Negro Life and History]. The celebration made a deep impression.... Easily understood, the idea was readily taken up at centers where some thought is given to social amelioration and wherever special efforts are being made to elevate the Negro. Ministers, teachers, social workers, and business men rallied to the support of the movement and made it a national success."[5]

By the early 1930s, Negro History Week was nearly universally observed in black segregated schools.[6] The weeklong holiday was so successful that the preeminent African American scholar of the twentieth century W. E. B. Du Bois referred to Negro History Week in 1940 as "the single greatest accomplishment" of the Black Renaissance era. Given the unprecedented blossoming in black art, literature, and scholarship during the interwar years—not only in Harlem but across the country and internationally—such praise by Du Bois speaks volumes to the waves made by this public history campaign created by Woodson then embraced and championed by African American communities.[7]

Yet while February 1926 is important to Black History Month's beginnings, it is also true that this monumental achievement flows from a much more expansive tradition stretching back across the African American odyssey in "the New World." Indeed, black people expressed concerns about historical interpretation in public and private ways well before the twentieth century. They did so because they recognized how stories told about the past influence the way we live our lives in the present as well as the way we imagine paths for the future. As a people of action, African Americans decided that they would have to create black history through their actions within the world around them as they struggled against antiblack violence and injustice and also as memory workers, through various methods of documenting and bearing witness to their experiences, past and present, and by writing new scripts of knowledge that would be accountable to those experiences.

Two distinct yet interrelated trajectories were foundational to the intellectual context from which Black History Month emerged. First is the legacy of black knowledge production in the United States, particularly as it was expressed in written form, which can be traced back to the antislavery texts penned by fugitive slaves and black abolitionists. The second extends from African American organizing traditions in the realm of public history and historical commemoration. Both legacies directly informed African Americans' creation of Black History Month. What's more, black memory workers' sustained production of historical knowledge, as well as their organizing opportunities for public engagement with that knowledge, formed a core vein in the intellectual arm of the African American freedom movement, beginning as early as the slavery era and certainly throughout the twentieth century.

I intentionally use the word *creation* to contextualize the origins of Black History Month. By doing so, I hope to underscore the role human agency plays in history, both in the occurrence of historical events across time and space and in the crafting of stories that attempt to detail such developments in narrative form. People's actions in the past and the occurrence of particular events were never inevitable. Likewise, human agency and all its imperfections drive the production of historical memory and written scholarship. So just as our social realities are constructed by people and what they do with power, the same is true of the stories we tell ourselves about the past, present, and future of our social lives. Such stories, whether written or oral in form, are also our creations.

It is important that all citizens hold themselves accountable as historical subjects, not only when we consider the role of human agency in the production of historical memory but also because of the influence history (both the literal past and the stories we tell about it) has on our collective lives. It demands that we be intentional in how we craft our relationship with such knowledge. For indeed, we are all historical subjects and always intimately formed through the stories we accumulate about the past. To quote James Baldwin, "*History* . . . is not merely something to be read. And it does not refer merely, or even principally, to the past. On the contrary, the great force of history comes from the fact that we carry it within us, are unconsciously controlled by it in many ways, and history is literally *present* in all that we do. It could scarcely be otherwise, since it is to history that we owe our frames of reference, our identities, and our aspirations."[8]

Recognizing the severe limitations of dominant historical knowledge, African Americans created what the late historian Charles H. Wesley called a "heroic tradition" of remembering history: They insisted on giving a black account of the past, even when their interpretations, additions, and reconstructions of critical historical details about the past conflicted with those of people in positions of power; even when such knowledge of the past was deemed seditious by white Americans. Again, I trace this heroic tradition back to the writings of fugitive slaves, runaway captives who chose physical escape from bondage and who also found ways to escape into their mind. For indeed, stealing one's own mind has always been the first step in the African American plot for freedom.

•

THE FREEDOM NARRATIVES of fugitive slaves constitute the first texts in African American letters, and they laid the literary foundation of the heroic tradition of black history and, eventually, Black History Month. Through such writings, self-emancipated black people sought to counteract the misinformation about slavery that perpetuated apathy among those who lacked an intimate relationship with the system. Absent testimony from black perspectives, most portrayals presented the peculiar institution as a mild, benevolent, and generally harmless system that benefited the otherwise "heathen" and "barbarous" African captives. Though deemed by US law to be the property of other people, escaped slaves insisted on speaking out and in doing so expressed insights bearing on the human condition that could be expressed only through the perspective of black political subjects in a world shaped by racial chattel slavery. And yet, their narratives exposed depths of the social world that had implications for everyone invested in the virtues of freedom and justice.

Through their literacy acts, escaped slaves presented themselves as more than financial losses to be recorded in their masters' ledger, their claims forming the basis of new interpretations of the political order and of human history. Fugitive slaves, as early black memory workers, chipped away at the ideas propping up white supremacy in their speaking and writing; they undermined it when they asserted themselves as "the piece of intelligent humanity who could say [and write]: I have been owned like an ox. I stole my own body and now I am hunted by law and lash to be made an ox again."[9] By bearing witness to their violent alienation from American society and documenting their interior lives, agency, and cultural practices, those former captives created a particular critique of the world from which emerged a new basis for historical interpretation and study. They exposed the hypocrisy in the very notion of American freedom; they exposed lies endemic to the prevalent racial ideologies; they articulated the most expansive vision of justice, which included the most dispossessed; they expressed their distinct interpretations of beauty and experiences of sorrow; and in attesting to their suffering at the hands of their enslavers, they exposed the pathologies of whiteness, such as its obsession with possessing and dominating, that have continued to mark the world.[10] In rendering alternative accounts of their lives and the social world, antebellum African Americans initiated a tradition of black study that formed the basis of a new heroic tradition in historical interpretation, indeed laying the foundation for what we know today as "black history."

When speaking about the facts of slavery as they lived it, fugitives such as Harriet Jacobs, James W. C. Pennington, and Frederick Douglass became subjects of history, not merely its objects. In addition to writing his life story in 1849 with the publication of *The Fugitive Blacksmith*, Pennington, a runaway slave from Maryland, also published *A Text Book of the Origins and History, &c. &c. of the Colored People* in 1841, while working at the African Free School in Newtown, Connecticut. Pennington did not just render bone-dry historical narratives or create listings of factual details absent clear critical social analysis, for the aim of his memory work was to help advance a deeper understanding of the social problems faced by those most vulnerable in American society and his labor was driven by clear political motivations.

Long before the proliferation of recent scholarship on capitalism and slavery, Pennington reminded nineteenth-century readers that the violence of slavery was not only or primarily physical but was rooted in "the chattel principle," which was his way of describing the political economy of race and antiblackness that enabled and undergirded the matrix of violence in the slave society. According to Pennington, slavery's evil lay not primarily in its physical brutality or cultural degradation; "the cart-whip, starvation, and nakedness, are its inevitable consequences," he argued. The essence of slavery's evil dwelled in the business of the slave trade itself and the terms of human sociality that animated its transactions; he pointed to the laws as well as the attendant racial ideology that gave them meaning. He declared, "The being of slavery, its soul and body, lives and moves in the chattel principle, the property principle, the bills of sale principle."[11] The principle that turns people into property was a symbolic violation that breathed life into the condemnation of black life through every major or minor transaction.

Pennington's nineteenth-century analysis of the conditions of chattel slavery is a shining example of black memory work serving as more than simple documentation. In his careful naming of slave capital, expressed in racial terms, as an evil premise in New World economic development, he went on to chart how the chattel principle shaped the content of historical narratives and archives: "No where does he [the enslaved] find any record of himself *as a man*. On looking at the family record of his old, kind, Christian, master, there he finds his name on a catalogue with the horses, cows, hogs and dogs. However humiliating and degrading it may be to his feelings to find his name written down among the beasts of the field, *that* is just the place, and the *only* place assigned to it by the chattel relation."[12] He addressed the construction of antiblack silences in historical narratives; he draws our attention to the written documents that would come to inform the expansive body of historical sources used to recover and analyze the past because that paper trail reflected the essence of the antiblack world in which he lived and the historical distortions he sought to disrupt. In doing so, he anticipated arguments by contemporary scholars who name the limitations of such historical sources produced by white people that defined African Americans as property and erased their interiority—a problem for which present-day historians continue to seek out methodological remedies as they engage in black memory work, as they seek traces of black agency and textured lives in historical collections produced in a social world ordered by white supremacy.[13] Through such analysis, the fugitive blacksmith, teacher, and social theorist clarified just why the black memory work he engaged in was so important: he understood his literacy acts, textbook, life writing, and political speeches to be vital contributions to an intellectual tradition set against the chattel principle and the racial order it secured.

Pennington's memory work and writing were literacy acts in the long war against the narrative condemnation of black people. His life writing and textbook are legacies of an insurgent form of black intellectualism, a tradition that grew steadily during the nineteenth century. It was especially well developed in the writing of the freeborn Civil War veteran George Washington Williams, who in 1881 published what is considered by many to be the first systematic treatment of African American history. By this I mean that he employed conventional practices of historical writing and research, whereas much of Pennington's writing was heavily informed by biblical interpretations and arguments. Williams was careful to provide information about where he had retrieved his facts and information, as a means of accountability; he provided evidence to demonstrate the rigor of his claims. More important, he not only sought to correct the history of the race but was explicit about the political stakes of his work. He critiqued claims by white scholars across academic fields who denigrated black life and culture. In framing his book, *History of the Negro Race in America from 1619 to 1880*, he observed, "Many writers of ethnology, anthropology, and slavery

James W. C. Pennington

have strenuously striven to place the Negro outside of the human family; and the disciples of these teachers have endeavored to justify their views by the most dehumanizing treatment of the Negro."[14]

In addition to their writings, African Americans engaged in activities of historical commemoration, often in very public ways, that expressed their new interpretations of the black past. Such public engagements with history were a complementary form of memory work that was informed by and helped stimulate the written traditions of black history. To trace this through line, we need to look no further than the most immediate precursor of Woodson's Negro History Week: the annual celebration of Frederick Douglass Day, which began on February 14, 1897.

•

AFTER READING A column in *The Evening Star* crediting someone else with founding Frederick Douglass Day, the retired educator and activist Mary Church Terrell wrote to the newspaper's editor, according to an undated manuscript, likely in 1924, to set the record straight. It was she and she alone, she said, who had established the annual commemoration of Frederick Douglass's birthday on February 14 in the public schools of Washington, DC, in 1897, just two years after the famous abolitionist had died of a heart attack. She declared, "With the exception of the trustees who voted for it, no human being dead or alive had anything whatsoever to do with establishing Douglass Day in the Colored Schools but myself." She added, "I have done very few things of which I am proud, but I am proud of the fact that it was entirely through my suggestion and motion that the trustees voted to set aside a portion of the afternoon of Feb. 14th in which to honor the memory of one of the greatest men this country have ever produced."[15]

The archival record substantiates Terrell's claim. She pointed the editor to the District of Columbia School Board's meeting minutes. There he would find details of the business transacted on January 12, 1897: "On motion of Mrs. Terrell the afternoon of February 14th, 1897, beginning at half past one o'clock was ordered set apart in the colored schools of the District in which to commemorate the memory of Frederick Douglass."[16] Terrell also played a major role in coordinating the first annual Douglass Day event for DC's colored schools, which occurred on Friday, February 12, when a ceremony was hosted in the assembly hall at the M Street School, the only black public high school in the city. At the event, Terrell accepted a portrait of Frederick Douglass from the leader's sons, which they gifted to the colored teachers and students of the DC public schools. In her remarks, she expressed a deep sense of purpose, receiving the gift "with reverence, with pride and with hope." Speaking to the students and teachers in the audience, she explained that there were many lessons to be learned from the life of Douglass, "a man who was a benefaction to his race and a blessing to the world," a leader "who set a high standard of life and dared to live up to it in spite of opposition, criticism and persecution." She declared, "As they see the light of knowledge, which is power, beaming from those eyes ... May they be constantly reminded of their duty."[17]

Mary Church Terrell made history when she compelled the local school board of the segregated education system in the nation's capital to formally set apart time to honor the life of a formerly enslaved man who was a fierce champion for black freedom, as well as women's rights, and who left a written record of what he saw and knew to be true—about himself, his people, and the world as they encountered it. It is important to note that while Frederick Douglass is widely celebrated today, his name and contributions to American political life were conspicuously absent from mainstream textbooks used in American schools at the turn of the twentieth century and for decades to come, even when one searches the most progressive among them—for even though some textbooks discussed the abolitionist movement, they named only white abolitionists, one textbook even citing Douglass's writing in its endnotes, only to discuss the white abolitionist William Lloyd Garrison in its main text.[18] This textbook, *Essentials in American History*, was published in 1905 by Albert Bushnell Hart, the historian who would be Carter G. Woodson's professor and dissertation adviser at Harvard University from 1908 to 1912. What's more, Douglass Day was taken up as a celebration in more than just the public schools; churches and black literary associations also observed the holiday, demonstrating the educational benefit of Terrell's actions beyond the school walls. In its first year, the Bethel Literary and Historical Association in DC hosted an event to observe Douglass Day at the Metropolitan African Methodist Church, noting, "Mr. Douglass was, in his life, greatly interested in this organization." Therefore, the association would make "Douglass Day a fixture in its calendar, and will observe it annually."[19]

Terrell once suggested, "Perhaps Douglass Day inspired Dr. Carter G. Woodson to establish Negro History Week many years afterward."[20] I suspect that Terrell's suggestion was more of a nudge; another respectful correction to the historical record. The connection she identifies seems undeniable, as Woodson was explicit in acknowledging that he had chosen the middle of February for the weeklong celebration because of Douglass's birthday (as well as Abraham Lincoln's). Furthermore, Woodson and Terrell were well acquainted and close collaborators. Both served on the faculty of the M Street School, the nation's first black public high school, which in 1916 would be renamed after the African American poet Paul Laurence Dunbar. Terrell began working at the school in 1887, and Woodson joined the faculty in 1911, as he completed his doctoral studies for a PhD in history at Harvard University. Readers might find it useful to recall that high schools were less common in the early twentieth century, especially for African Americans. Black communities continued to fight for access to high school education up and through the Jim Crow era. Therefore, institutions such as Dunbar High School carried much more prestige in communities than readers today might think. Dunbar's prestige was also due to the intellectual and political activity of the school's educators, many of whom had advanced degrees and who led important local and national organizations, including the NAACP and various black women's clubs, such as the National Association of Colored Women's Clubs. What's more, Woodson and Terrell were part of a broader community of African American teachers who were deeply interested in the study of black history and culture.

During Woodson's time working in DC schools, local educators organized to expand access to knowledge about the black past even beyond Douglass Day celebrations. Leila Amos Pendleton and John W. Cromwell, both DC-based public school teachers, published textbooks on black history in 1912 and 1914, respectively. Furthermore, while Woodson partnered with four other men to establish the Association for the Study of Negro Life and History while doing research in Chicago, in September 1915, African American teachers in DC organized a yearlong series of professional development workshops focused on deepening their studies and teaching about black life and culture. Mary Church Terrell would have been part of these efforts, just as Woodson and W. E. B. Du Bois each led workshops on black history for DC's local educators.[21] The following year, when Wood-

Mary Church Terrell

son published the first issue of *The Journal of Negro History* in January 1916, Mary Church Terrell was one of the contributing authors, and she would continue to contribute original essays to the journal in years to come.[22] She also helped plan the annual meetings of Woodson's Association, where scholars, educators, and community members gathered to discuss new scholarship related to black life and culture while also planning for its dissemination around the nation and the world.[23]

Such vibrant intellectual currents among African American teachers and their involvement in building and maintaining various social and civic organizations greatly influenced the social foundations of what became the national commemoration of black life and culture. The road that paved the way to Negro History Week and eventually Black History Month was the product of many minds of black memory workers. In stating this, my intent is not to minimize Woodson's role as the founder of the holiday, for there can be no doubt that his

Frederick Douglass Day clippings from *The Evening Star*, January 13 and February 12, 1897 sustained commitment to institution building around researching and disseminating knowledge about black history was the most significant source responsible for the staying power of the weeklong celebration. However, when we contextualize Woodson's work within the organizing traditions around black history prior to 1926, we gain a deeper appreciation of collective struggle, of the ways educators, scholars, and activists worked together to reinterpret black life on their own terms, and of the cumulative nature of the black freedom struggle, whether on the activist or the scholarly side of the movement. We also encounter a more detailed account of the kind of collective labor, by which I mean the literal work, often happening behind the scenes, that went into the creation of this tradition and its maintenance over such a long period of time. We gain a more nuanced account of the journey, which is also instructive for the road ahead.

Woodson's prior work helping launch Omega Psi Phi fraternity's Negro History and Literature Week in April 1921 is also important to the story of Black History Month. Omega Psi Phi was one of four historically black intercollegiate fraternities, and it had been committed to racial uplift ever since its founding at Howard University in 1911. Its Campaign for the Study of Negro History and Literature ran from 1921 to 1924, as it engaged communities around the country through programming informed by African American history, literature, and the arts. The springboard of this national initiative was a stirring address Woodson gave in December 1920 at the fraternity's annual meeting at Meharry Medical College in Nashville. His address, entitled "Democracy and the Man Far Down," convinced the organization's leadership that a week devoted to the historical and cultural achievements of the race would be a worthy cause for a national program. Therefore, during the month of April 1921, Omega Psi Phi required all its chapters, numbering just under twenty, to host Negro History and Literature Week. Celebrations took the form of public programs in churches, schools, and events partnering with literary societies and other community organizations.²⁴

After its success, the fraternity's leaders continued their campaign for a second year. In February 1922, writing to Omega Psi Phi men around the country through the fraternity's publication, *The Oracle*, the organization's leaders stated, "Few of us realize how really little we know of ourselves as a race. Yet if we are to survive and live, race consciousness must be awakened; and there is no surer way to awaken race consciousness in a people than by familiarizing them with the history, traditions and achievements of their race." In preparation for the campaign, scheduled for April 2 through April 8, 1922, the organization declared, "Let us then adopt as our slogan for Negro Week the old adage, 'Know thyself,' and launch forth into the campaign the first week in April with the determination that we and all Negroes shall know more about the achievements of our race and will be thereby influenced to accomplish more in the future."²⁵ A committee was appointed in the months leading up to the third year's celebration, as the fraternity hoped to outline a strategic plan for implementation, given the campaign's momentum. Their charge was to "develop [definite] plans for fostering the study of Negro History in the schools and colleges of the country."²⁶ Omega Psi Phi brothers in the field of education, spanning state and regional lines, served on the committee. The list included Carter G. Woodson, as well as Omega Psi Phi educational leaders such as Garnet C. Wilkinson,

Carter G. Woodson

the assistant superintendent of colored schools in the District of Columbia.

As the fraternity began to expand and establish new chapters, its primary focus was on infrastructure, and at its national meeting in December 1924, Woodson insisted that the initiative be run under the auspices of his organization. The Association for the Study of Negro Life and History published books and an academic journal; it also hosted annual meetings with an increasingly broad reach, all focused on researching, preserving, and disseminating knowledge about black life and culture. The expansive membership base of Woodson's association, many of whom were teachers and women, enabled the program to have a larger reach, as its planning was not beholden to fraternity support. No celebration took place in the year 1925. Then, in February 1926, the Association for the Study of Negro Life and History sponsored Negro History Week for the first time. Again, Woodson intentionally chose the month of February. After all, Douglass Day celebrations were already quite popular in black schools, especially in DC, thanks to the organizing efforts of community leaders such as Mary Church Terrell.

Expanding from Douglass Day to Negro History Week in 1926, the schools of Washington, DC, and many other cities around the country celebrated the commemorative holiday for the first time. On February 5, 1926, *The Washington Tribune* printed the following announcement under "School News":

NEGRO HISTORY WEEK.
Under the direction of a general committee appointed by First Assistant Superintendent G. C. Wilkinson, the public schools of divisions 10–13 have prepared to observe Negro History Week by a meeting of teachers, to which the public is cordially invited, and by daily exercises in each school building.

The public meeting will be held on Tuesday, February 9, at 2:45 p.m., in the auditorium of Dunbar High School. The program for this meeting will consist of musical compositions by Colored composers and of short talks on phases of Negro History by Dr. Charles H. Wesley, Dr. Carter G. Woodson and Mr. Neval H. Thomas. The musical numbers will be contributed by Miss Estelle Pickney, Miss M. L. Europe, Mr. James B. Lomack, Mr. Wesley Howard, Mr. Joseph A. Walker, and Mr. A. W. Burleigh. First Assistant Superintendent G. C. Wilkinson will preside.

The programs for each building, though planned along individual lines, will feature the Negro's part in the making of America, the Negro achievements in art and letters. Every effort is being made to bring before the children this heritage of the past and to awaken in them a duty and responsibility for the present and future. To this end two things are being stressed: ideals of noble character and ideals of worthy citizenship.[27]

•

WOODSON'S 1926 CREATION extended from organizing and educational traditions that were quite expansive in African American life. This observation can be found in the words of Du Bois, who couched his discussion of Negro History Week in that broader context. When reflecting on debates pertaining to segregated schools, he urged that black students "ought not to forget the 5th of March,— the first national holiday of this country, which commemorates the martyrdom of Crispus Attucks. They ought to celebrate Negro Health Week [founded by Booker T. Washington in 1915] and Negro History Week. They ought to study intelligently and from their own point of view" the past and present realities of black life, including "the slave trade, slavery, emancipation, Reconstruction, and present economic development."²⁸ In his statement, Du Bois traced a tradition: Douglass Day, then Negro History Week extended from a longer practice of self-initiated public history efforts by African Americans in the United States, where they worked to commemorate the lives of people and important historical events from the black past, especially when they understood such people and events to be deserving of broader recognition for their contributions to the nation or the advancement of human civilization.

Both Mary Church Terrell and Carter G. Woodson operated in a tradition of black historical consciousness. Their efforts were anticipated by William Cooper Nell, a journalist and antislavery activist who was a contemporary of Douglass, though he was born free in Boston, Massachusetts. Nell is credited with establishing Crispus Attucks Day on March 5 to commemorate the Boston Massacre of 1770, when Attucks, a man of mixed-race heritage, including black and native ancestry, became the first of a group of protestors killed when resisting the increased presence of British soldiers.

Woodson wrote an article for teachers and students about Crispus Attucks Day in 1947, noting how the event that had ended in the death of Attucks "became the 'Boston Massacre,' a tale of horror which increased hatred of the British with each retelling." The incident had such importance among American patriots that "The Fifth of March was observed each year thereafter with a public demonstration until the peace of 1783, after which the Fourth of July was substituted as Independence Day"; hence Du Bois's proclamation that the first American holiday was a day of commemoration that, intentionally or not, recognized the sacrifice made by a black man for American freedom.²⁹

For patriotic black abolitionists, Attucks's story was an important one to tell in the face of ongoing black oppression. People such as William Cooper Nell drew upon the legacy of Attucks as a historical basis for making demands for equal citizenship and opportunity in the United States. Therefore, it became a cause for concern when the Boston Massacre and Attucks's name became minimized in the story of the US fight for independence, conveniently erasing the black (and native) presence from the narrative. Writing nearly a century after Nell's organizing, Woodson noted that white historians had minimized the importance of Crispus Attucks, which he interpreted as part of the broader resistance to including black people in the national story. He told readers of *The Negro History Bulletin*, "A Professor of the University of Pennsylvania once questioned the Editor's playing up of Crispus as a hero, saying that he was only a roustabout." Likewise, "A Harvard professor once called the Editor to account also for emphasizing the martyrdom of Crispus Attucks, pointing out that he was not the only hero in the Boston Massacre," and they did so even though Woodson had "the documentary evidence to show that Crispus Attucks was the leader in the attack; and, therefore, while not the only hero, he was the hero of the day." He added, "The most trustworthy accounts of the event support this contention of the priority of the martyrdom of the sable descendant of despised Negro and Indian forbears."[30]

To work against such threats of erasure and hold the public accountable, William Cooper Nell noted the legacy of Crispus Attucks during the antebellum era, hoping to expose the contradictions inherent in American freedom as it continued to be predicated on black enslavement. He helped resurrect the commemoration of the Boston Massacre, and, more specifically, he encouraged the celebration of Crispus Attucks Day. Speaking on Crispus Attucks Day on March 5, 1862, he asserted, "When the authorities of the town of Boston voted to merge the 5th of March celebration into the 4th of July, it would have been very well, and no need for its revival as a special commemoration, had the people not so entirely, from that day to this, forgotten that the colored man was one of the 'all men created free and equal,' and that he had with them shared the dangers of that struggle which resulted in the severance of the American colonies from the domination of monarchical England."[31] He argued that there would be no need for Attucks Day as a separate celebration from July Fourth if the United States had not fallen prey to the great amnesia that had become so commonplace in public memory and that had conditioned the national identity, whereby black people had been written out of the nation's history and thus narratively framed as undeserving of equal rights and protections. Such rhetorical provocations would continuously be made, especially by advocates of Negro History Week. African Americans, including Woodson, continued to express hope for a day when such separate commemorative holidays would not be necessary and when whitewashed histories would be replaced with transformed curricula unscathed by antiblackness and racist ideology. However, pending such thorough transformation, they recognized the persistent need for such insurgent intellectual traditions and public history organizing.

THE TRADITION OF public commemorations did not begin or end with Crispus Attucks Day. As the wind of the antislavery movement spread across the Atlantic world, African Americans clung to historic emancipation dates in the diaspora as a way of reflecting on how far black people had come since being forcefully brought to the Americas. They circulated historical information about the events, using written texts, cultural resources, and rumor, as they continued to engage in the unfinished work of abolition. Indeed, free black people in the North recognized their consanguinity with black men and women still in bondage. They insisted that even as they gained freedom, they maintained a shared vulnerability with all black people, including those still in chains. The historical transcript notes celebrations on July 5 to commemorate the abolition of slavery in New York in 1827; August 1 to commemorate the end of slavery in British colonies in 1834; and while there were no documented public commemorations of Haitian independence, the historical transcript documents how African Americans framed the significance of those subsequent events of black emancipation in relation to Haitian independence, which was gained by enslaved people defeating European forces and declaring the nation's freedom on January 1, 1804.[32]

James McCune Smith, a man born enslaved in Manhattan who had become the first African American to earn a medical degree (in Glasgow, Scotland), recalled the first Emancipation Day celebration in New York. He was fourteen years old when the state passed its Emancipation Act on July 4, 1827. However, African Americans commemorated their freedom on July 5 in order to avoid white backlash against black celebrations falling on the same day as (white) American independence. The one-day delay, in many respects, symbolized the distance between American freedom and the freedom of African American people. Smith recalled that black people had lined the streets of New York City to celebrate their crossing over from slavery to freedom. He also noted the diversity of black people in the crowd; they represented "every State in the Union, and not a few with gay bandanna handkerchiefs, betraying their West Indian birth: neither was Africa itself unrepresented, hundreds who had survived the middle passage, and a youth in slavery joined in the joyful procession." Smith proclaimed, "That was a celebration! A real, full-souled, full-voiced shouting for joy, and marching through the crowded streets, with feet jubilant to songs of freedom!"[33]

Emancipation Day celebrations were a reminder of progress toward an incomplete goal—a time to reflect on, celebrate, and refuel for a continued black freedom struggle. Smith knew that better than anyone else; even after July 4, 1827, his own mother continued to be enslaved by the white man who had fathered him.

Since she had been born enslaved in South Carolina and owned by a citizen of that state, a loophole in New York's law abolishing slavery allowed for her prolonged captivity. That complicated family dynamic was one shared by many black people. Participants in Emancipation Day celebrations were connected to African-descended people still enslaved in various parts of the Americas, some in more intimate ways than others.

Early commemorative events, when African Americans engaged in public celebrations of black history, anticipated Emancipation Day celebrations during and after the Civil War. The latter included African American communities commemorating the Emancipation Proclamation, following its signing on January 1, 1863; and similarly, Juneteenth celebrations, which commemorated the delayed arrival of emancipation to enslaved people in Galveston, Texas, on June 19, 1865.[34] Such celebrations were often planned by churches and other religious institutions, as those organizations were deeply integrated into the social fabric of African American communities. For instance, in 1892, leaders of the National Baptist Convention provided instructions for Juneteenth celebrations, especially since that year's holiday fell on a Sunday. They called for communities to hold "a GRAND REUNION of the OLD and YOUNG FREEDMEN," which was to commence by having the church bell rung "by the oldest member of the church" at 5:00 a.m. They also proposed appropriate themes and scriptures that might inform the minister's sermon. More important, they encouraged communities to hold an "Ex-slave reunion" where "Everybody that knows anything about the evils of slavery" could come forward and bear witness to what they remembered of the violent institution, thus passing on their memories to inspire continued work to uplift the race. The program stressed the importance of continued educational work in schools and colleges, identifying education as a key method of addressing "the disadvantages under which the negro was 'turned loose' at the close of the war." In addition to the sermons, bell ringing, dinners, and educational fundraisers, the Baptist leaders encouraged the convention's members to "have a good old fashion shout and give thanks to God for our freedom all day long."[35]

WHEN I READ the printed advertisement for the 1892 Juneteenth celebration, I was struck by the call for "a good old fashion shout" as an accompaniment of testimonies commemorating black emancipation and reflections on the history of slavery. It reminded me of Zora Neale Hurston's writing about "the shout" within the cultural context of African American religious life and the history that had shaped such characteristics of black expression. Indeed, the shout referenced by the Baptist leaders could be traced back to hush harbors and praise houses in the woods, back to the African derived ring shout—a flash of the spirit that was, in form, a diasporic gesture, performance, and artifact translated across many linguistic and geographic contexts.[36] But more important, as Hurston noted, "Shouting is a community thing. It thrives in concert." Building on her observations of black religion, she continued, "It is the first shout that is difficult for the preacher to arouse. After that one they are likely to sweep like fire over the church."[37] The connections among Hurston's writing in the 1930s, the commemorative celebration in 1892, and Emancipation Day celebrations in the 1820s were a reminder that "the shout" was itself a historical artifact: a performance that carried memory and cultural knowledge. And like that ritual, the roots of black memory work—or the first shout of black history, to speak metaphorically—almost certainly occurred much earlier than the lineage traced in this essay.

Black history has always been about more than what is written down. The memories shared by the old and young freedmen in

Texas, the "full-souled, full-voiced shouting" recalled by Smith, the songs and dances recorded by Hurston, and the words and feelings lined out by Miss Butterfield during the Black History Month programs of my youth point to a kind of memory work that defies the "world of paper" that typically confines our methods of researching and studying the past.[38] I would be remiss if I did not make this point while reflecting on the historical consciousness of black people, as I explore remnants of what has been passed down as knowledge about the black past and committed to memory in African American communities over generations.

Black memory work is about power: the power to determine how we interpret our lives in the past and present; the power to describe the textured realities of black cultures on our own terms; and it is a tradition of historical knowledge production and commemoration in which the quest for freedom is understood to be an animating feature of black social life. History, for black people, by necessity became more than a record of past events and the names of people spelled out on paper. It was also a means of cultivating the spiritual strivings of a people who were left for dead, socially and politically, but who refused death, choosing instead to study their past and present to chart paths toward more dignified lives for the future.

Black history is also a weapon to be deployed in a protracted war. African Americans are just like all other communities of the human species in their possession of history and culture. Their possession of heritage is thus quite ordinary. However, memories preserved in black communities have led generation after generation to recognize that they face extraordinary forces invested in the constant denigration, silencing, and erasure of their heritage as a means of justifying and prolonging their subjugation. Such external threats result from the fact that black people's oppression has been so deeply woven into the social fabric of the modern world. Thus, African Americans' cause for historical commemoration and study was always political in nature. To borrow from Black History Month's founder, it was a matter of life and death: a fight against powerful forces that sought to make black people "a negligible factor in the thought of the world."[39]

Critical study of black memory work is necessary if this tradition is to evolve and maintain its resilience in the face of both present threats and those that are likely to arise in the years ahead. Indeed, one of the enduring lessons of the journey outlined in the previous pages is that retrenchment and attempts to erase black history are persistent. In fact, they are just as persistent as calls to remember and bear witness among the persecuted. *I'll Make Me a World* seeks to clarify why the struggle continues to be worth the trouble, despite the persistent attacks from powerful forces.

To be clear, I caution against simply taking a defensive posture in our collective efforts to study and provide more honest interpretations of the black past. The best models of memory work in the African American tradition have always been about more than responding to external threats. We must also be disciplined enough to think outside the noise of whiteness and naysayers, as such forces create distractions seeking to direct our attention away from more pressing aims. There is a time for correcting myths for pragmatic purposes; however, there are also times when our creative work must focus inward, on our own imagination, when we must intentionally operate outside the terms and boundaries set by the oppressive forces in high places. Black memory work can not only be about negation; there must also be a positive project—an assertion of our own communal beliefs even if they carry little weight in convincing skeptical or hostile parties. To allow such external threats to be the primary forces that shape black history, or our advocacy for Black History Month, is likely to compromise the integrity and rigor of the work. Given the stakes of this knowledge, scholars and advocates of black history must continue to evolve in our thinking. We must push ourselves to grow in what we study from the black past, how we study it, and toward what ends.

Failing to take seriously the work of black memory, especially during this desperate hour, would be a dereliction of duty. Woodson once described black historians and memory workers as warriors on the front lines; as culture keepers whose job it is to protect our gifts. He painted a picture of black memory workers "standing like the watchman on the wall, ever mindful of what calamities we have suffered from misinterpretation in the past and looking out with a scrutinizing eye for everything indicative of a similar attack."[40] He understood the stakes of this work to be high. It was spirit work, not just about representation on paper or the recollection of facts. Those were merely the elements of a protocol to create a more expansive ceremony. Woodson understood that as a people from whom so much has been taken, our memories, our songs, our stories as African Americans are our greatest power. They are gifts—first to ourselves and then to the world.

Studying the black past has always been about investing in the present and future lives of black people. By choosing to provide an account of their own histories, African Americans set out to craft narratives about the past that were honest, clarifying, and usable. *I'll Make Me a World* is about the inner life of this creation story, about the characteristics of black social life that gave way to the traditions of Black History Month, as well as the intellectual and political imperatives that have led black people to work so hard in sustaining the tradition for the last one hundred years.

Our stories are like wings. It was only through our stories that generations of black people came to know of their gift: that we can fly. Black memories taught us that even among the lowly, the 'buked and scorned, flight was possible. This is a lesson worthy of repetition. So in the pages ahead, I will do my best to line it out.

PART II

THE NEGRO DIGS UP HIS PAST

Searching for Black History in the Everyday

If the past is another country, then I am its citizen. I am the relic of an experience most preferred not to remember, as if the sheer will to forget could settle or decide the matter of history. I am a reminder that the twelve million crossed the Atlantic Ocean and the past is not yet over. I am the progeny of the captives. I am the vestige of the dead. And history is how the secular world attends to the dead.[1]

—SAIDIYA HARTMAN, *LOSE YOUR MOTHER: A JOURNEY ALONG THE ATLANTIC SLAVE ROUTE* (2008)

IN 2018, I WAS SEARCHING through archives at Jackson State University, hoping to find coverage of Negro History Week celebrations in Mississippi's segregated schools. In my quest for ephemera and written accounts, I stumbled upon a bound set of letters—some typed, some handwritten—by African American teachers that forced me to ponder the deeper cultural and political significance of black memory work to the souls of black folk. The letters, from 1949, documented gross inequities in the state's school system. They also revealed unexpected details about the ordinary lives of black teachers and students. In their own words, African American educators outlined details from their everyday realities, thus documenting social facts of black history, stories from their social worlds that went beyond the names of monumental figures or details about iconic events. They rendered vivid descriptions of their daily lives that would otherwise be forgotten.

One particular letter in neat cursive handwriting, by Miss Mary Ross Jones, made a lasting impression on me. Miss Jones described the overcrowding at her school just one mile north of Jackson. Eight educators worked "in a three teacher type school . . . with four in the three room school and four in a small open church." The school had "the large enrollment of approximately four hundred and eighty children," yet there were no partitions to divide the open church into separate classrooms because, as she explained, the large number of students made such organization physically impossible. However, the image of eight educators working in a school fit for three teachers with nearly five hundred children was not what caused the hairs on the back of my neck to stand on end; it was Miss Jones's detailed account of what was required of her every day to operate the school in the small open church that caught my attention as I sat, pressed for time, rapidly skimming through uncatalogued historical materials held in plastic containers on the top floor of the university library.[2]

Miss Jones explained, "Fridays we are asked to make changes by moving seats and giving a general cleaning for Sunday. And on Mondays we change the seats back for teaching. . . . Sometimes during the week we are asked to arrange the church for night service. . . . Therefore, we have to move our bulletin boards, charts, and other class room materials down and put it up each morning." And yet regularly scheduled worship services were not the only thing that interfered with the school day. Miss Jones also described how sometimes she, her colleagues, and students had "to arrange for a funeral during school hours." It was that detail that left me dead in my tracks.

Black schools, dating back to the nineteenth century, often began in churches. I was aware of that. However, I never stopped to consider what that meant in practice for teachers and students. In addition to pushing me to notice more detail and nuance, Miss Jones's story forced me to sit with the deeper meaning of the history I was pursuing, namely that there was and continues to be a distinctive intimacy between death and black memory work in African American social life. African Americans' pursuit of knowledge about the black past, as a foundation of liberatory education, is inextricably linked to their struggles to attend to and acknowledge their dead. It's not just about listing their names among those who have passed on but about giving an account of the substance of their lives and asserting their value in a world that has perpetually condemned black people both in life and in death. Researching, studying, and commemorating black history, for African Americans, became a ceremony of the living to honor and remember the deceased—to insist that black people's lives were valuable and that those lives had been filled with lessons and knowledge, as well as beauty and hard truths about the world. Black people have used knowledge of the black past to restore honor to their predecessors; and by asserting that past black lives were valuable, the creators of black history recognized the value of black lives in the present and future.

In fact, the memory of black people's unfortunate intimacy with death and their violent erasure from history shaped a conviction among African Americans about the necessity of memorialization.[3] The practice of remembering and studying stories that account for the lives of those who have died is not something black people can take for granted. The silencing of black life and history, through white supremacy's predatory practices of extraction and systematic erasure, has long been worked out through various actions that have violated the dead, indeed through the desecration of their memory, the denial of their struggles and contributions. Yet black memory workers—including historians both formally trained and untrained, teachers, storytellers, and artists—have found ways to attend to the deceased and to clear a path for the gift of their stories. As I see it, Black History Month emerged as a commemorative practice to memorialize the richly textured political and cultural life black people created despite their unnatural relationship to death precipitated by antiblack violence.

I have returned to the scene in Miss Jones's classroom several times since encountering it, because I continue to see traces of a relationship between African Americans' struggle to preserve and study the black past and their insistence on honoring the dead in a world that denigrates them. Part of the cultural and political significance of black history and Black History Month stems from the power struggle surrounding what knowledge we choose to carry forward from black lives in the past in service of our efforts to live freer and more dignified lives in the present and future. Thus, black death and dying, historically speaking, has been top of mind for black memory workers. The words and deeds of various African American figures over the course of history, some who are recognizable and others, like Miss Jones, who are lesser known, provide important examples to explore this distinctive quality in the black historical tradition.

IN COMMEMORATING the hundred-year journey of Black History Month, I intentionally turn to Miss Jones's classroom—an unfamiliar scene in African American life—for three primary reasons. The first is that her letter reflects the everyday life of ordinary black people. A major contention in *I'll Make Me a World* is that there is a need for deeper engagement with black histories that move beyond commemorating the lives of monumental men and women and for wider recognition of historical narratives that focus on the everyday. My goal is not to disavow individuals of rare achievement but to insist that commemoration of the latter should not come at the expense of a wider appreciation of the ordinary. As expressed beautifully by the Guyanese historian and political leader Walter Rodney, the survival of black people on this side of the Atlantic is one of the greatest miracles in modern history, and "every day black people in the Americas perform the miracle anew."[4] Attending to the details that gave form to the everyday aspects of black life and the practices that helped sustain African American communities is critical to rigorous historical interpretations of the past.

Early celebrations of black history were often structured on a historical model that valorized great black men and women for pragmatic reasons. Such stories provided counternarratives that were indisputable. They could be held up as "a living, breathing, convincing argument against the claim that the Negro's intellectual capacities fit him only for slavery," to borrow from the formerly enslaved educator and textbook author Edward A. Johnson, who offered these words in his 1890 book *A School History of the Negro Race in America from 1619 to 1890.*[5] Black memory workers such as Johnson told the story of black genius and rare achievement, including stories of great precolonial African civilizations, especially Egypt and Ethiopia, to answer questions about whether black people were intelligent or capable of leadership and to demonstrate that they, too, had created cultural gifts that had contributed immensely to the greater good of humanity. They insisted that ancestors such as Crispus Attucks, Phillis Wheatley, Benjamin Banneker, Frederick Douglass, and Sojourner Truth were irrefutable evidence that discredited widespread racist lies about black people's supposed intellectual inferiority and unfitness for citizenship. The greater public, especially black youths, needed to have close contact with such stories to help fend off the threat of the antiblack myths so endemic to national narratives and widely circulated forms of racial representation.

Early black memory workers understood the stories of great achievers and other variations of black folk heroes to be sources of inspiration and aspiration—antidotes to miseducation that could fly in the face of everything white people wanted black people to think about ourselves. When advocating for more stories of great black men and women in 1935, Mary McLeod Bethune likened those stories to the statues of great men along the highways of ancient Rome used to inspire Roman youths. Black children, she asserted, also deserved monuments in the form of historical narratives that commemorated the lives of their great men and women. And by "gazing upon their faces," she believed, black youths "might be stimulated to greater achievement and accomplishment."[6]

However, just as early advocates of black history radically reconsidered and responded to fundamental historical questions—such as "Whose life can we learn from?" and "Whose life is important?"—we should continue to evolve and grow in our responses to such queries. One of the greatest lessons left behind by black memory workers is the need to develop the courage to make intentional and ethical decisions about how and what we remember; we should be intentional when choosing the heroes of our day-to-day lives, in our approaches to telling their stories, and through the methods we employ to bring out the value and meaning of their lives.

Miss Mary Ross Jones did not achieve something recognizably "great" by the traditional standards used to evaluate worthiness for historical commemoration and study. Nevertheless, she and her classroom story represent the kind of narratives I refer to in this book as *black histories of the everyday*, stories of ordinary people and the intimate realities of their lives that are worthy of deep study and memorialization for future generations. These are everyday stories that when analyzed and treated with care help us achieve new understanding about the texture of black people's realities. I believe this more expansive lens should be applied not only during the month of February but also in our study of the past more generally. In the pages ahead, I hope to model a commitment to pursuing the gifts of beauty, truth, and deeper knowledge of human complexity by examining the lives of ordinary black people and by turning to lesser known scenes in history as sites in which to dig up valuable knowledge about the black past.

Contrary to popular practice, this commitment to studying the lives of ordinary black people reflects the origin story of black history as a field, as well as the emergence of Black History Month. It was the stories of ordinary people in Carter G. Woodson's life—his formerly enslaved relatives, illiterate black coal miners, "the Negro washerwoman," "the workadays," and other "undistinguished Negroes," to borrow his language—in addition to stories of black genius and heroism that inspired him to think beyond white conceptions of human history. It was black histories of the everyday that inspired and helped sustain the movement he led to popularize the study of black life and culture.[7]

We would do well to remember that Black History Month emerged as a critique of the narrow, racist hierarchies that determine what counts as history. It modeled more just and radically inclusive ways of remembering the past. In keeping with this heroic tradition, contemporary advocates of black memory work might continue to think more expansively about our commemorative practices and approaches to studying history in the present.[8]

When I look at this story of Miss Jones and her students—a story of black resourcefulness in which African American educators made beauty in all the ways they could despite their meager material resources—I see both the realities of black suffering and the resilience of a people in search of human flourishing despite their living in a world in which their subjection was enshrined. I know that both things can be true. What occurred in Miss Jones's classroom is a story of ordinary people making do with what they had in the meantime yet plotting for the achievement of brighter days ahead.

The second reason I found Miss Jones's story to be important was its explicit reference to black death and mourning, which I understand to be essential for understanding the cultural and political stakes of black history in the social life of African American people. As the African American studies scholar Karla F. C. Holloway noted, "The anticipation of death and dying figured into the experiences of black folk so persistently, given how much more omnipresent death was for them than for other Americans, that lamentations and mortification both found their way into public and private representations of African America to an astonishing degree." She traced how the prevalence of death in black life, beyond "inevitable end-of-lifespan events," shaped a response among black Americans, where they "worked this experience into the culture's iconography and included it as an aspect of black cultural sensibility." Indeed, "African American cultural practices—music, literature, and visual arts—all used the facts of black death and dying as their subjects."[9] In agreeing with Holloway, I assert that black history, as a field of study shaped by African American memory work and cultural insights, was also birthed through and marked by a preoccupation with the realities of black death. In such a context, black history functioned, even if not solely or entirely, as a practice of mourning shaped by accumulated grief. It is a ceremony of knowledge production created by the enslaved and then refined and evolved by their progeny as a resource for living, where lessons from the black past may be studied to help mitigate and transform present-day realities in which black people are forced to live "in a context of anticipated death, brutal violence, and enduring dispossession."[10]

Miss Jones's account prompted me to consider the fact that a reckoning with death is always at the forefront of black life, even in the most unexpected ways, even in schools and classrooms, and even as students study in preparation for the future. My mind ran away with itself. I began to imagine what it must have been like for black teachers and their students as they studied lessons in reading, arithmetic, history, and science to then have to transform their classroom, a site of living and learning, to one fit for mourning and the final rites for a community member who had passed on. I traced a through line from the story of Miss Jones's classroom in the 1940s to the scene of a funeral in the Sea Islands off South Carolina just after the legislative end of slavery in the 1860s, in which one woman described witnessing "a group of children, school books in their hands, standing around the grave singing their A, B, C over and over as they stood waiting for the preacher to arrive." The woman felt this act to be "another proof" that for those recently freed people—those children and their loved ones—their educational strivings were never merely an academic pursuit but also an expression of their spiritual strivings as a people. The recitation of lessons learned in school—a school possibly run out of a church—was deemed so consecrated and revered among a people to whom education had been so long denied that the children's singing of the alphabet was akin to a sorrow song, a spiritual in its own right.[11]

Miss Jones's story also forced me to think about the prevalence of death, or the threat of death, in some of the most prominent stories in black history, which I learned about as a young student. There was no way to fully learn about Martin Luther King, Jr., and Malcolm X without also learning about how their lives had been ended prematurely. There was no way to learn about the Black Panthers without learning about the long list of assassinations used to politically neutralize the Black Power movement. There was no way to appreciate the activism of Fannie Lou Hamer without learning about the realities of sexual violence she was subjected to as a black woman in Jim Crow Mississippi, and which contributed to the deaths of so many black women in the shadows. There was no way to critically study the emergence of "the New Negro" without also noticing the "nadir" in African American history, a period marked by the specter of lynching; without seeing the NAACP's banner, bearing the words "A Man Was Lynched Yesterday," hanging over the story of black intellectual vitality, imagination, and collective struggle as it unfolded during the Black Renaissance era. There was no way to learn about transatlantic slavery without also learning about the unimaginable horrors of the Middle Passage and the millions of people who met unspeakable ends en route, as well as the many other millions who survived only to be forced to struggle to create meaningful black lives amid an unnatural, perpetual recurrence of black death and dying.

Reckoning with death—and particularly with the lives and actions of people who have passed on—is central to the work of history, though we rarely discuss our studies and commemoration of the past in such terms. All human societies, ancient and modern, revere the dead. They preserve stories about them as key resources in forming social worlds in the present, using them as guides for imagining a future.[12] It is a fact of life. As one philosopher explained, "To be human means above all to bury"—to mark our relationship to the dead and carry forward, through stories and commemorative acts, the lessons accrued from past lives to shape future generations. For "humanity is not a species (Homo sapiens is a species); it is a way of being mortal and relating to the dead."[13]

Yet while attending to the dead is a key expression of our humanity, African Americans recognize how the denigration of their deceased predecessors functions as a key weapon to curtail black freedoms in the present. Indeed, Europeans' and Euro-Americans' attempts to erase an entire race of people's history through the desecration of tombs, histories, and names sought to prevent black people from tending to their dead as a means of disrupting the passing on of their heritage and the formation of social and political life among the enslaved and their descendants. Yet African Americans understand that how we value the dead says something about how we value their living progeny; this struggle is at the heart of black history and the story of its emergence as a distinct body of knowledge about the past.

As an effort to resist erasure and think beyond white conceptions of the past, black history became a key expression of what the historian Vincent Brown called mortuary politics, in which the "relations between the living and the dead" become a site of organizing, activism, and protest precisely because "those relations emerge as a source of struggle."[14] Attempts to erase the identities and history of enslaved captives, and therefore of their descendants, both in the social world and in the material artifacts that represent that world, made the relations between African Americans and their predecessors, from one generation to the next, a perpetual site of political struggle. Time and time again, African Americans contested social forces and capitalist projects that violated the remains of their predecessors and desecrated the memory of them (at times quite literally, when we think of the burial grounds of enslaved people or the selling of their bodies after death as research cadavers).[15]

African Americans' ability to relate to their ancestors has been tested across generations, and given the violent rupture in memory caused by the Middle Passage, it is a struggle unlike any other ethnic or racial group has experienced with such prolonged intensity. As such, a long line of black memory workers has struggled to correct the historical procedures of forced forgetting and erasure, eventually establishing a formalized culture and a set of scholarly protocols around their labors.

Black history as a New World creation came about as a disruption to the deathly violations of black social life enumerated above. Such awareness shaped the political impulse to restore honor to the deceased, becoming central to the work of black culture and African American historical consciousness. Writing of such cultural politics, the Pulitzer Prize–winning author Alice Walker once observed, "We are a people. A people do not throw their geniuses away. And if they are thrown away, it is our duty as artists and as witnesses for the future to collect them again for the sake of our children, and, if necessary, bone by bone."[16]

To be clear, black history is not just about remembering the names of people who have passed on or maintaining evidence that they existed. The more important aspect of this memory work is studying the texture and substance of their living and to do so honestly is to also reckon with how those lives ended. It is about noticing their individuality as well as their relationship to the collective. In elaborating on Walker's observation, I would also insist that black history is about more than responding to erasure, forced forgetting, and flattening of African-descended people; it is also about insisting on more nuanced understandings of their experiments with human life, and pursuing the wisdom that awaits in the stories of both extraordinary achievement and quotidian reality.

Commemorating and reinterpreting the lives of the deceased played a major role in generating the force and momentum that helped grow the black historical tradition as an intellectual project in service of the black freedom movement. Readers will recall the early establishment of Crispus Attucks Day in the antebellum North by black abolitionists as an effort to correct his erasure in the story of American independence, and they will also remember how Mary Church Terrell established the practice of celebrating Frederick Douglass Day on February 14 in black public schools in 1897, two years following Douglass's death. As I see it, black history has always been a key expression of black mortuary politics. For indeed, "history is how the secular world attends to the dead," to borrow from African American studies scholar Saidiya Hartman, and this has been especially true for black people.[17]

Mainstream history, written by white historians in the United States throughout the early twentieth century, condemned black life in ways that justified the killing and oppression of black people.[18] The connection between narrative condemnation in history and literature and the violence enacted upon African Americans led Carter G. Woodson to proclaim in 1933, "There would be no lynching if it did not start in the schoolroom." What's more, while scholars of black history set out to document and bear witness to the injustices black people experienced, which too often ended in unjust killings and early deaths, this area of study has always been about reinterpreting and reframing the lives of deceased ancestors, heroes, and communities of the past. The social life African Americans created amid the unnatural prevalence of early death in their communities is connected to universal aspects of human societies while also being driven by particular motivations in response to the distinct social antagonisms black people face in the afterlife of slavery.[19]

Miss Jones's story was important to me for a third and final reason; that is, the presence of black youths in her classroom and their proximity to the social realities of death and dying in African American communities. That detail reminded me that history is a primary means through which African Americans have cared for those who have passed on, but it is also connected to a deep investment in future generations. Thus, while death is present in Miss Jones's story, so, too, is a commitment to life and emergent black futures. By attending to the dead, African Americans worked to carry forward and sustain a heritage for the young and those not yet born. Indeed, black youths were always cited as a primary motivation of African Americans' struggle to preserve and correct narratives about the black past.

The children in Miss Jones's classroom represent the future-oriented frame of *I'll Make Me a World*, even as the conditions of their lives demanded that they attend to the past. In keeping with this reality, I have worked to model a set of dispositions and practices for those of us among the living who desire to be more intentional in our relationship with the black past—identifying things we can do and teach to subsequent generations as we attend to history through study, commemorative practices, and preservation, understanding these things to be essential to our pursuit of greater justice and freedom in the future for all people, especially black people. What's more, I would contend that how we attend to the dead is intimately connected to how we attend to the young because both require a commitment to heritage, as the maintenance of our heritage is essential to the preservation of life.

While it was the details of Miss Jones's letter that reminded me of that lesson—about the intimacy between the dead and the living in the work of black history—this assertion can also be found among black thinkers and champions of black history across time and space, before and after Miss Jones's letter written in 1949. The lessons can be traced through the ideas of prominent thinkers such as Zora Neale Hurston, Arturo Schomburg, and Alice Walker, as well as my own teachers in more recent times. In the pages that follow, I will elaborate on how and why nuanced study of the black past and an honest reckoning with black death have been so central to African Americans' pursuit of justice and human flourishing. I believe that such an honest analysis of black history and the politics that shape it is necessary to appreciate what continues to be at stake in this work, even one hundred years after the first national commemoration of black history.

GOING BACK AND collecting what is left of our predecessors—the stories of their lives, their names, and any remnants of their social worlds—has been a key strategy in forging and sustaining black political life in a world deeply predicated on black suffering. Such remains, both material and intangible, speak to black achievement and black struggles, and they affirm to subsequent generations that they are not alone in their suffering, that what they see happening around them is no figment of their imagination. Such remains help us see and know the truth of our lives in greater context. This philosophy of black history was sketched out just months before the inaugural celebration of Negro History Week. Two months prior to the first celebration in February 1926, Arturo Schomburg's famous essay "The Negro Digs Up His Past" appeared in

The New Negro: An Interpretation, the historic anthology of essays, poems, and stories by Black Renaissance writers compiled by the philosopher and Howard University professor Alain Locke. In his essay, the Afro–Puerto Rican bibliophile described a philosophy of black history that has persisted over the last century, and his language builds on a historical consciousness exhibited by black people well before his time.

Schomburg's theory of black history was based on the idea that African Americans must dig up and reconstruct their past as a people in order to chart a path for a better future, and he insisted that "History must restore what slavery took away, for it is the social damage of slavery that the present generations must repair and offset."[20] Importantly, he described the project of black history as a self-initiated pursuit. More than mere objective scholarly inquiry, the emergence of black history is fundamentally a political project of self-determination and self-definition, one in which "the Negro," himself, excavates, preserves, and studies the black past as an antidote to imposed miseducation. To be clear, his point was not to suggest that only black people should study and write about black history; however, scholars such as Schomburg, Woodson, and their contemporaries made it abundantly clear that the political stakes of such work were immediately relevant to the lived experiences of African-descended people; black history was to serve as an intellectual foundation for their political struggles waged in the present. Schomburg's archaeological appeal outlined a praxis—that is, a theory and practice—for studying the black past that was framed as an integral part of black people's political response to the problem of widespread antiblackness in the Americas resulting from transatlantic slavery and its attendant racial ideologies.

For Schomburg, black historical excavation, preservation, and study were means of black worldmaking. By outlining that praxis, he gave language to a tradition of black memory work that had been practiced and experimented with by African-descended people before him. For instance, he worked closely with other black history collectors in New York City and other parts of the diaspora in the previous decades, even cofounding the critically important Negro Society for Historical Research in 1911 alongside the African American journalist John Edward Bruce, a man who had been born enslaved in 1856 and who had begun his education as a fugitive slave.[21] Schomburg's theorizing about how and why the Negro must dig up his past was thus less a novel idea and more the naming of a long-standing intellectual tradition. In fact, Schomburg cited black memory workers of previous generations as his guides, noting that "the Negro historian to-day digs under the spot where his predecessor stood and argued." That historical impulse formed a core part of black consciousness in the educational lives of African-descended people as far back as the slavery era.

The instinct to dig up the black past can be found in the stories of enslaved people secretly reading newspaper accounts about the Haitian Revolution to their fellow captives. It can be traced in the stories of early-nineteenth-century black youths such as Alexander Crummell, whose parents shared stories about their memories of life before the Middle Passage. It can also be traced to the writings of fugitive slaves who produced counternarratives of black life, such as Harriet Jacobs and James W. C. Pennington, both of whom became schoolteachers.

Commemorating the black past can also be traced to the actions of enslaved black people prior to literature written by fugitive slaves, notably in a complex story found in the archive of slavery in which a group of enslaved women nearly incited an insurrection on the slave ship *Hudibras*, traveling from Africa to the Americas in 1786. The event transpired after a woman who was "universally esteemed" among the captives unexpectedly died aboard the ship, leading her fellow bondswomen to insist on being the last to view the body and to witness its proper laying to rest.

I find this to be an appropriate place to elaborate on Schomburg's archaeological appeal, because where else should one go to dig up the black past, if not to a grave beneath the earth or in the sea? What is it precisely that one hopes to find in such sites if not the remains of what was once a fleshly body and artifacts from past lives? The story of the *Hudibras* is yet another reminder of death's inconspicuous presence in history in general, yet the large amount of space it holds in the annals of black history. It also highlights more directly the role that death plays in histories of black political life formed in the wake of slavery.

WE HAVE NO record of the name of the woman who died on board the *Hudibras*. Identifiable markers of individuality and culture were rarely recorded in written accounts left by white enslavers. African captives experienced the erasing of their identities as one of the many violent acts employed to reduce them to fungible objects. The historical erasure experienced in real time—as captives' names reflecting diverse African linguistic and cultural customs were replaced by English, Spanish, French, Dutch, and Portuguese names—is further underscored by the fact that slavery's records, which we rely on to tell the story of enslaved people, are marred by such silences and forced forgetting. Yet while we have no name for the woman, unusual details were preserved about her life because of the events occasioned by her untimely death.

William Butterworth, a seventeen-year-old English boy from Leeds, England, took copious notes about the woman's leadership and the spiritual nourishment she provided to her fellow captives. We have his name because it is through his written account—that of a free, white man—that we gain access to that enslaved African woman's story, a reflection of race and power in the world of literature as it expanded through the slavery era. Yet according to that white observer, the African captives and their enslavers applied conflicting values to the woman's life that reflect the core struggles at the heart of black history as conceived of by African Americans living in the time of slavery and then in its wake.

As Butterworth observed, the deceased woman had been "the soul of sociality, and, amongst her country women, an oracle of literature." When that popular woman was alive, she would "sing slow airs" and "recite such pieces as moved the passions"; in doing so, she aroused "joy or grief, pleasure or pain," all "in order to render more easy the hours of her sisters in exile." Butterworth also described the systematic and formalized manner in which the women organized themselves, as their leader addressed them in a language unknown to him. When allowed to use the quarterdeck during their time out of the ship's hold, the women "formed themselves into circles, the youngest constituting the innermost circle, and so on, several deep, the most aged always being found outermost." At the center of the innermost circle could be found the orator and songstress: "her attitude, kneeling, nearly prostrate, with her hands stretched forth and placed upon the deck, and her head resting on her hands." She delivered sermons and songs in this posture, according to Butterworth, with "the other females joining in responses, or a kind of chorus, at the close of particular sentences." Over time, Butterworth surmised that the woman's orations "might be speaking of friends far distant, and homes now no more." It's likely that he gained some understanding of the women's songs and sayings through broken translations by an enslaved boy named Bristol, as the young boy understood the languages spoken by the captives while also being fluent in English. The boy had been given the name Bristol because he was owned by a man who had ordered that he be taken back to the city of Bristol, England, where he would be gifted to a friend of his enslaver.[22]

To the ship's crew, the woman, who to the white enslavers bore no name, was valued based on cold calculations of European currency: numeric values assigned to her body based on her age, stature, and childbearing abilities that would lead to future earnings for the men and women who might claim her as their property. Yet the other African captives had alternative means of assessing her worth based on the history and people from which they came. In fact, the deceased woman was a keeper of the very heritage that stood at odds with the ideas of her enslavers. This is underscored by Butterworth's descriptions of the woman lining out songs and leading speeches among her fellow captives, in which he suggests that she helped her fellow bondswomen stay connected to a history and sense of humanity based in the homelands from which they had been taken.[23]

Because of her stature among them, the captives experienced her death as a "severe loss." While her death represented a loss of capital to the enslavers, who valued her only as a commodity, to the other African captives, her death was not based on such inhumane evaluative measures. To them she was a keeper of their knowledge, someone who had helped sustain their interior lives despite externally imposed conditions meant to suffocate their souls. Indeed, that woman, who surely had a name that was widely known by the enslaved, helped them remember their "soul value," to borrow from the historian Daina Ramey Berry.[24]

Deaths aboard slave ships were common. That was especially the case for African captives, but also for their white enslavers. Sickness, shipwrecks, violent uprisings, unspeakable violations (of the body, mind, and spirit), death by suicide and infanticide, drowning, starvation, a lack of fresh water, and many other factors contributed to the death toll aboard the ships, leading one historian to refer to them as "floating dungeons."[25] Such deaths, as excessive as they were, were understood as a cost of doing business.

To be clear, while enslavers intended to kill the African captives socially by stripping away their names and violating their kinship ties, among other means, their physical death was mostly incidental. After all, slave traders did not go into the business of trafficking people in order to kill the people they claimed as property. While slavery and racism were illogical in many ways, that wasn't one of them. Captives' deaths were akin to "collateral damage," in a present-day commercial term. As one scholar, Saidiya Hartman, clarified, "Incidental death occurs when life has no normative value, when no humans are involved, when the population is, in effect, seen as already dead. Unlike the concentration camp, the gulag, and the killing field, which had as their intended end the extermination of a population, the Atlantic trade created millions of corpses, but as a corollary to the making of commodities."[26]

Yet irrespective of how much or little the woman who died aboard the *Hudibras* was valued by her captors, her demise was experienced as a great spiritual loss to the enslaved; and her final rites became a struggle symbolizing the greater meaning that death would carry amid the black freedom struggle in the New World. Given the woman's "universally esteemed" status, combined with the reality that many of the enslaved believed their white enslavers to be cannibals, there was a heightened agitation among the women as they were forced back into the hold while the deceased woman's body lay unattended on the deck.

According to Butterworth, it was around five in the evening, and the enslavers were waiting for the next flood tide to carry out the interment. However, the women did not trust the white men with the beloved woman's corpse. Before going belowdecks, "her companions expressed the most heart-felt sorrow. It was loud, deep, and impressive; and they often whispered in her ear," believing that "the spirit still continued in, or hovered about, its former habitation, that it retained all its power, and would execute their commands, in the representation of their wishes, to be remembered to their friends in the other country, when they should meet again." Yet despite their outcry, the female captives were forced belowdecks.

While locked in the hold, the women let out "loud and generous murmurings," which expressed the thoughts going through their minds. They demanded to see the body of their sister lowered into the water with their own eyes. They feared that they had been "sent below, in order that [the white men] might begin to eat their dead favourite." The women did not cease protesting until they were permitted to see the woman's body consigned to the sea. Fearing an uprising, the ship's captain eventually saw fit to oblige them, allowing several of them to come above, and "in their presence, the corpse was lowered into the water."

The corpse of the captive African woman for whom no name was recorded was not unindividuated flesh, even as she and her fellow bondswomen underwent a process that sought to reduce them and their future generations to property. The captives insisted that she was a woman bound up in a social world of meaning, history, and culture that carried value for the people around her. Though the burial was not in keeping with their customs, it was carried out with "more decency ... than generally appeared in the funeral of a slave." Then, and only then, "the murmurs subsided."

The struggle of those women to have the last viewing of the captive's body was their way of insisting on having the final say over who she was and the value of her life. Their act of protest anticipated a tradition of black memory work that would proliferate in the centuries to come.

I CONSIDER STORIES such as the one above to be integral to the intellectual and political traditions that informed the early development of what we have inherited as Black History Month. The traditions that informed the commemorative practice have many beginnings, reaching back before the emergence of Negro History Week in 1926, as the previous chapter showed. Its origin story extends from the political life created and sustained among African-descended people such as those on the *Hudibras*, just as it persisted in gatherings of black social life in the hush harbors and the secret places to which the enslaved escaped to think, imagine, and be otherwise after they arrived in America. While the stories of those people and their actions were not recorded in US history books and taught in US schools, black people held on to pieces of those histories in their own ways.

Black history and all the ways in which African Americans have strategized to preserve, study, and commemorate it developed as part of the mortuary politics of the enslaved and their descendants. Given the particularities of slavery, black people have been forced to reckon with the fact that our present struggles extend not only to what is said about those of us among the living but to what is said (and not said) about the people we came from, those who are among the dead. The women aboard the *Hudibras* who insisted on offering an alternative narrative account of their fellow captive, like subsequent generations of black historical subjects, refused such methods of social domination through a range of practices, memory work and the preservation of life through heritage being principally among them.

THE BLACK WRITER and anthropologist Zora Neale Hurston expressed deep concern for how African Americans employed history and memorialization when attending to the lives of black artists and leaders who had passed on. Her concern was motivated by a desire to preserve black history in service of future studies by subsequent generations. In 1945, she wrote a letter to the historian and sociologist W. E. B. Du Bois, proposing that Du Bois, as "Dean of American Negro Artists" (a title of endearment Hurston gave the scholar), lead an effort to organize "a cemetery for the illustrious Negro dead." Her proposal echoes the mortuary politics embodied by the women aboard the *Hudibras* and elaborated by Schomburg; indeed, the same conception of the black past I experienced through my encounter with Miss Jones's letter.[27]

Nearly twenty years after the first Negro History Week celebration and exactly thirty years after Woodson founded the Association for the Study of Negro Life and History in 1915 as the first professional organization committed to such an academic endeavor, Hurston believed that more needed to be done. She feared that many important aspects of black history and culture might be lost. In appealing to Du Bois, she insisted that we "let no Negro celebrity, no matter what financial condition they might be in at death, lie in inconspicuous forgetfulness. We must assume the responsibility of their graves being known and honored." The absence of such a "tangible thing allows our people to forget, and their spirits evaporate."

While Hurston was especially interested in black artists and writers, her concerns also extended to black political leaders and freedom fighters. When describing who should be represented at this cemetery for the illustrious Negro dead, she insisted, "There one ought to also see the tomb of Nat Turner. Naturally, his bones have been since gone to dust, but that should not prevent his tomb being among us, Fred Douglas [sic] and all the rest." Her concern about loss and erasure is substantiated by the stories of those two radical abolitionists, the former having led the bloodiest slave insurrection in US history, the latter having successfully escaped slavery and then having become the most influential black political voice of the nineteenth century. Hurston's warning is substantiated because to this day there continue to be questions about the scattered remains of Nat Turner. Following the 1831 insurrection, Turner was captured, and the whites of Southampton, Virginia, dismembered his body, taking some pieces of him for scientific research and others for trophies. In 2016, an inquiry surfaced about Turner's skull possibly being in someone's private possession. Thus, contrary to Hurston's assumption, it seems that Turner's bones had not completely "gone to dust" but may very well continue to be among us.

I remember when I first learned of Turner's story, including his death and dismemberment. I was in third grade, and my class was preparing for our school's annual Black History Month program. Turner became the center of a lesson in my third-grade classroom, as a black folk hero, when Miss Shirley Todman, an African American teacher from North Carolina, told my classmates and me his story after becoming concerned that we were not taking our rehearsals seriously. Sitting at her desk, she gave us an impromptu lecture on Turner. I can still see the big picture window immediately behind her, through which was visible the school's rear playground, featuring a blue metal swing set, monkey bars, and the tall iron jungle gym we loved to climb during recess.

To contextualize our assignment, which was to memorize Eloise Greenfield's poem about the night flyer Harriet Tubman, Miss Todman explained how our freedom had been bought and paid for by the people whose lives we were commemorating. She insisted that we had to remember and study the bravery of these people. We were to study the courage and collective struggle demonstrated by their stories and hopefully be inspired to put some of what we learned into practice in our own lives. She stressed that the world they lived in and the world we had inherited could be quite hateful toward black people. She also told us that Nat Turner's story was evidence of this.

That was my first time hearing Turner's name—and I would never forget it. Turner wasn't just killed after fighting to free the enslaved, Miss Todman explained. She looked at us as she dragged her nails, covered in gold polish, down her outstretched arm, describing how "they took parts of his body. They made purses and hats and clothes from his skin." I remember thinking that such a thing could not possibly be true. I had previously learned something about the violence experienced by enslaved people; however, the story Miss Todman shared was not just violent but evil in a way that was impossible for my eight-year-old mind to grasp. It would be some time before I fully understood the meaning of that kind of violation of the enslaved. As a third-grade student, I did not fully understand how such disregard and violation of human life was part of the process of maintaining the social hierarchies between enslaved and free, between black and white, in the United States. The lesson embedded in Miss Todman's lecture, I eventually grasped decades later.

For some reason, I carried my skepticism of Miss Todman's story into adulthood. Even as a child, I knew that she was one for dramatics and hyperbole. Her stories, though true, felt embellished. However, I remember my shock when reading details about the Southampton insurrection as a graduate student and being slightly ashamed to learn that Miss Todman had indeed been telling the truth all those years ago. To this day, Greenfield's poem occasionally pops into my mind, reminding me that "Harriet Tubman didn't take no stuff / Wasn't scared of nothing neither / Didn't come in this world to be no slave / And wasn't going to stay one either."[28]

Just as Miss Todman's lecture about Turner was true, Hurston's anxieties about black erasure and dismemberment, both literal and symbolic, were justified. The scattered remains of Nat Turner are evidence of this. It is also reflected in the fact that generations of black students would be denied access to historical information about his life and those of other black freedom fighters. Yet the lessons of Turner's life were taught to me by Miss Todman, even in the absence of a proper burial of his corpse. Together, these stories represent the threat of inconspicuous forgetfulness named by Hurston and, simultaneously, black people's persistent efforts to commemorate their leaders who have passed on, even in the face of America's collective amnesia. Despite efforts to the contrary, African Americans have kept Nat Turner's memory alive.

I now recognize that people such as Hurston, as well as my third-grade teacher, carried on in the same tradition described by the nineteenth-century African American historian George Washington Williams when writing about Nat Turner. In his 1881 textbook, Williams wrote that while "no stone marks the resting-place of this martyr to freedom . . . The image of Nat Turner is carved on the fleshy tablets of four million hearts." He argued that although Turner's story was generally kept from African Americans by formal written histories and school textbooks, his memory persists because "the women have handed the tradition to their children, and the 'Prophet Nat.' is still marching on."[29] I recall reading that passage for the first time and immediately thinking about Miss Todman and our preparation for my third-grade Black History Month program. Then, after studying the history of African American education more broadly, I began to think about the many thousands of black teachers who kept the memory of Turner alive because they understood him to be an integral part of their history as a people, even as white historians wrote him off as demented and deluded.[30] I learned that, like Miss Todman, the black textbook author and Washington, DC–based schoolteacher John W. Cromwell described the gruesome story of Turner's death to black students. In an article published in *The Journal of Negro History* in 1920, Cromwell described how "[Turner's] body was given over to the surgeons for dissection. He was skinned to supply such souvenirs as purses, his flesh made into grease, and his bones divided as trophies to be handed down as heirlooms. It is said that there still lives a Virginian who has a piece of his skin which was tanned, that another Virginian possesses one of his ears and that the skull graces the collection of a physician in the city of Norfolk."[31]

The burial ground imagined by Hurston was to be a place for commemorating black histories. However, she didn't propose just a burial ground for black leaders, artists, and writers who had passed on; the site she proposed would also serve as a gathering place. She suggested avoiding a chapel, unless sufficient funding was secured to build a chapel grand enough for such a purpose. To avoid some pitiful imitation of historic chapels around the world, Hurston proposed an alternative: "Let there be a hall of meeting, and let the Negro sculptors and painters decorate it with scenes from our own literature and life. Mythology and all." She said that the place could serve multiple purposes, but of course, "funerals can be held from there as well." She dreamed of a place of black learning and literature for those among the living that would commemorate the beautiful experiments with human life exhibited by those who had come before.[32]

Whenever I read Hurston's proposal, I find myself wondering which sculptors and painters she had in mind. Did she imagine the colorful murals of Aaron Douglass gracing the walls of a Cemetery for the Illustrious Negro Dead? Perhaps she gazed upon the murals Douglass had painted in the interiors of several buildings at Fisk University more than a decade prior. The silhouette paintings often depicted a long memory of African people: their achievements prior to enslavement as well as their struggles and triumphs over the course of their odyssey in the Americas. And what of the sculptures? Did Hurston envision the striking sculptures of her fellow Floridian Augusta Savage on display in the cemetery's Hall of Meeting? After all, in the 1920s Savage became known for sculpting busts of prominent black figures, including W. E. B. Du Bois and Marcus Garvey, the Jamaican-born founder and leader of the Universal Negro Improvement Association. However, while those sculptures were celebrated, it was the beautiful sculpture of Savage's nephew that had gained her the most acclaim. In the piece, called *Namin*, Savage rendered the form of a young black boy in a manner that expressed her sophisticated study of black form, expressions, and features. Having been deeply immersed in the world of Black Renaissance artists, Hurston certainly had plenty of black artists to choose from as she imagined such creative works of history for the gathering place conjured up in her mind.

In her letter to Du Bois, Hurston explained that such a project was not only timely but also time sensitive. An expansive amount of land would be necessary, and she proposed "so much as 100 acres." After all, they would have to account for the inclusion of black achievers in the future. Furthermore, she hoped that such an expansive plot of land would help "to prevent white encroachment" and that it might allow for the creation of "an artist colony if ever the need arose." Having been raised in Eatonville, a self-contained incorporated African American community in Florida, Hurston was a strong advocate of black self-determination. Her caution was also motivated by the challenges of white paternalism African American communities and memory workers experienced while operating in a racially stratified society. She expressed a deep concern about preserving control over such a consecrated space, having personally been forced to kowtow to white funders when pursuing support for her work as a writer.

Hurston's cemetery never came to fruition, and there is no evidence of Du Bois ever replying to the proposal. It is possible that he found the idea too extravagant or not the best use of time and money during the mid-1940s, as the world was still steeped in the blood shed during World War II. Nevertheless, black people continued to make history, and black communities continued to honor the dead even though Hurston's project did not succeed, doing so in a variety of ways: through Negro History Week celebrations, by producing new scholarship about black life and culture, and through various acts of commemorating the black past.

The prescience of Hurston's proposal is painful to think about, as I reflect on it eighty years from the date her letter was written, and sixty-five years after her death in 1960. Hurston's fear, unfortunately, became her fate. She died alone and poor and was buried in an unmarked grave. For more than a decade, she was relegated to the forgetfulness of which she had warned in her letter. However, the same historical impulse that had informed her proposal and the substance of so much of Du Bois's scholarship carried over into the consciousness of generations of black people who came after her.

In 1973, the Georgia-born black writer Alice Walker went on a quest to find the burial site of that great author and keeper of black culture. Posing as Hurston's niece, she traveled to various places where her literary aunt had lived, written, and studied in Florida, hoping not only to find answers about her last days but also to place a headstone on Hurston's grave in the old segregated black cemetery in Fort Pierce, Florida. It was as though she had read Hurston's letter located in Du Bois's archive, though she made no mention of it in her important 1975 essay, "In Search of Zora Neale Hurston."

Walker's quest to find Hurston's unmarked grave after more than a decade proved challenging. She described the scene of an old, unkempt cemetery covered by weeds and bushes and infested by snakes.[33] After sifting through the field, Walker stumbled upon a sunken rectangle in the dirt, just about where the groundskeeper had described the location of Hurston's burial site. Having successfully identified the final resting place of Hurston, the Georgia-born writer went back into town to purchase the best headstone her money could buy. It was a tall black one that the seller referred to as "Ebony Mist," on which Walker had the following words engraved:

ZORA NEALE HURSTON

"A GENIUS OF THE SOUTH"

1901–1960

NOVELIST   FOLKLORIST

ANTHROPOLOGIST

This grave in the old, segregated cemetery was nothing like the grand historic site Hurston had dreamed of. The headstone also lists the incorrect year of Hurston's birth, as 1901 instead of 1891. Yet something tells me that the story of that acclaimed black woman writer—"a genius of the South" in her own right—hunting down Hurston's burial site to honor her memory while helping reintroduce Zora Neale Hurston's writing to new generations of readers would be seen as an act of commemoration more meaningful than any lifeless shrine could offer.

I was in the eleventh grade when I first read Hurston's 1937 novel *Their Eyes Were Watching God*. That same year, a film based on the book, produced by Oprah Winfrey and Quincy Jones, aired on television. I was lucky to have attended a high school where black life and history had been valued parts of the academic culture. For that was certainly not the norm in most schools in California or other parts of the country, and it has become even less so today, amid the new waves of attacks on black history in American schools motivated by "antiwoke," "anti-DEI," and "anti-CRT" campaigns led by Republican legislators and the interest groups with which they are aligned.

Hurston would likely cut her eyes at the thought of her home state of Florida—and several others—having now banned her most famous novel from being taught in its public schools. Yet she would likely find little shock at the action among the general public, given the skepticism she expressed about desegregated schooling after the Supreme Court ruled in *Brown v. Board of Education* in 1954. Her criticism of desegregation plans would bring her under attack by African American leaders advocating for integration.[34] However, decades after failed attempts at desegregation, many African Americans find themselves in a similar place of skepticism when it comes to questions about who should have control over the education of black youths. A close reading of Hurston's proposal to build a Cemetery for the Illustrious Negro Dead reveals her concern for the teaching and passing on of black history as an important basis of liberatory education, an education that would be even more difficult to obtain in court-ordered desegregated schools in which white parents were hostile to the very thought of black children sitting next to their own.

•

THE SPIRIT OF Hurston's proposal can be traced through various museums and monuments around the country. The Legacy Museum in Montgomery, Alabama, immediately comes to mind. This museum underscores the historical relationship between lynching and the failures of the US justice system to protect the lives of black people equally with those of whites. What I appreciate most about this museum is the National Memorial for Peace and Justice on the grounds just outside the museum building. This memorial recognizes the lives of ordinary black people who were lynched across the United States, and the museum includes small deposits of dirt from all the places where recorded lynchings occurred. I see this installment as an example of reckoning with black history beyond the lives of the "illustrious" and the monumental; a revised implementation of Hurston's proposal, one that invites us to extend our collective conception of who counts as being worthy of historical study and recognition. Just as Hurston and others before her reframed the memory of Nat Turner despite the utter disregard for his life by mainstream white society, I see the effort to recover and reinterpret the lives of black victims of white mob violence, both the named and unnamed, as evidence of the continued evolution of the ethics driving the practices of black memory workers.

Hurston's proposal also comes to mind when I think of the National Museum of African American History and Culture in Washington, DC, a 420,000-square-foot, ten-story structure that doubles as a shrine to the simultaneously terrible and beautiful history of black people in the United States. The museum renders a history of the country's constitution from a black perspective. I read it as a physical manifestation of an idea proclaimed by Hurston's contemporary Richard Wright when he declared that "the Negro is America's metaphor." In channeling that declaration, the museum reflects the way the material and cultural realities of African Americans expose deep-seated, often underexamined realities of the US social order, especially as it pertains to the violent contradictions in the national identity when it comes to matters of race. Black memory workers have always known this to be true, though many others have refused to see it. The "Blacksonian," as some affectionately refer to the museum, makes such contradictions in the national culture difficult to overlook.

When I think of that ten-story golden creation, I am reminded of the mortuary politics that have long informed the struggle to preserve and commemorate black history. I have visited the museum twice since its opening in 2016, and two artifacts always come to mind when I reflect on the experience: Harriet Tubman's shawl and Emmett Till's casket. The regal shawl worn by one of the most iconic freedom fighters in black history stuck with me partly because of the lessons of my third-grade teacher, Miss Todman. And after some reflection, I realized that Till's casket also stood out to me because of a classroom encounter with a black educator. Emmett Till's story is forever etched in my mind because my college professor and mentor Robert L. Allen traced his own political awakening to witnessing Till's mutilated body for the first time in 1955 while delivering *Jet* magazines as a teenager in Atlanta, Georgia.

The shawl prompts me to think of the covering Tubman provided to so many enslaved people as she guided them, as fugitives, on their way to freedom. That's what I see when I think about that material object gifted to Tubman by Queen Victoria of England in 1897. I also consider the spiritual protection Tubman herself must have had to complete so many missions successfully, given the odds against her doing so. When I look at Tubman's shawl, I hear Miss Todman and my third-grade classmates reciting Greenfield's poem about Harriet Tubman not taking "no stuff" and her heroic journeys through the woods with slave catchers on her heels, risking everything to save others. I hear my twenty-five classmates and our teacher reciting in unison, "Nineteen times she went back South / To get three hundred others / She ran for her freedom nineteen times / To save Black sisters and brothers."[35]

It's likely that some might see the regal, hand-stitched silk lace and linen shawl to be at odds with the popular image of Tubman. This "woman named Moses," as African Americans during her time came to call her, is often depicted toting a rifle, wading through swamps, and leading 150 black soldiers in the Combahee Ferry Raid in June 1863, when they freed seven hundred enslaved people. However, I see no conflict between her heroic efforts and the femininity symbolized by the shawl because Tubman, like so many other black women of the tradition she represents, helped establish a new standard of womanhood that troubled Victorian notions of what a woman ought to be, do, and think. Perhaps it is also this depth and complexity that draw me to the image of Tubman in the shawl. Beyond my memory of Miss Todman's class, I also imagine Tubman in old age, sitting in all her glory, wearing this piece of clothing, and in doing so challenging all that it represented. I recall the title and substance of Paula Giddings's important book, *When and Where I Enter: The Impact of Black Women on Race and Sex in America*. Indeed, black women leaders such as Tubman disrupted racialized and gendered norms through their political, cultural, and intellectual actions; and those actions were informed by the insights black women had gleaned from their overlapping experiences of oppression as women who are both black and overrepresented among the most economically disadvantaged.

I learned no poems about Emmett Till during my youth, though I certainly learned his name. In fact, I would hear the name Emmett Till again and again over the course of my intellectual journey and before seeing his casket at the National Museum of African American History and Culture. Like the publicized chase and killing of the seventeen-year-old Trayvon Martin in February 2012 in Sanford, Florida, the lynching of Emmett Till in Money, Mississippi, in August 1955 was a life-altering event that awakened the consciousness of a generation of black young people. The memory of his death and the promise of his life would be told again and again in black history. Stories like his served as a motivation to engage in the ongoing struggle to study and preserve knowledge about the black past.

Emmett Till was lynched after a white woman falsely accused him of whistling at her—an accusation she later admitted to having lied about. Her confession, which came more than half a century late, made no difference in the outcome of Till's life, and his story marked the collective psyche of African American youths of the 1950s, driving a great many of them to political action. Just as the poet Elizabeth Alexander refers to her own sons and the other young people who came of age in the wake of Martin's death as "the Trayvon Generation," we might think of young people who came of age in the wake of Emmett Till's widely publicized killing as "the Emmett Generation."[36] There were no 911 audiotapes of Till's killers as they hunted him down; however, Mamie Till-Mobley's decision to have an open-casket funeral and to allow *Jet* magazine to print images of his mutilated body invited the world to see what those white men had done to her fourteen-year-old son. The image of his tortured and bloated face circulated, and his death stirred outrage across the nation, especially among other African American youths.

At every inflection point in my life and career I can trace much of my own growth to the teachings of those steeped in the tradition of black memory work, beginning with my elementary teachers such as Miss Butterfield and Miss Todman and continuing with Professor Robert L. Allen at UC Berkeley. I name these educators partly as a way of modeling the tradition of bearing witness that they taught me, but also because they represent the kind of everyday black people and stories that have been central to sustaining the insurgent intellectual tradition that gave form to Black History Month and that have helped sustain the best iterations of this commemorative practice over the last century.

Professor Allen was a student of the Emmett Generation. He shared the story with me and my classmates in his course on Black Men in America during the spring semester of my sophomore year in 2008. Professor Allen, a historical sociologist and 1963 graduate of Morehouse College, had been a student at the historically black Booker T. Washington High School in Atlanta, Georgia, when Emmett Till's murder took place in 1955. He was nearly the same age as Emmett when he witnessed the horrifying image of the grotesquely disfigured boy in his casket, and, like many others, he was forever changed by what he saw. In an oral history interview, he recalled, "The young student generation coming along, and I think almost everybody who saw those pictures of Emmett Till, they said, 'No, we're not going along with this anymore. No more. No.' That event [Emmett's lynching] turned so many people around because so many saw it in *Jet*. It's just astonishing when I think back about that. Because parents were hiding those pictures from their children. They didn't want them to see how horrible it was. But there I was delivering it to their doors."[37]

It was a painful reminder for the Emmett Generation, as it was for the Trayvon Generation, that black youths were also—or perhaps especially—vulnerable to extreme forms of antiblack violence. Booker T. Washington High School was a standing memorial to the local black freedom movement, an ongoing struggle of which the school's soon-to-be most prominent alumnus, Martin Luther King, Jr., was at the forefront. In 1924, three decades before Till's murder, Dr. King's grandfather, together with other local leaders, had protested and filed a lawsuit to force the city of Atlanta to allocate resources for the creation of Booker T. Washington as the city's first black public high school, just five years before his own grandson's birth. As in many other southern cities at the time, African American youths were denied access to a public high school education, although high schools were widely available for white southerners. Some cities had several white high schools with no provisions for African Americans.[38]

The historical significance of that high school makes me wonder how the teachers at Booker T. Washington supported their students as they were forced to process Emmett's death in relation to their own lives. Yet without having any direct answers to this question, I do know that many high school students in Atlanta received a political education by local black college students engaged in the Civil Rights Movement. Allen noted that when describing having to cross the campuses of Spelman College,

Morehouse College, and Atlanta University to attend his segregated schools.

Though not of the Emmett Generation myself, I was taught and mentored by an educator who framed the political stakes of his scholarship and teachings through the memory of Till's death. It was partly Professor Allen's story that caused me to sit with the casket of the fourteen-year-old boy at the National Museum. Seeing through the lens of my professor's childhood memory, I was constantly reminded of the larger stakes of black historical preservation and study—that sustained truth telling about the black past was essential for helping new generations recognize injustice when they see it and that it is critical that these generations learn the strategies employed by oppressed communities to resist the various ways in which people in power work to maintain their subjugation.

I found myself thinking of Professor Allen's childhood story when I taught his 1969 book, *Black Awakening in Capitalist America*, in an African American history seminar at Harvard in the fall of 2023, just months before Allen's unexpected death the following July. As that memory crept into my mind, I was reminded that black deaths continue to be a key motivation for black study, even as black study, in its truest form, is fundamentally concerned with the preservation of life and an investment in black futurity. The lesson became even more pronounced for me when I attended Professor Allen's memorial service held in the very same university building where I had first learned that Allen was a child of the Emmett Generation.

During the service, I learned that Professor Allen had been a young man in his early twenties sitting in the Audubon Ballroom in New York City when Malcolm X was assassinated there in 1965. He had been working as a social worker for the Welfare Department in Harlem, having graduated from Morehouse College just two years before. I do not recall Allen ever sharing that particular story, though we had studied speeches by Malcolm X in class nearly twenty years prior and just seven floors down from the site where we were gathered to celebrate his life.

Professor Allen's commitment to clarifying the social and historical realities of black life made even more sense once I learned that he had been a witness to Malcolm's death. In fact, Allen's first piece of published writing was his account of Malcolm's assassination for *National Guardian*, a leftist newspaper that had hired him as its first black reporter. By that time, Allen had quit working for the welfare office, having observed it to be thoroughly oppressive and invasive of black families in Harlem—as similar offices were for black families across the country. As a new reporter, he covered African American political activism, including the Black Panther Party for Self-Defense and other black nationalist organizations. Through his documentary work, he began laying the foundation of what ultimately became his analysis of black life in the United States as an "internal colony," wherein he described African Americans as a colonized people within the heart of the empire and described the way in which corporate elites worked to co-opt the leaders of the black freedom struggle to neutralize the movement's radical potential.[39]

Allen continued researching and writing in the wake of Malcolm's death. He eventually went back to graduate school and even started a bookstore in Harlem called Browser Books. The bookstore failed, but according to Allen it had been a wonderful educational experience, as it had given him lots of material to read. During that time he also worked remotely as a research assistant for Dr. Benjamin Elijah Mays, the president of Morehouse College. It was touching to read the warm exchanges between Allen and Mays from 1968 because I had previously been unaware of their personal relationship, though the connection now carries a great deal of significance to me personally as someone who would become an academic fellow in a program named in honor of Mays.[40]

The same semester I learned that Professor Allen was a child of the Emmett Generation, he encouraged me to apply to the Mellon Mays Undergraduate Fellowship (MMUF) program at UC Berkeley. He handed me a pamphlet for the newly established program on that ordinary day as I lingered after class to discuss ideas for my final paper, which I'd planned to write on the Million Man March of 1995. Professor Allen explained, "This is supposed to be for students in the humanities and social sciences, but I think it will be good for you." He knew I was technically ineligible for the program because I was a business administration major; however, he encouraged me to apply anyhow and even offered to provide me with a letter of support. The fellowship, funded by the Mellon foundation and named after Benjamin Elijah Mays, was originally created as a pipeline program committed to diversifying the professoriate by supporting students from historically marginalized backgrounds to matriculate from college, through doctoral programs, and ultimately into tenure-track faculty positions. I know beyond the shadow of a doubt that I would not be a professor today had it not been for my experiences in the Mellon Mays community and had Professor Allen not encouraged me to continue down the path of pursuing questions about black life and culture that were immediately relevant to the lives of the community I came from. I think of this often now as concerted efforts to dismantle programs such as Mellon Mays occur alongside attacks on black history, as part of broader efforts to gut diversity, equity, and inclusion programs in higher education. That Allen was personally connected to the educational leader for whom the fellowship had been named—a fact that my humble mentor would never mention—makes the entire exchange seem that much more significant in hindsight.

Allen's commitment to studying and writing about black history can be traced back to his encounter with Emmett Till's death, as well as his witnessing of Malcolm X's assassination ten years later, in 1965. However, it was also cultivated through his engagement in the Black Freedom Movement, in which he participated as a student activist, as well as his educational experiences at Morehouse College, where he took courses with the historian and Spelman College professor Howard Zinn, as well as his ongoing relationship to Benjamin Mays. In that way, he was formed through black history. He was shaped not only by historical events that occurred during his lifetime but also by his everyday encounters while living in a segregated black world in Jim Crow America.

Two years before Black History Week was formally expanded to Black History Month, Allen discussed Malcolm X's assassination with University of Michigan students as he framed the intellectual and political work of black studies. A 1974 article in *The Michigan Daily* covered Allen as an invited speaker for a "Black History Week" series on campus. By that time, Allen was a professor of African American studies at San Jose State University, at a time when many departments were being formed in colleges and universities across the country, resulting from black students' demands beginning in 1968. He was also working full-time for *The Black Scholar*, an academic journal founded in 1969 that published articles based on research and political events related to the newly formed academic field.

During his Black History Week lecture at the University of Michigan, he declared, "Malcolm X is dead, but his ideas have only now begun to live." He went on to explain that "Racism—whether in the Congo, in Mississippi or in Vietnam—was derived from the same source since those discriminated against are victims of an international power structure." He insisted that that revelation about the interrelationship between racism and capitalism and the "need to completely restructure the current power system is part of the political heritage Malcolm X left to us."[41] He told the students at the lecture that their desire to understand and fight against this social dilemma plaguing the world around them would require deep study of the black past.

Through his scholarship and teachings, Allen created a shrine to Emmett, just as he venerated the memory of Malcolm. His studies of the black past were not about worshiping the dead but about a commitment to studying and remembering the lessons the dead have left for those of us still living. Through such actions, he insisted that Emmett and Malcolm had lived valuable lives. The same lesson was communicated through Alice Walker's memory work for Hurston and the work my first teachers of black history did for various figures of the black past, and it is the work I seek to do for ordinary people, like black educators, who have kept this tradition alive.

I see educators such as Professor Allen, Miss Jones, and Miss Todman, as well as the unnamed "oracle of literature" on the *Hudibras*, to be among "the illustrious Negro dead." Their stories invite a friendly amendment to Hurston's proposal: that we take account of black histories in the everyday, which entails creating a more expansive vision of where to look for black achievement, noteworthy accomplishments, and lessons for how we might live good lives that align with a vision of collective flourishing. I also see a clear relationship between the scene in that overcrowded, open church classroom in Mississippi, the tradition of commemorating black history at the heart of Hurston's proposal, and the hundred-year journey of Black History Month. Across all these examples is a collective declaration by black people, through words and deeds, that their lives are worth living despite their unimaginable conditions and that they are worth honoring despite widespread condemnation. More important, these cases, across time, emphasize that the repetition of this claim is a necessary act, a disciplined practice that must be maintained. For indeed, sustained storytelling to this end has played a key role in black people's fight to preserve their heritage and tend to their humanity. While they were minor figures in the pantheon of black history, they were major figures in the lives of ordinary people and in local contexts; the stories of these ordinary people represent a tradition of African Americans striving to create a new world with the best of their resources, their imagination, and their confidence in the value of their lives.

•

LIKE MANY BEFORE me, my first lessons in black history became equipment for living. Eight months after my first Black History Month program in 1993, I would be tasked with applying what I had learned under Miss Butterfield's tutelage of me and my preschool classmates in a moment of bereavement. However, I was now in kindergarten, and this time my recitation would not take place at the school board's auditorium but in a chapel at Forest Lawn Cemetery for the funeral of my twenty-two-year-old father, Jarvis Ray Givens II. His death was not the result of inhumane treatment aboard a slave ship; it was not due to a political assassination in Southampton or New York City; nor was it caused by the racialized and gendered torture inflicted by a white mob in Mississippi; or perhaps it is more appropriate to say that such scenes of subjection, in this particular instance, were not the immediate cause of death. Instead, my father was shot and killed during a gang-related altercation outside a party in Long Beach, California, in October 1993. As fate would have it, his death occurred just blocks from where his own father, Jarvis Ray Givens, Sr., had been shot and killed twelve years prior.

When making arrangements for the funeral, my family decided I should play some role. Their memory of my participation in Miss

Butterfield's Black History Month program likely motivated that decision. However, Dr. King's speech was not appropriate, nor was the poem "I Am the Black Child," which Miss Butterfield had taught me and my classmates for our preschool graduation ceremony. While we were sitting in my grandmother's kitchen, they decided I would recite the Lord's Prayer, which Miss Butterfield had taught us for morning devotion. Every day that prayer was wedged between our reciting of "Dreams" by Langston Hughes and our singing of "Lift Every Voice and Sing." I recall rehearsing the words while standing in front of the stove that was about my height, as the adults sat around the wooden table planning out logistics for the final rites of my father and the repass that would follow.

Unbeknown to Miss Butterfield, my black history lessons would now be repurposed to honor the life of my father. The ceremony would be a memorialization of a much humbler life, one distinct from memorializations of freedom fighters such as Nat Turner or of Zora Neale Hurston as "a genius of the South," and it was categorically different from those of the "shining black prince" of African Americans, as Malcolm X was eulogized by the actor and activist Ossie Davis. However, the facts of my father's life and death are nonetheless part and parcel of the black past: a young man whose early death represents those of too many African Americans who have died at the hands of gang violence precipitated by government officials' aggressive neglect of impoverished urban communities.

I recently came across two photographs from the scene at my father's funeral. I am told by my mother that the pictures were likely taken by my late cousin Marcel Bradly, whom my family affectionately referred to as "Fish." In the first image, I am standing in front of the blue casket and several floral arrangements.

My black slacks, white dress shirt, tie, and suspenders look very similar to the clothes I had worn for Black History Month earlier that year; and my head peeks just above the open casket as I speak into the microphone before an audience of bowed heads. My maternal grandmother hovers over my left shoulder. She is dressed in a floral print blouse, a long black skirt, black stockings, and black shoes. Crowning her head is a black-and-gold hat. She holds a copy of the obituary in her left hand, and she appears to be whispering encouraging words in my ear, or maybe she's just leaning close so that I know I'm not alone. Opposite my grandmother, bending over my right shoulder, is a friend of my father, a man named Charlie Mac, who often visited me in the years following the funeral. He wears an adult version of my outfit, sans suspenders. I recognize some people in the audience from their profiles—an uncle here, a cousin there—but mostly all I see is me standing there, reciting my solemn request for covering the way Miss Butterfield had lined it out for me and my classmates, the way her teachers had taught her.

In the second image, I am being escorted by my grandmother back to our seats. We are midstride, passing my paternal grandmother on the front row. She is wearing a solid black dress with her light brown hair pulled neatly into a bun beneath a black hat with a wide brim and a bow on the side. Her sister and mother—my great-grandmother, whose house we'd often visit after church—sit beside her. In the photo, I can see their heads turned toward me as I pass them. In the center of the frame, where I stood in the previous photo, is the open blue casket, where the crossed hands and forehead of my father's corpse are noticeable.

The sight of this image is not morbid to me, though the circumstances were terrible. When I see these photographs, I am reminded

Homegoing service of Jarvis Ray Givens II (October 22, 1993)

of immeasurable pain and suffering, and I am also reminded that my family, like many African American families across the nation, faced and confronted such dire events clad in a cultural armor passed on to us, resources that many generations of people had been forced to create and repurpose in order to carve out lives for the future. When I see these photos, I am reminded of the many lessons I learned from Miss Butterfield, just as I am reminded of the many church members who visited my grandmother in the days leading up to the funeral and after. They gathered around her as she mourned "the passing of the firstborn"—friends and church family, especially white-gloved ushers from the Gospel Memorial Church of God in Christ.

She, too, passed through the blood-stained gate, as did many before her—a heartbreak W. E. B. Du Bois also shared, having lost a black son in a world that was cruel and callous toward black children, even before birth. Du Bois penned the first African American mourning story in *The Souls of Black Folk*. Writing at the turn of the century, he described his son being born "within the Veil" as "a Negro and a Negro's son." I wonder if at some point my grandmother experienced the same "awful gladness in [her] heart" as Du Bois, when her loss and heartbreak were balanced by a little relief. Perhaps her soul also whispered to her, "Not dead, not dead, but escaped; not bond, but free." Having been well practiced in mourning the deaths of children who died too soon, many women gathered around my grandmother during that time to perform a ritual of grieving that had been rehearsed to exhaustion. Once again, to quote Du Bois, "the chamber of death writhed the world's most piteous thing—a childless mother." And though the circumstances were different, the songs "Strange Fruit" and "Lord, How Come Me Here?" still seem to me a melody in the background. For "even if the story is grief-stricken, the act of memorializing retains a particular aspect of a culture's narrative, and for blacks in the Americas, some notion of racial memory and racial realization is mediated through the veil of death."[42]

The images from my father's funeral, when placed in a thoughtful context, also provide a glimpse at black history in the everyday. My point here is not to suggest that death was an all-consuming factor in my life or that of my family, but more to offer that this scene of my family's gathering after the death of my father also represents the range of important sites to be excavated for interpretation and study. It is a reminder that knowing the past is not only about the flattened details of names and events but also about the social facts of life that constitute our pasts. It is about seeking to understand how black people worked to build social worlds based on care for one another, which includes details about how they succeeded and, at times, failed; times when they thrived and also when they could barely eke out an existence. It is about understanding the relationship between moments of joy and moments of mourning, between the Black History Month program and the homegoing service, both events in which black cultural resources were put into practice as a way of commemorating black lives. These, too, are sites where African American people might dig up their past, where we might explore deeper knowledge about the lived experiences of black communities and how they worked to live out their beliefs, their politics, and their heritage.

In our pursuit of black histories of the everyday, we must also have the courage to look at scenes that cause discomfort, just as we might study events and lives that are immediately inspiring. Such work requires a holistic assessment if it is to be useful, especially for black people whose lives are most closely aligned with the kind of scenes depicted in these photos. Indeed, rarely do black people have the luxury of looking away and refusing to remember. How else could we have faced this world without resources honed by our sorrows and strivings from the past? It is these resources—this equipment for living—that are always at stake in our struggles to preserve and study black history.

PART III

WHEN TRUTH GETS A HEARING

Unveiling the Labor and Legacy of Black Memory Work(ers)

> One of the most cruel things that one could do today would be to forget or ignore pioneers such as these early Negro historians. One of the most praiseworthy things one could do would be to recognize the enormous importance of their keeping the light of truth flickering until it could be kindled by greater resources and many more hands.
>
> —JOHN HOPE FRANKLIN, *NEGRO DIGEST*, FEBRUARY 1966

JUSTICE WALKED INTO THE COURTROOM, and everyone stood. She wore a long, horizontally striped robe, a crown graced her head, and a white shawl was draped over her shoulders. Her purpose, on this occasion, was to hear the case to be made for and against "the Negro." Testifying on behalf of the plaintiff was Truth, as well as a long list of witnesses, including Grace, Mercy, Womanhood, Haiti, and History, all of whom could attest to what the accused had and had not done in the past and present. Truth had been tasked with searching written records of the modern world and antiquity. The record was vast, and it stretched well beyond the Americas and before 1492.

The opposing counsel was led by none other than Prejudice. She was joined by Injustice. They had their ax to grind. They sought to prove that "the Negro" had never accomplished anything of merit, that he was inferior to the white race, and that segregation was therefore justified. Black people's position at the lower rung of society was attributable to their intellectual inferiority, their criminality, and their licentiousness. The barbarism they displayed, from their time as heathens on the African continent to their carryings-on in the slums of New York City and the ghettos of Washington, DC, was evidence in and of itself. Their position in American society and in the world, Prejudice and Injustice argued, was exactly what it should be. Whatever achievements they had accomplished had more to do with their proximity to the white race than anything to do with their own gifts. The Negro was a child race, to be saved only by the paternalism of those greater and more capable. So went the arguments of early-twentieth-century white social science scholars of race, which informed the position of those seeking to keep the Negro "in his place."

Yet only Justice could render a verdict. This was her courtroom. She would render a decision only after hearing the facts of the case. And for the first time, Truth would have her say on the matter, helping to settle the dispute once and for all. Too long had she been forced to sit on the sidelines and allow so many less qualified evaluators determine the course of action. It was time she had a hearing.

Justice, Truth, Injustice, Prejudice, Representative of the Negro, Grace, Womanhood, and many more virtues and historical actors were all characters in a stage play entitled *When Truth Gets a Hearing*, written and directed by the African American school founder, labor activist, and black history enthusiast Nannie Helen Burroughs in the 1920s.[1] The cast were all students at Burroughs's National Training School for Women and Girls, which she had founded through the Women's Convention, Auxiliary of the National Baptist Convention, USA, in 1909 in Washington, DC, with support from individual black donors in the nation's capital. The play, almost lost to history, is but one example of the ways in which the black past was engaged, studied, and preserved in black communities during the early years of the black history movement, the same time that Negro History Week was founded and quickly spread across the country. As a curricular device, Burroughs's play was instructive; as a piece of art it provided an entryway to black history for those who might not engage other forms, such as essays and traditional history books; as a documentary performance, it forced those in the audience to consider how black people's agency to define themselves had been hijacked for centuries but could still be reclaimed. For indeed, the characters in the play actively performed the recovery work, and Burroughs's writing of the script based on her study of emerging scholarship by scholars such as Carter G. Woodson was evidence of such black reconstructions of the past. Burroughs operated in a tradition of black memory workers that is quite extensive in the African American tradition, and she represented a critical mass of black teachers who made up a majority of such faithful laborers.

The National Training School served primarily working-class students from across the United States, though it also enrolled students from various countries in the African diaspora. The program was based on a "practical" approach to educating black women and girls, which meant preparing them to be successful in the limited jobs within their reach: as domestic workers, caterers, laundresses, hairdressers, and typists. During the early twentieth century, most black women and girls worked as domestic servants and agricultural workers. As noted by the historian Evelyn Brooks Higginbotham, "By 1930, nine-tenths of all black working women were still in farm or domestic work, the only change being that the majority were now employed in the latter field," whereas in the earlier part of the twentieth century the majority had worked as agricultural laborers.[2] Given that context, Burroughs took a practical approach to women's education, often likened to that of Booker T. Washington. It was her position that black women and girls were going into certain occupations without being prepared to do their jobs efficiently, often lacking the skills to navigate emergent technology in those industries. Recognizing how susceptible they were to high turnover rates in those lines of employment, Burroughs insisted that poor preparation only exacerbated their vulnerability. She committed herself to advocating for better labor conditions, including better pay for those women, while also preparing them to do their work effectively and with a deep sense of self-worth. She insisted that one's occupation did not determine one's value in the world, and as a black Baptist leader, she professed that it certainly did not determine one's value in the eyes of the Almighty.

Yet the National Training School's curriculum was not so rigid in its focus on preparing the young women for industrial and domestic roles that it abandoned other subjects more aligned with classical education. Burroughs took a holistic approach to developing students, blending the liberal arts with industrial training. What's more, the school required its students to study black history and culture. Indeed, the recurring performances and tours of *When Truth Gets a Hearing* were one of many ways Burroughs incorporated knowledge about the black past into the school's academic culture.[3]

The National Training School regularly observed Negro History Week while also integrating knowledge about black history and studies about contemporary black social issues into the curriculum year-round. By the late 1920s, the school was one of approximately one hundred institutions that had adopted Carter G. Woodson's textbook *The Negro in Our History* as part of their curriculum.[4] All students were required to take a course in black history and demonstrate competency in the subject. In a June 1929 profile of Burroughs's school, *The Pittsburgh Courier* wrote, "An examination is held, both written and oral" and "students then write orations on Negro achievements, and by a process of elimination the two best orators from each class are selected." The school held an annual oratorical competition based on those speeches, usually during Negro History Week, and three winners were selected and awarded prizes. Those elements of the school's curriculum cultivated academic identities among students that were grounded in black history and a concern with contemporary black life.[5]

A student's account from 1929 also emphasized the centrality of black history and culture to the school's academic identity both in February and year-round. She wrote, "This school teaches History and Negro History, and the students are tremendously inspired by learning the truth about their own race. We know now that our race has been going on in the building of world civilizations." The young woman then explained that the National Training School had adopted Woodson's textbook for instruction and furthermore that the school had "a real library . . .

set apart for the Study of Negro Life and History." Of the school's oratorical competition, she wrote, "If you want to see us in our glory visit us on Appreciation Day, February 22nd, and hear us tell what the Negro has done for the world." She continued, "When it comes to this race history the Training School Girls have the world beat, not including Dr. Woodson.... We know our material."[6]

Nannie Helen Burroughs had long been a champion of black pride and race consciousness; indeed, long before Negro History Week's inauguration or the debut of *When Truth Gets a Hearing* in the late 1920s. Her pedagogy was driven by her political commitment to her race and passion for social justice. Her heightened racial consciousness and pride can be detected as early as in a 1904 article condemning skin-bleaching creams and cosmetic products that altered the physical appearance of black women and thus further stigmatized physical features associated with African ancestry. In "Not Color but Character," the school founder insisted that black women who used such products suffered from a vicious form of

Negro History Library at the National Training School for Women and Girls, ca. 1929

miseducation. She declared, "What every woman who bleaches and straightens out needs is not her appearance changed, but her mind."[7] What's more, she had been educated by black teachers who had emphasized the importance of black history in the lives of African American youths, in schools where young students such as Burroughs were taught to study the life and contributions of notable black men and women in order to emulate the courage and commitment to racial uplift they modeled. For instance, in 1896, Burroughs graduated from the M Street School in Washington, DC, the only black high school in the nation's capital, at the same time that Mary Church Terrell was leading the effort to establish Frederick Douglass Day in the DC public schools. The colored schools of DC began celebrating Douglass's birthday immediately following his death in 1895, though it wasn't officially recognized as a districtwide holiday until 1897.[8]

Burroughs also understood herself to be a diasporic subject. She was a black woman who recognized her suffering in the United States to be intimately connected with the struggles of black people around the world. In February 1915, she wrote an essay, "What the Belgians Did to the Negro," for the National Training School's newspaper, *The Worker*, detailing key aspects of European colonialism, particularly the exploitation of African labor so central to that violent phenomenon. She also identified the connections between antiblack violence on the continent of Africa and in the United States, describing how "our villages" were being burned in the Congo just as black people were the targets of violent lynchings in America.[9]

Burroughs, who thought internationally about the black freedom struggle, was an active member of the International Council of Women of the Darker Races, a study group of black women leaders—primarily educators—focused on gaining a deeper understanding of the challenges facing women of color (of the African diaspora and otherwise) around the world. The women, including the educators Janie Porter Barrett in Virginia and Margaret Murray Washington in Tuskegee, Alabama, were based mostly in the United States but also included at least one woman abroad, the school founder and Pan-Africanist Adelaide Casely-Hayford in Freetown, Sierra Leone. In the early 1920s, the women issued a collective statement emphasizing the urgent need to study black history in schools. They declared, "Men like Douglass, Langston, Bruce, and Revels; women like Sojourner Truth, Frances Ellen Watkins Harper and Harriet Tubman, to say nothing of more recent characters of prominence should be as well known by our youth as men and women of any other race, even if their names do not occur quite so often in print. If we as teachers do not think to do this, who will do it?"[10]

Through her studies and deep involvement in black women's groups and African American institutions, Burroughs's black consciousness continued to mature over the years. In fact, one might say that she was ahead of her time. Many of her political views anticipated the declarations of black pride and black studies typically associated with the Black Power era decades later. In a 1927 article, she professed to her students and anyone who would listen that "No race is richer in soul quality and color than the Negro. Some day he will realize it and glorify them. He will popularize black."[11]

Popularizing the "soul quality" of black people and cultivating a deeper appreciation for the race's history was exactly what Burroughs set out to do with her play, *When Truth Gets a Hearing*. It was a dramatization of the black freedom struggle in the United States, though it also incorporated strong references to Ethiopia, Liberia, and Haiti, displaying Burroughs's international assessment of the black condition. Through a skillful use of satire and black cultural resources, especially music, she integrated key elements of the black past into a stirring performance. The play ended "with Justice on the throne; with Opposition, Prejudice and Injustice banished from the Court, and the Negro race girding on spiritual weapons to go forth to fight its battles for its God-given rights."[12]

When Truth Gets a Hearing received glowing reviews from prominent black scholars, according to the *Afro-American* newspaper. The poet and activist Alice Dunbar Nelson was impressed by the strong performances of the training school students on stage, writing that "the girls spoke clearly and delightfully." There was "no mealy-mouth mumbling, but enunciation and articulation that was a delight to the ear." The students' acting "was natural and graceful and some of it quite dramatic." But most of all, she wrote, "the singing was excellent." The Labor Chorus was a key feature of the play. They sang "a number of carefully selected spirituals," one of the highlights being "A quartette of deep full voices singing, 'Nobody Knows the Trouble I've Seen,' [which] brought forth a storm of applause."[13]

W. E. B. Du Bois traveled to Philadelphia from New York City to see *When Truth Gets a Hearing* and was blown away by it. He wrote to Burroughs, "There was such a crowd last night that I did not try to get to see you. I thank you for the opportunity of seeing your pageant. I was astonished and gratified to note the way in which it gripped and interested the audience." Dunbar Nelson shared Du Bois's astonishment at the audience's reception. At certain moments, she said, "We could have wished the audience were less enthusiastic, for often they voiced their approval so vigorously and whole-heartedly that some of the lines were lost." Carter G. Woodson, a longtime supporter of Burroughs, also had a chance to see the play and gave it a full-throated endorsement, declaring "The pageant is a clever dramatization which, because of its humor together with its serious appeal, takes high rank as a visualization of the history of the Negro." He was so impressed with the students' performance and the substance of Burroughs's play that he invited them to be a featured part of the annual meeting of the Association for the Study of Negro Life and History in November 1929 in Washington, DC.[14]

I have read Burrough's unpublished script of *When Truth Gets a Hearing* several times, first in the Rare Book and Special Collections Reading Room at the Library of Congress, which houses Burrough's personal papers and her school's records. I have also taught the play in my course on the history of African American education, and I reviewed the text in preparation for writing this book. Each time I read it, I notice something different; the thing I enjoy most is how well the script represents Burroughs's quick wit and humor, her personality and mind shining through in the development of various scenes. In one scene, Justice invites the "Representative of the Negro" to state their case; and before speaking, the Representative breaks out into song. According to Burroughs's script, Prejudice cuts her eyes at the Representative and politely asks the judge to make her stop: "Justice, will you please stop the Negro from singing here? This is no church." Ever well tempered and fair, however, Justice replies, "Each witness, you included, will be permitted to present his testimony in any way he sees fit. (Singing continued)." This early scene of the play introduces a series of heated courtroom exchanges in which the record of the race is put to the test and musical performances express black memory and feelings. Knowing the power of music, especially when paired with the complicated history covered in the play, Burroughs catered to the tastes of African American audiences across the country, enabling them to experience outrage in some moments and laughter in others as she and her students guided them through a dramatized interpretation of their history that was both honest and inspiring.

National Training School for Women and Girls students performing in *When Truth Gets a Hearing*, ca. 1929

BURROUGHS OPERATED IN a long tradition of black memory workers, a collective of people in various walks of life who helped sustain a historical enterprise dedicated to researching, preserving, and bearing witness to the black past. While she was not a traditionally trained historian or archivist, she was responsible for bringing knowledge about black history to many audiences around the country, especially to her students at the National Training School. *When Truth Gets a Hearing* was performed before thousands of people. It ran in local school auditoriums, churches, and theaters in cities such as Washington, DC, New York, Baltimore, and Philadelphia and even in various parts of California. National Training School students also traveled with their school's founder to various conferences and conventions of historically black organizations, performing their play before groups such as the National Baptist Convention's Golden Jubilee meeting in Chicago in September 1930.[15]

There is no one way to remember the black past; no one method of memory work has been responsible for sustaining the tradition. Likewise, there is no one qualification or credential that makes a black memory worker's contribution meaningful. While I recognize that there are degrees to which diverse memory workers engage the processes of historical production and the dissemination of knowledge about the past, I also know that a failure to acknowledge this range of actors would be a false representation of the way history and historical knowledge function, especially in the African American tradition. Furthermore, contrary to popular understanding, the historical enterprise has always included a large assortment of activities in which narratives and detail are engaged to achieve certain educational or social ends.[16] For the black historical enterprise in particular, the work extends far beyond individuals with advanced degrees who write books and teach in universities. As a matter of political necessity, African American people created black historical knowledge well before they were allowed to enter higher education in significant numbers and even before the establishment of black history as the academic discipline it became in the twentieth century. It is for these reasons and more that I turn to more expansive language.

The language of black memory work(ers) is used by a diverse group of caretakers of black stories, books, material artifacts, political traditions, performances, and cultural resources passed from one generation to the next, enabling us to recover insights from the black past. I was first introduced to the language of black memory work by African American women archivists who wrote about their work of preserving historical collections as part of a longer tradition of African-descended people constructing and caring for black archives in the afterlife of slavery, where antiblack biases in the historical profession, universities, and public memory have devalued and erased black history.[17] These women continue in the tradition of the black history collectors and archivists who preceded them, including Arturo Schomburg, Dorothy Porter Wesley, and Vivian Harsh, among others.[18] The language of black memory work is also informed by scholarship that distinguishes between black memory and state memory, the latter being shaped by the interests of nation-states and people in power. Black memory (and those working for its preservation and study) generally formed in opposition to state memory, given the long-standing realities of black suffering at the hands of the nation-state and of citizens in varying positions of privilege because of their proximity to whiteness; it formed as a critique of national narratives that elided the realities of black people's suffering and that erased their contributions to the nation and the broader realm of human experience.

Here lies the polemic nature of black memory and the political commitments of black memory workers. "The ulterior motive of black memory," to quote the African American studies scholar Michael Hanchard, is "to make claims in contemporary life about the relationships between present inequalities and past injustices." He continued, "Black memory has mostly served the purpose of keeping visible the actual or imagined experiences of black peoples that would have been otherwise forgotten or neglected, and in this manner black memory can be characterized as a collectively instantiated process, distinct from the personal memories of individual black persons."[19] Thus, to borrow from Burroughs, the political and intellectual uses of black memory have been to allow truth to have a hearing in the hope of advancing broader political projects in the pursuit of freedom and justice. For this reason, even when black memory workers focus on remembering and memorializing an individual black person, it is generally done in service of remembering something about black people collectively; the study of individual black lives is still concerned with knowledge about the past that can serve black people's shared interests in the future. Black memory and the work of remembering it and passing it on are constructed from within the black interior, though much of what it documents has to do with external social forces that seek to undermine black social life. They are always a collective process, a historical enterprise forged by and through community.

Black memory workers are found throughout the African American freedom movement in the United States from the time black culture and black consciousness developed among the enslaved as critical culture and critical consciousness set against a world order structured on black enslavement. This is a message that bears repeating, a message that every generation of black memory workers must learn and relearn. Writing during Negro History Week in 1966, the historian John Hope Franklin observed, "It came as something of a shock . . . to discover—even during the period of slavery—that there were Negroes who began to write the history of their people."[20] Those early black memory workers engaged in such literary tasks because they recognized how closely aligned the devaluation of black lives in historical narratives was with the devaluing of black lives in the world in which they lived. The former provided instruction about and justification for the latter. Burroughs's play and the performances of her students arose from that legacy of truth telling. Negro History Week and Black History Month became a formalized practice based on that project.

I position Burroughs as a black memory worker because her story provides the space to delve into the hidden labors of preserving and commemorating the black past. I want to stage a conversation about the veiled labor of black memory work in the past and present, which I hope to make more explicit in conversations about preserving black history and celebrating Black History Month in the future. Burroughs's story allows me to emphasize the central role black educators played in popularizing the study of black life and culture in schools and communities around the country, thus demonstrating the important role African American teachers play as black memory workers. A second point is that Burroughs's play serves as a reminder that the preservation of black history and memory takes many different forms. Indeed, creative works have long aided in the movement to research, preserve, and encourage the study of the black past.

Last, I turn to Burroughs's story because I am interested in unveiling the black memory work that led to the recovery of her legacy after her death in 1961. While she labored tirelessly to give the truth about black life and culture a hearing, her story was almost lost to history. The tale of her reemergence as a historical figure provides many lessons for how we might better appreciate the work of black history today. The story of black historical preservation points to the larger challenges faced by black memory workers, which have direct implications for the stories we have access to in the present. Sitting with such challenges presents an opportunity to take meaningful action in how we organize around the work of black history throughout the year, especially during Black History Month in 2026 and beyond.

•

SHORTLY AFTER ALICE WALKER went looking for Zora Neale Hurston in 1973, Evelyn Brooks (now Higginbotham) went searching for Nannie Helen Burroughs. Both were young scholars under the age of thirty, and both were African American women in pursuit of the submerged histories of other black women thinkers. Walker and Brooks were early pioneers in an intellectual movement that would establish the fields of black women's studies and black women's history. While knowledge about the black past had long been silenced, the social hierarchies of gender and sexuality had also led to extreme forms of erasure when it came to the lives of black women in the historical record, even in written scholarship about African American life and culture. Reflecting on her childhood, Higginbotham recalled, "From childhood I was taught Negro History, as it was called in Woodson's and my father's time, and yet I was taught very little about black women. I found particularly unsettling that this omission paralleled the omission of black people in American history."[21] While Walker found an unmarked grave in an abandoned segregated cemetery in Florida, she would stumble upon an old school building packed with boxes filled with letters, photographs, and other traces of Burroughs's life and the school she had founded. What had once been the National Training School for Women and Girls, founded by Burroughs in 1909, had now become a tomb of black history.

What sent Evelyn Brooks (Higginbotham) on her quest for Burroughs in the first place? The school founder had died in May 1961 at the age of eighty-one; by the time of her death, the National Training School's prominence had faded, and Burroughs was remembered by only a small contingent of black elders in Washington, DC. Few people knew the name of the outspoken black woman who, from an early age, had forced members of her community to recognize "How the Sisters are Hindered from Helping" in the work of bringing about more justice in the world. In fact, Brooks hadn't heard of Burroughs until her mother, herself a retired DC educator, had told her about the school's founder while Brooks was searching for a black woman to be the subject of her dissertation as a doctoral student.

Brooks was an early laborer in the field of black women's history, when scholars during the 1970s, particularly African American women, worked to unveil the role women had played in the Black Freedom Movement. Those black memory workers unearthed social, intellectual, and institutional histories that reflected the intersectional lives of black women as political subjects.

Their scholarship expanded the parameters of knowledge about the black past, pushing us to see the broader role women played in every aspect of black life, while also delineating their long-standing traditions of institution building as well as the distinct vulnerabilities black women experienced because of their race, sex, and class, including the exploitation of their labor from the slavery era through the twentieth century, their encounters with sexual violence, and more.

Brooks first pursued a master's degree in history at Howard University alongside notable doctoral scholars such as Rosalyn Terborg-Penn (PhD, Howard University, 1977) and Sharon Harley (PhD, Howard University, 1981), who helped formalize the field of black women's history through their own research. Writing of her time as a graduate student, she recalled one particular seminar during which she had truly begun to realize the importance of black women's history: "In my second and last year of the Master's program Rosalyn and I took a research seminar together under Professor Arnold Taylor. I wrote my final paper on the decline of blacks in agriculture. Rosalyn wrote on African Americans in the women's suffrage campaign during the nineteenth and twentieth century. When we were asked to report in class as to our research progress, I marveled each time she discussed her topic. I had no knowledge of this story and could not help but recognize the importance of her contribution to scholarship."[22] She was encouraged by her peers to pursue a doctoral degree. They insisted that she find a black woman no one had written about, then make that woman the subject of her dissertation. Harley and Terborg-Penn also invited Brooks to contribute to a historic volume they coedited, *The Afro-American Woman: Struggles and Images*, published in 1978, just one year before they and several others founded the Association of Black Women Historians. Through her essay in *The Afro-American Woman*, Brooks reintroduced Burroughs as a major contributor to the self-help tradition among African Americans, highlighting especially her leadership in the realm of black women's education.

Brooks's discovery of Burroughs was serendipitous. She had initially planned to write about a more easily recognizable figure, such as Mary Church Terrell or Mary McLeod Bethune. After all, they were women her professor, Rayford W. Logan, at Howard University spoke highly of. Brooks recalled that Professor Logan had raved about those two women and had even invited her to contribute an entry on Terrell to the *Dictionary of American Negro Biography* (1982), of which he was a coeditor. But when Brooks's mother learned of her daughter's quest, it brought back memories of a powerful woman she hadn't heard about in some time. She informed her daughter that "There was a woman at your grandfather's church, you should write about her, her name was Nannie Helen Burroughs, and people don't know about her now but she was great."[23] She urged her daughter to consider that woman, who had built her own school, championed the rights of working-class black women, and advocated for the teaching of black history.

One of the first things she did as a doctoral student, having enrolled in the University of Rochester's history program in 1975 as the only black student and single mother in the history department, was visit the former location of the National Training School for Women and Girls, which at the time was being used for a private elementary school. During that visit, she realized that studying and preserving black history, especially black women's history, meant fighting against environmental factors that threatened the very existence of such knowledge. She gained access to Trades Hall, a school building built during Burroughs's tenure, and immediately gasped as she looked at hundreds of boxes piled to the ceiling and scattered around the room. She couldn't believe her eyes. As a former staff member of the Moorland-Spingarn Research Center, which housed archives and special collections at Howard University, she knew what was required to ensure that historical materials were properly cared for and stored for long-term preservation. What she saw—the records of Burroughs and her school piled to the ceiling, rotting, and decaying—was a tangible example of how black history could be lost forever.

Brooks would complete her 1984 dissertation, entitled "The Women's Movement in the Black Baptist Church, 1880–1920," at the University of Rochester, in which she detailed how Burroughs and other black women leaders had figured prominently in the organizational politics and social impact of the largest religious sect among African Americans. The papers she found in Trades Hall were critical to that research. However, before writing her dissertation, she supported the process of getting Burroughs's papers acquired by the Library of Congress, thus ensuring that the materials would be secured for future research. When recalling those details, she wrote, "I immediately emphasized the need for acid-free folders and a climate-controlled setting, since the conditions in the Trades Hall were extremely deleterious to preserving the papers. I also told [Principal Aurelia] Downey that I had previously worked at the Moorland Spingarn Research Center and trained at the National Archives, where I developed knowledge of and skills in the preservation and processing of manuscript collections. My job, I informed her, was to become familiar with the contents of such collections in order to help researchers. Finally, I recommended the Library of Congress as best suited for a collection of this magnitude and for making the papers quickly available to the public. Downey welcomed my advice and over the course of 1976 and 1977 donated the papers."[24] What's more, she volunteered her services to help process the Burroughs collection at the Library of Congress during the summer of 1978, enabling her to become familiar with the historical materials before they were available to the public.[25] So not only did Brooks preserve Burroughs's legacy through her written scholarship, which culminated in her important book *Righteous Discontent: The Women's Movement in the Black Baptist Church, 1880–1920,* in which she coined the now widely used phrase "the politics of respectability," she also helped preserve and assemble an archive of a prominent black woman who had meant so much to African American people across the country during a critical phase of history. It is because of Brooks's labor as a black memory worker and her contributions to advancing the field of black women's history that Burroughs's story can be studied and taught by future generations of students, educators, and champions of women's rights.

THE STORY OF Brooks's recovery of Burroughs's legacy is a reminder that the broader enterprise of black history goes beyond the writing of books and the circulation of narratives about past lives and events. The work is layered, and the production of history includes many processes that can potentially contribute to erasure and silencing. Therefore, being vigilant about the processes of historical production is essential to sustaining and expanding the tradition of black history. In a moment when black history is being attacked and threatened in the public sphere, it is important that those of us who advocate teaching truth apply a more capacious understanding of black memory work in the hope of demystifying the politics of history.

When we discuss black history, whether in classrooms or in community spaces, it is important that we not only discuss the stories of the black past—the details of what happened—but also detail the work required to dig up, study, and preserve such knowledge. We must also educate ourselves about how we are able to know what happened and what's required for our communities to continue knowing. The labor of black memory workers is often placed out of sight. It can be easily taken for granted; however, allowing such work to be veiled and tucked away behind the scenes only leaves vulnerable communities at risk of further silencing, distortion, and erasure.

Knowledge can be removed from our reach through the scrubbing of websites, the banning of books, and the censoring of curricula, as present events make clear. In such instances, vulnerable communities can be placed at an even further disadvantage when we do not have a deep understanding about the intersections of power and the production of history. As we move into the next century of Black History Month, one can only hope that the labor of black memory workers will be prioritized in community conversations—from discussions about young people's career aspirations to the projects we support through fundraising efforts. The work of preservation is critical to remembering the black past, whether it be securing a historic site designation for the National Training School for Women and Girls by the National Park Service or the preservation of Burroughs's papers at the Library of Congress. For various reasons, we don't have the luxury of assuming that just because someone existed or some event transpired, a record of them will remain. Loss, theft, misplacement, discarding, forgetting, and destruction all pose enduring challenges for the preservation of black memory.

We must continue to insist that black archives remain available to subsequent generations. Doing so will ensure that black memory workers of the present and future can return to the black past to ask new questions and revise old narratives, thus enabling the continued growth and evolution of the tradition we have inherited from the laborers of black history who have passed on. As eloquently stated by the late historian John Hope Franklin in February 1966, "One of the most cruel things that one could do today would be to forget or ignore pioneers such as these early Negro historians. One of the most praiseworthy things one could do would be to recognize the enormous importance of their keeping the light of truth flickering until it could be kindled by greater resources and many more hands."[26]

The tasks involved in preserving the black past are many, yet the laborers and resources are few. Sustaining this worthy tradition requires coordinated action and intentional planning for both immediate needs and those likely to emerge in the future.

•

PRIOR TO LEARNING of Evelyn Brooks Higginbotham's encounter with Burroughs's papers, I had my own awakening about the unique challenges black memory workers faced in the realm of archives and historical sources. My early research into the history of African American teachers forced me to recognize the urgency of black memory work and what it means that such labor continues to be shaped by material circumstances that come with living in a world structured by the legacy of racial chattel slavery. This work is impacted by source materials that reflect antiblack ideas of past historical periods. The environment in which historical research is conducted is conditioned by the accumulated impact of underfunding historical scholarship and preservation efforts focused on African American communities over generations, thus reflecting broader structural inequities. What's more, remembering the black past is challenged by the scattered existence of source materials that reflect black perspectives (as opposed to other people's memories of black communities). In my quest to study African American teachers in the slavery and Jim Crow eras, I learned that producing scholarship about black lives in history is often threatened because the devaluation of black lives in the social order directly translated to their devaluation in the decision-making processes about which historical materials are deemed worthy of collecting and preserving by past and present history professionals. I also learned that while there are certainly classes of people and institutions that have committed themselves to preserving materials relevant to black life—especially historically black colleges and universities' librarians and black archivists—they often face many structural limitations, having to do the work with few resources and within predatory and dispiriting funding landscapes.

While searching for traces of the political and intellectual work of African American educators, I found the records of black teachers, who made up nearly half of African American professionals through the greater part of the twentieth century, to be in a precarious state. Such encounters were recurring, forcing me to see patterns that many other researchers had recognized well before me. They reminded me that historical silences are reproduced because of the current limitations of archives, which are formal repositories of historical documents, mostly written text, that reflect past lives, communities, institutions, and events and that are usually held in special collections in libraries, research centers, and other independent organizations. As explained in his field-shifting book, *Silencing the Past: Power and the Production of History*, the Haitian American scholar Michel-Rolph Trouillot described the four key moments when silences enter the process of historical production: "The moment of fact creation (the making of sources); the moment of fact assembly (the making of archives); the moment of fact retrieval (the making of narratives); and the moment of retrospective significance (the making of history)."[27] Thus, the lack of archival sources can contribute to broader historical omissions, and they accumulate as a result of past decisions made by history professionals who failed to prioritize the preservation of documentary materials that reflected the interior lives of black people and communities. I would add that silences also form as a result of aggressive neglect of the archival collections that do exist and that document the lives of black people.

My first trip to conduct archival research on black education presented an unexpected opportunity to reflect on the distinct challenges of black history as it pertained to archival silences, particularly as it relates to the educational life of African American communities. In July 2013, I encountered the autobiography of Sandy Rufus Youngblood, a fifteen-page account in which Youngblood discussed his family's enslavement, his coming of age during Reconstruction, and ultimately his journey as a public school teacher, principal, and then college professor in South Carolina, Georgia, and Oklahoma. His intimate story of bondage and educational striving was handwritten in the back of an old estate ledger. It wasn't until later that I could recognize the irony of that detail—the fact that a black educator's life story was inscribed in an instrument developed to increase the efficiency of recordkeeping during the slave trade. My appreciation of that detail came years later, as I continued studying and reading about the challenges and possibilities of writing about the black past, particularly when focusing on black lives during and immediately after slavery.

Youngblood's autobiography, penned in September 1914, centered around his father, Edwin Youngblood. He recalled being a fourteen-year-old boy when Edwin lay on his deathbed in 1876. His father's final wish was that he "Be a good boy and get an education."[28] I felt drawn to the intersubjectivity between the son and his formerly enslaved father, who had been "deprived . . . of the advantages of making himself what he desired to be," in Youngblood's words. I was interested in what appeared to be a shared understanding about the role education would play in challenging the past and present issues that circumscribed black life—how education was passed on as a community value in the African American consciousness during the days, years, and decades immediately following slavery.²⁹ The final exchange between Youngblood and his father marked him for the rest of his life. The educator pointed to his father's final request as a defining moment in his personal journey and professional trajectory as a teacher.

Youngblood was born into slavery in Colleton County, South Carolina, on April 16, 1862. His mother, Judy, who preceded his father in death, was "a good woman of a Christian family." His father, Edwin, became a farmer after emancipation. While slavery had deprived Edwin of the opportunity to learn to read and write, having been reduced to the property of another person in a state with the longest precedent of antiliteracy laws that criminalized black education, he dreamed that his only son would know a different reality.³⁰ Sandy Youngblood went on to obtain a BA from Claflin University in 1889, having begun his career as an educator while pursuing the degree.

In 1885, Youngblood earned his first teaching certificate, eventually going on to impact thousands of students and

Sandy Rufus Youngblood

"Autobiography—S. R. Youngblood," September 2, 1914

teachers over the course of his long career. He worked as a schoolteacher in Orangeburg, South Carolina, and Greene County, Georgia, before becoming an instructor of sixth-grade English in the college preparatory program at Claflin University, where he later served as an administrator and professor.[31] In 1910, he joined the faculty of Oklahoma Colored Agricultural and Normal University (now Langston University) as an instructor of English language and literature.[32] He also worked as a principal in the public schools of Oklahoma City.

The archive that remains of Youngblood's life reveals him to have been a gifted speaker and lecturer. He regularly gave talks throughout his professional career, especially at commencement ceremonies and teachers' association meetings. His orations covered a variety of themes relating to black education: the ongoing attacks against it, innovative pedagogical methods, questions about black citizenship, and the importance of history.[33] Yet even after decades of teaching, it was Youngblood's final encounter with his father that anchored his outlook. The deeper meaning and purpose of his vocation, it seemed, was framed through its connection to his father's history of captivity. For indeed, Edwin's life reminded Youngblood that black education was and continued to be a contested privilege. And that reality was symbolically reflected in the tension between Youngblood's story and the material artifact in which it is now preserved.

The significance of Youngblood's story is amplified when read in relationship to the ledger in which it is written. Youngblood's repurposing of that financial instrument to write his life in was a literacy act with layered meanings. For indeed, the ledger was essential to the management and administrative processes of slavery. It was used to record ships' inventories during the Middle Passage as well as keep the books of individual plantations. Though the ledger used by Youngblood was filled with empty pages, it was no tabula rasa when the educator encountered it. The ledger was a "scriptive thing," an item of material culture that carried an explicit script, prompts for how it was to be used and interacted with in the racialized world of property.[34] As one historian notes, "Bookkeeping practices developed as part of a trans-Atlantic print culture," and embedded in this print culture was a ritualized condemnation of black life in literary form.[35] For indeed, "The business of slave trading produced two interrelated but distinct bodies of archival material—one quantitative, and the other largely textual. The former comprised the ledgers, bills of lading, and other instruments of accounting by which traders monitored and measured their investments."[36] Every entry that accounted for enslaved Africans as property reinforced the chattel principle that reduced African captives to cargo.

Scholars of transatlantic slavery became critical to my interpretation of Youngblood's autobiography. These memory workers are often forced to rely on records left by slave traders to produce new stories about the enslaved. Yet black people appear in these sources mainly as commodities. They appear as numbers, captive bodies, fungible beings denied individuality.[37] Black scholars such as Vincent Brown, Marisa Fuentes, Thavolia Glymph, Saidiya Hartman, Jennifer Morgan, Julius S. Scott, Stephanie Smallwood, Hortense Spillers, and others have led the way in discussing both the challenges and the possibilities of reconstructing black life worlds, given the limitations of the archive that remains. Furthermore, these black scholars have clarified that the archive of slavery is problematic not only because captives' identities were violently erased in the documents but also because of the aggressive neglect of sources that privilege the perspectives and interior lives of the persecuted.

Writing of her experience searching through archives to locate the stories of those who endured the transatlantic trade, Saidiya

Hartman noted, "The account of commercial transactions was as near as I came to the enslaved." She continued, "In reading the annual reports of trading companies and the letters that traveled from London and Amsterdam to the trade outposts on the West African coast, I searched for the traces of the destroyed. In every line item, I saw a grave. Commodities, cargo, and things don't lend themselves to representations, at least not easily." This erasure of black interior life has proliferated and been amplified across the generations, because "the archive dictates what can be said about the past and the kinds of stories that can be told about the persons catalogued, embalmed, and sealed away in box files and folios."[38]

A kind of double erasure took place. The enslaved are silenced in the archive that remains while also having suffered through the violent events the archival documents imply. What's more, the violence endemic to these sources continues to reverberate. Limited archival materials exist for those who seek to study the experiences of the enslaved, and they are forced to rely on those records, even as such documents of transatlantic print culture render distorted images of black people, representing enslaved people primarily as numerical values, as cargo, as chattel. In such records, black people are dismembered, reduced to hands, wombs, and flesh to be bought and sold—people who were property absent an interior life, described with no names, framed as objects with no heritage, as things lacking the capacity to be self-possessed. This context is important for appreciating the life writing of Edwin Youngblood's son, the child of former slaves who became a teacher and one of the first leaders of freed people.

We know that Youngblood's parents and other ancestors would have been "taken into 'account' as quantities" in ledgers of the plantation and the slave ship.[39] Here, readers may recall James W. C. Pennington's concerns about slavery's archive elucidated in his 1849 autobiography, *The Fugitive Blacksmith*. He observed that

Plantation ledger listing inventory of enslaved people, 1850

Capell Family Papers, Louisiana and Lower Mississippi Valley Collections, LSU Libraries, Baton Rouge, Louisiana

"Autobiography—S. R. Youngblood," September 2, 1914

when the African American scholar approaches archives from the antebellum era, "No where does he find any record of himself *as a man*. On looking at the family record of his old, kind, Christian, master, there he finds his name on a catalogue with the horses, cows, hogs and dogs. However humiliating and degrading it may be to his feelings to find his name written down among the beasts of the field, *that* is just the place, and the *only* place assigned to it by the chattel relation." The violence done by the ledger in black life did not end with emancipation. For even after slavery was abolished, wealthy white landlords and shop owners continued to use it as a tool of antiblack domination, as a record book for marking up and unfairly increasing the debts owed by black farmers and sharecroppers, many of whom were illiterate and unable to contest such economic exploitation.[40]

Sandy Youngblood's decision to write his life over the grid of a ledger challenged past (and present) black subjection. Furthermore, his literacy, life, and self-narration belonged to a heroic tradition of black memory work that was the foundation of black liberatory education—indeed, a tradition that critiqued the social order and the use of the ledger as a tool of antiblackness. Despite the chattel relation codified through instruments such as the ledger, literate ex-slaves such as Pennington insisted on paper that their life held value beyond the arbitrary logics of slavery's capitalism. That was the cornerstone of the educational heritage forged by black people, one based on memories of black life beyond their subjugation in the United States. It was a heritage that emerged in the time of slavery and was carried over to the postemancipation era. Youngblood's narrative in—but not of—the ledger confirmed that he and his predecessors were more than fungible laborers to be owned and controlled by others. The competing narratives reflected the embattled reality of black history. For indeed, the black past is a creation of memory workers who refused white supremacist conceptions of human history. It is a tradition of memory and memorialization that arose from the freedom dreams of the enslaved and their progeny.

YOUNGBLOOD'S AUTOBIOGRAPHY WRITTEN in the ledger was contained in a box labeled "Oversized Items" in the S. Rufus Youngblood papers at Emory University. I found the document only after the curator of African American collections, a black man named Pellom McDaniels III, encouraged me to spend time with the Youngblood materials. He told me that until very recently, Youngblood's small yet rare collection on black pedagogy, made up of lectures, letters, photographs, and personal materials, had remained unprocessed since his death in 1938, a fact that revealed the distinctive challenge plaguing black collections in the post–Civil War era; that even when black people leave behind rich historical collections, they continue to be buried and rendered effectively invisible.

The delay in preserving Youngblood's historical materials drove home an important lesson in my development as a black memory worker: that one cannot assume archival abundance in the afterlife of slavery. Even when African Americans have produced an extensive written record, the history of racialized exclusion within the academy, black economic precarity, and other forms of structural neglect have led to the loss and inaccessibility of archives. This situation exemplifies what the African American studies scholar Sarah Lewis calls "negative assembly," the excision and exclusion of details, ideas, and historical materials to "block scrutiny or skepticism about the foundations of white racial supremacy and the racial order it secured." Thinking with Lewis, I assert that though African Americans during Reconstruction and after had greater access to literacy, more opportunities to narrate the self or to plead their own cause, the loss and erasure of historical materials did not cease. The threats to black history are structural, as well as exacerbated and extended by concerted efforts to undermine knowledge of the black past, such as state legislation banning books on black history and forbidding the teaching of African American studies.

Until now, Youngblood's story has never appeared in my published scholarship. However, I have found myself returning to his story often, especially his handwritten autobiography in the back of that old estate ledger. It constantly pushed me to rethink the political stakes of my work as a scholar of African American educational history and my commitment to honoring the tradition of black memory workers of the past. This particular historical source—both the material object and the substance of Youngblood's writing within it—symbolized, for me, the many opposing forces that constrain black memory work as well as the source of inspiration that continues to animate creative efforts to dig up and remember the black past.

Having become well informed about the hostile environment in the world of historical research, black memory workers seek to mitigate the damage of the powerful practices of erasure that inhibit important truths from being heard. Despite the odds against them, these laborers have continued to craft new ways of preserving black history, constantly seeking out creative means because they had a conviction that the black past would always have a role to play in the worlds to be created in black futures. It was partly Youngblood's story and archive that inspired my commitment not only to write about black educational history but also to advocate for the ongoing work of preserving historical collections that reflect the educational heritage of black people. His account is a poignant reminder that continued historical scholarship on black life will continue to require discovery and proper stewardship of black collections and, as in all aspects of black education, those seeking to carry on this tradition will have to "overcome the oncoming attacks that will be made upon [them]," to quote the words of Youngblood himself.[41] That educator, through his actions, helped me understand that we must continue to dig up the past and at times read against the grain of the archives that exist, even rearranging them to see new patterns and achieve greater understanding.

•

SINCE I ENCOUNTERED Youngblood's archive, a key part of my historical method has included the work of *archival assembly*: the discovery, preservation, and (at times) rearrangement of historical collections to address erasure and archival silences that obstruct the advancement of historical knowledge for the greater good. This is something I find to be necessary when pursuing submerged histories, particularly black histories of the everyday. This approach to historical research emerged from my reading of Youngblood's materials; however, it was solidified as I studied Carter G. Woodson's national partnership with African American teachers to popularize the teaching of black life and culture in segregated schools, especially through his national campaign for Negro History Week. It was there that the stories of people such as Burroughs and Woodson converged with the lessons I learned from Youngblood's autobiography.

When writing my dissertation, I learned that the national expansion of Negro History Week had been the result of grassroots organizing by African American teachers who worked in direct partnership with Woodson. After finding several examples of his partnership with the professional networks of African American teachers, particularly organizations formerly known as "Colored Teachers Associations," I decided to seek out the records of those institutions to connect the dots of this story. I noticed a great degree of consistency in the language black students and teachers had used to characterize their lessons in "Negro history," which made me interested in determining how such information circulated across communities scattered throughout the nation in both rural and urban contexts. After identifying the records of Colored Teachers Associations as the most reliable set of historical sources to document this, I sought out records across state lines, hoping to demonstrate the breadth and depth of Woodson's collaboration with African American educators and thus elevate the important intellectual and political legacy of black teachers. By that point, I was convinced that the legacy of black schoolteachers was underappreciated in the stories told and retold about black education prior to the desegregation era of the mid–twentieth century and furthermore that African American teachers had gone unacknowledged for the critical role they had played in the Black Freedom Movement. Those teachers worked diligently, over the course of generations, to nurture the political and intellectual imaginations of black youths who later became leaders who changed the direction of US history during the twentieth century.

However, locating the materials of Colored Teachers Associations proved to be more challenging than I had expected. What I found while traveling to more than a dozen states and Washington, DC, was deeply concerning. Some records had been catalogued and were easy to access. The majority, however, were unprocessed, meaning that they were stored physically in research collections without having been catalogued, making them undetectable in library systems and archival databases. A large quantity of the materials existed in bits and pieces, scattered among various historical repositories and personal collections. Sometimes I was told that the materials did not exist—after driving from New Orleans to Jackson, Mississippi, on a hunch—only for a nearly complete collection to later be discovered in an old plastic bin, tucked away in an archive; unprocessed, but there waiting to be engaged and accounted for. Sometimes the magazines, journals, and bulletins of Colored Teachers Associations sat on shelves in libraries as ordinary reference materials, despite their physically fragile state and historical significance. But there were also beautiful moments of serendipity, like the time a ninety-two-year-old black woman named Annie Mable McDaniel Abrams, a former teacher and staff member of the Arkansas Teachers Association, personally shared her bound copy of the organization's journals during a conversation in her home, just blocks from the historic Central High School in Little Rock.

Recognizing the disorderly nature of the archives, I decided that my work as a scholar included the custodial task of securing the long-term preservation of these collections—to ensure that an archive will remain available to subsequent generations of scholars, who will exceed my work and indeed my lifetime. Like many other black memory workers of today and the past, I realized that advancing the tradition that made my work possible and that continues to inspire leaders and freedom dreaming in African American communities would require thinking beyond the conventions of the historical profession and the current configurations of archives.

And so since 2018, I have been building the Black Teacher Archive (BTA), which entails locating, cataloging, and digitizing the serial journals and publications of Colored Teachers Associations (CTA). In October 2023, the Black Teacher Archive became available to the public as an open-access online portal of digitized historical documents that allow for in-text searching. This work is being done in collaboration with two colleagues, the scholar and writer Imani Perry and the archivist Micha Broadnax, each of whom draws on the tradition of black memory workers in their own way.

Containing over fifty thousand pages of written materials by African American educators through the Jim Crow era, the Black Teacher Archive is the largest digital repository of material on

Imani Perry, Annie Mable McDaniel Abrams, and Jarvis Givens (June 2023)

African American teachers and education. Based on our estimates, approximately 2,500 issues of CTA journals were published. Of this number, we have located, digitized, and processed nearly 2,000 issues. The publication dates range from 1907 to 1973, and the journals, representing the national CTA as well as affiliates in fifteen states and Washington, DC, were collected from more than eighty-five historical repositories. We have also digitized eighteen volumes of Colored Teachers Association histories written by leaders of those organizations during the 1960s as they were forced to merge with white professional groups and were effectively integrated out of existence (and public memory). Given the scattered existence of the physical materials across the country, BTA has taken shape as a digital archive that does not, and cannot, exist as a physical collection.

Now that the Black Teacher Archive has been assembled, black memory workers can ask new kinds of questions about the past when it comes to the role teachers played in all aspects of African American life and engage in deeper analyses of the social and political realities of black education in the United States. For instance, given the digital form of this collection, we are now able to search tens of thousands of pages of historical material on black teachers and schools using specific names, keywords, and topics (*desegregation, literacy, Negro history*, etc.). This search capability enables analyses that were previously nearly impossible when these materials were scattered across the country. One of the specific benefits of this collection is its documentation of Negro History Week's foundational years from 1926 up until its expansion to Black History Month in 1976. It is worth noting that Black History Month does not appear in these journals because by the mid-1970s, Colored Teachers Associations, which had collectively existed for more than a century, had recently been merged with white teachers associations as part of the national effort to advance desegregation in American public schools in the wake of *Brown v. Board of Education*.[42] Their dismantling had a devastating impact on African American communities and on black teachers as a professional group, an aspect of African American history that has recently been examined more closely.[43]

IN SEARCHING THE records of black teachers for "Negro History Week," one finds hundreds of references in these journals. The details included reveal the way black teachers across the country used Negro History Week to support their efforts to develop black students as learners and future leaders. What's more, these records make clear that the spread of Negro History Week (and later Black History Month) would not have been possible without black teachers and their leadership through the Jim Crow era.

In 1935, for instance, black teachers in West Virginia described Negro History Week celebrations across the state, noting that nearly twenty thousand black students had participated in programs focused on black achievements in the past and present. According to *The Bulletin*, the official publication of the West Virginia State Teachers' Association, professors at West Virginia State College partnered with the state supervisor of Negro schools to coordinate a special program in fifteen black high schools in the southern part of the state. The program focused on black history in West Virginia, methods of historical research, and plans for more thoroughly incorporating black history into West Virginia schools, especially since many high school graduates would go on to be teachers in the lower grades.[44] Decades later, Negro History Week continued to be widely celebrated in the schools of West Virginia, especially Frederick Douglass High School in Huntington, where Carter G. Woodson had once been a student and later a principal. In 1953, the West Virginia State Teachers' Association reported that the commemorative holiday was "a red letter event on the calendar at Douglass High School." The school's ninth-grade English class, taught by Miss Myra E. Fairfax, opened the week's celebration with a radio skit dramatizing the life of Frederick Douglass. The students also celebrated the life of Carter G. Woodson, even leading a fundraiser for the Association for the Study of Negro Life and History, which Woodson had founded in 1915.[45]

Celebrations of black life and culture were often collaborative efforts among multiple institutions. That was especially the case in communities where Historically Black Colleges and Universities (HBCUs) were located. In 1946, a group of Georgia educators planned an elaborate calendar of events for Negro History Week that included college students, scholars from various campuses across the state, public events, and curated learning opportunities for local students in elementary and secondary schools. Students in Albany State's Negro History class and scholars in the Department of Social Sciences created an exhibit, "The Negro in American and World Culture," that included historical materials ranging from large gold-framed photographs of historical figures and written descriptions of important events in black history to a collection of artistic wood carvings and material artifacts from the Congo. Several local schools created student assignments based on the exhibit, and guest lectures by professors from Morehouse College and Fort Valley State College were also featured in the week's events.[46]

In 1947, more than twenty years after the inauguration of Negro History Week, black teachers in North Carolina discussed why that era's focus on black history and culture had been so important. One history instructor at Fayetteville State Teachers College stated, "For almost 250 years the Negro was buried in slavery and all but forgotten. Since slavery he has continually been climbing up the rough side of the mountain, asking the white man to give him, at least, an opportunity." The educator continued, "The noble deeds of Negroes are conspicuous in American histories by their absence" while "Daily newspapers usually magnify our crimes and minimize our virtues." Given such hostility in the world of ideas and representation, he urged teachers across the state to continue championing Negro History Week, insisting that "Acquainting young people with the accomplishment of their race is sowing seeds of racial pride in fertile soils." He framed Negro History Week as part of a movement to transcend the racial myths used to justify the unequal treatment of African Americans, a movement to refuse to countenance racial myths that had the power to miseducate black students.[47]

Teachers developed creative ways to align Negro History Week celebrations with learning goals. They used the study of black life and culture to help students develop skills that would be transferable to other subject areas and increase students' broader academic development, including creative writing, public speaking, and critical thinking about pressing social issues in the past and present. In Chesterfield County, Virginia, educators expressed a desire to improve students' communication skills during the 1952–1953 school year and subsequently created a radio program centered on the voices of their students. The program was the perfect opportunity for children to share what they were learning about black history and culture over the local airwaves during Negro History Week. The February broadcast, entitled "What Catherine Learned," featured students at Hickory Hill School in Richmond, who prepared short speeches detailing what a student named Catherine had learned about "the Negro" through her studies. A photograph was included in the *Virginia Education Bulletin* depicting the students standing around the table, scripts in hand, preparing to record their segment for the radio broadcast, all dressed up for their big day. The teachers explained how in the days prior to arriving at the radio studio, the students had rehearsed by recording themselves in class using a tape recorder, which had enabled them to listen to themselves and offer feedback to one another on how to improve their performance in oral communication and public speaking.[48]

Hickory Hill students getting ready to record Negro History Week broadcast, 1953

In 1964, students at Lamar Elementary School in Del Valle, Texas, observed Negro History Week by studying historical narratives and social science data, as well as black art and music that reflected "the path of the Negro heritage," according to the school's teachers, and concluded their program by focusing on black achievements in the present. The school's chorus also staged a play they prepared with their teacher, Miss Minnie C. Overton, entitled *Out of Darkness Comes a New Day*, that dramatized historical developments in black history. A group of students who participated in the week's program appear in a photograph featured in *The Texas Standard*, the official publication of the Colored Teachers State Association of Texas. The students can be seen posing in front of a bulletin board bearing the words "Negro History Week: A Basis for the New Freedom," the tagline being the theme of Negro History Week advertised by the Association for the Study of Negro Life and History that year. A photograph of Carter G. Woodson appears in the center of the frame, between the students; the founder of Negro History Week had died fourteen years prior.[49]

Black teachers in Texas explained that more expansive knowledge about the black past was an important basis of the African American freedom movement and that through Negro History Week, black students and teachers were "calling attention to the contributions of Negroes to the cultural, economical and social development of America and the world." They stressed, "This is especially important in this new day of freedom when protests are so widespread against the lack of inclusion of Negroes in planning, employment and other facets of national world living." Furthermore, they said, Negro History Week was an invitation for teachers and students to participate in a broader campaign to

Lamar Elementary School Negro History Week student participants, 1964

challenge antiblackness in mainstream curricula because it helped communities expose "the lack of proper treatment of the Negro ethnic group in textbooks, American mass media, and other items of publicity and propaganda."⁵⁰

These stories of Negro History Week stretch far and wide in the records of black teachers. They are most prevalent in the records from the southern states, in which the majority of black people lived during the first half of the twentieth century; however, they also appear in northern states, if more sparingly. For instance, the New Jersey Organization of Teachers of Colored Children described Negro History Week activities in 1942 in its spring bulletin circulated to members. The coverage included a review of a new book edited by Howard University professor Sterling A. Brown and two of his colleagues entitled *The Negro Caravan: Writings by American Negroes*. The bulletin recommended the work as an excellent source for reading and teaching about the history of the race.⁵¹ Black teachers in New Jersey had long sought literature on black life and culture to be used with black students. For instance, alongside Burroughs's National Training School on the list of institutions using Carter G. Woodson's textbook by the late 1920s was the Bordentown School, an independent black industrial and manual arts school in the southern part of the state.⁵²

Despite there being a smaller number of black teachers in states such as New Jersey, Massachusetts, and New York, we know that the early black history movement made its way to those parts of the country and beyond. Sometimes the work was carried on not only by black teachers but also by students. I was reminded of this by a written exchange between a student in Salem, New Jersey, and Carter G. Woodson in the 1920s. A high school student, Vaughn C. Mason, had met Carter G. Woodson and purchased a copy of his 1928 textbook, *Negro Makers of History*, likely at an event hosted by African American teachers in New Jersey or possibly in nearby Philadelphia, in April 1929. Mason later wrote to the author, thanking him for the book and sharing that he had taken the text to his high school teacher, who was unfamiliar with scholarship on Negro history. In that instance, it was a student who took the initiative to inform his teacher that there were books about the black past that documented the contributions of African-descended people to human civilization. Responding to Mason's letter on June 13, Woodson wrote, "My dear Mr. Mason: On returning to my desk I find here your letter. I am delighted to know that you find the book interesting and that it made an impression on your teacher. With best wishes, I am, Yours very truly, Carter G. Woodson, Director." While Salem, New Jersey, maintained segregated elementary schools, in which mostly black teachers taught black students, the city's high school enrolled both black and white students, but employed exclusively white teachers. Therefore, it is very possible that Vaughn Mason may have been exposed to black history prior to his time in high school by black teachers involved in New Jersey's black teachers association, which would explain the personally signed copy of Woodson's textbook in his possession.

Vaughn C. Mason's story is not found in the Black Teacher Archive. It was shared by my colleague Professor Pamela Mason after she stumbled upon her late father's personal copy of *Negro Makers of History*, which still had Woodson's letter tucked into the cover. My point is that even as the Black Teacher Archive helps expand our thinking about the world of black education, specifically the labor of African American educators, it has its limits. The voices of African American students, who were active participants in the tradition of black memory workers, is not immediately represented. However, through supplementary materials, such as Vaughn's old textbook and personal correspondence with "the Father of Black History," we can continue to develop a more expansive perspective on the black past. This letter is a testament to why continued preservation is important and the fact that the possibilities for such work are often hidden in plain sight: in the attics of our family houses, in a storage room of an old school, in old suitcases filled with things our late grandmothers and grandfathers collected because they understood them to be meaningful pieces of the past they deemed worthy of holding on to.

THE BLACK TEACHER ARCHIVE is important because it enables contemporary black memory workers and researchers to recover details about important events such as Negro History Week. However, it also enables us to explore more obscure social facts of the black past, such as details of everyday aspects of African American life, thus enabling us to increase our understanding of how black people built and sustained community institutions, formed relations, and crafted solutions to the challenges they faced. I was reminded of these more expansive aspects of the Black Teacher Archive when my first teacher of black history, Miss Myron Ruth Butterfield, discussed her memories of an event called Field Day.

Readers will recall that it was Miss Butterfield, my preschool teacher, who introduced me to Black History Month in 1993, as she prepared my classmates and me to recite excerpts from Martin Luther King, Jr.'s "mountaintop" speech. During my conversation with Miss Butterfield in 2019, she shared many details about her early education in Grenada, Mississippi, during the 1940s and '50s. In addition to her memories of Negro History Week, she discussed Field Day as being among her fondest memories as a student, a program collaboratively planned by the black educators in her county. During the gatherings, black schools from different towns came together for academic competitions, food, sporting events, and student performances. And just as Negro History

Week celebrations can be traced in the Black Teacher Archive, so can lesser known events such as Field Day programs. While unfamiliar to most readers today, such events were an important part of the cultural life of black segregated schools.

At six years old, Miss Butterfield began her formal education in a school built on land owned by a family of black farmers. She attended the school from first through eighth grades, from the mid-1940s though the early 1950s, before transitioning to high school in Calhoun County. She recalled her earliest teachers as being very nice people, stern but caring. She also recalled her teachers coordinating plays and events in which students were required to recite speeches, perform plays, and demonstrate other academic achievements accomplished over the year. She recalled, "I used to be a good speaker.... I wasn't shy or nothing. It got where I would speak at . . . a program called Fields Day. All the schools would meet up, and they would have a cookout and they would have programs that we'd be a part of. And spelling contests and all that." Miss Butterfield's memory of Field Day is traceable across black rural schools during the Jim Crow era. Indeed, many references to Field Day events can be found in the Black Teacher Archive. As explained in 1934 by a black educator in Mississippi, Field Day was also a time when schools came together at the end of the school term to celebrate their collective accomplishments. Writing in the publication of the Mississippi Teacher Association, he noted, "The teachers and pupils have done some few things so well that they want others to know about it, thus they come together to show what they have done and how they did it."[53]

Miss Butterfield's account of Field Day highlighted an example of black history in the everyday that challenges the flattened descriptions of African American education in the Jim Crow South as separate, unequal, and nothing else. Her memories of black educational life in Grenada, Mississippi, provide details about things that were valuable to those communities, experiences they created that affirmed black youths and nurtured their development despite the material inequities that existed between white and black schools. Field Day is an example of the kinds of experiences African American teachers curated for black youths to feel valued, empowered, and part of a community that nurtured their educational aspirations, even in the context of a school system that was explicitly antiblack.

Field Day celebrations did not occur during Negro History Week, nor were they explicitly about black history. Yet they represent the kind of enriching events and relationships that characterized black education during Jim Crow, reflecting the kinds of social facts to be studied in black histories of the everyday. Events such as Field Day can easily be lost to history; however, such mundane experiences in black life are just as important to remember as the names of black inventors and political leaders or famous songs and artwork. They are descriptive of the distinct ways black people cared for one another and made room for laughter and spiritual nourishment amid the chaos and violence of Jim Crow. These are important lessons. They provide equipment for living—in the past, present, and future. Such stories are also worthy of studying and committing to memory.

The possibilities of recovery in the records of the black past are vast. And there is much to be learned from the ways black teachers used the content of black life and culture to develop skills and leadership among African American youths. Take for instance, an unexpected encounter with the eleven-year-old Alice Walker in a 1955 issue of *The Herald*, the official journal of the Georgia Teachers and Education Association. In the journal, the contribution of the future Pulitzer Prize winner appeared among those by many other students participating in academic competitions in the rural schools of Putnam County, Georgia, in a program very similar to the Field Day described by Miss Butterfield and other teachers in Mississippi. The story is a beautiful reminder that long before Walker went looking for the grave of Zora Neale Hurston in the hope of marking her final resting place and reintroducing her literature to the world, she was an ordinary black girl in a rural community made up of other very capable and skilled black people. Like so many other great achievers, she went on to do extraordinary things, largely because of the sacrifices made by everyday people in her community who helped inspire her and cultivate her gifts.

The article documenting Walker's elementary school program, entitled "Notes from the Field," is a detailed description of a Dramatic Festival and

Dramatic Festival and Student Activity Day, Putnam County, Georgia, 1955

A Negro History Week Display, Bells Chapel School, Mrs. Mary S. Hogan Principal.

Student Activity Day in Putnam County's black segregated schools. The event took place across two days, February 28 and March 3, and it included a play performed by teachers entitled "Manless Wedding," an exhibition hall in which schools showed displays from their Negro History Week lessons, and students' participation in several academic and athletic competitions. The winning Negro History Week display came from Bell's Chapel Elementary School, and it was entitled "The Road Has Been Rugged—We Are Still Climbing." However, among the student competitions one finds the name Alice Walker of the East Putnam Consolidated School listed as the second-place winner in two categories: interpretive reading and oratorical contest. No information is included about the content of her dramatic reading or her speech, but given the schools' recent Negro History Week celebrations, it is likely that her performances engaged some aspect of black history and culture.[54]

In the records of Colored Teachers Associations, we find not only the words of prominent black figures such as Mary McLeod Bethune, James Weldon Johnson, and Carter G. Woodson—for indeed, such monumental men and women do appear—but also the stories of ordinary teachers and black youths in the context of their communities. We find them learning and striving to make a new world despite a social context that said they had never accomplished anything and were undeserving of equality and being afforded the same respect as others. We find the early life of a young writer, reading and speaking to her community, finding her voice among a chorus of many. In that early publication, for which Alice Walker took home second place in her local dramatic arts festival, we are pushed to understand that our geniuses are rarely, if ever, of their own making; they are often formed and nurtured by relationships that inspire them to achieve the things they accomplish that contribute some good to the world and its cultures.

People such as Walker who go on to do extraordinary things

are often the products of ordinary communities whose members are seeking to live meaningful and dignified lives despite hostile environmental factors. In an autobiographical account, Walker recalled some of the history of her early school community in Putnam County, Georgia, detailing how local white citizens had viewed black schools with contempt, even targeting these schools with violence. Her father, Willie Lee Walker, was a sharecropper who helped organize the first African American school in Eatonton, Georgia, which was later set ablaze. The story had been passed on to Walker, who recorded it in her journal, recounting how her father had walked around town talking to parents, raising money to build the school and how local whites had later burned it to the ground. Racially motivated acts of school arson had been recurring events in African American communities across the South since the nineteenth century. Black school burnings were especially widespread during the Reconstruction era, when more than 630 black schools in the southern states were set on fire. In detailing that one event among the many, Walker described how her father "had to humble himself to get use of an abandoned shack" for the school to operate in until another structure could be erected.[55] Time and time again, African American communities continued to rebuild and remake their worlds as they advanced their cause. They did so in the same way that black people continued to recover and hold on to their memories, even though their history had been taken away and discredited in cyclical fashion, only to be reconstructed by the many hands of committed black memory workers and laborers over generations.

The violent opposition to black education was part of the social context in the black schools of Putnam County, where African American teachers and community members worked to carve out meaningful learning environments in which they could inspire black youths and cultivate their aspirations as future leaders, professionals, responsible citizens, and black memory workers. Indeed, it was in those spaces that Walker learned that she came from a people who valued one another and had a history worthy of studying and holding on to. It was among those everyday people and at events such as Field Days and dramatics festivals planned by rural teachers that Walker learned what it meant to be "a people"; that "A people do not throw their geniuses away. And if they are thrown away, it is our duty as artists and as witnesses for the future to collect them again for the sake of our children, and, if necessary, bone by bone."[56]

Genius can be found among individuals as well as in the collective. Knowing both things to be true is a vital lesson for black memory workers. Like Zora Neale Hurston, Alice Walker is a "genius of the South" who came from a people for whom genius abounds, where their faith and their gifts (or faith in their gifts) were the only things that sustained them on their journey along a rugged road—a road that they were climbing in 1955 and that we are still climbing today. There is much to be learned from studying the lives of black achievers of the past as well as the communities from which they emerged. However, to know their truths requires our refusing to discard them. It requires that we hold on to the stories and pieces of them that remain. When possible, we must collect them "bone by bone" and put them into a place commensurate with the value they hold for us. It requires us to do all that we can to place them beyond the reach of immediate harm and degradation. That was the mission that informed Zora Neale Hurston's Cemetery for the Illustrious Negro Dead, it was that of William Cooper Nell's Crispus Attucks Day, it was the Atlantic Ocean for the female captives aboard the *Hudibras* who refused to allow their dead favorite to be defiled by their enslavers, and it was Negro History Week for the many teachers and students around the country who worked to cultivate a collective memory of the black past. It is also the Black Teacher Archive and so many other creations by black memory workers who have refused to throw our geniuses away or allow their spirits to evaporate, to borrow from Hurston.

Until recently, Walker was unaware that any record of the 1955 Dramatic Festival and Student Activity Day existed, though she carries fond memories of her early years in black segregated schools as sites critical to her intellectual and creative development. When my colleague Imani Perry shared the record from the Black Teacher Archive with Walker in 2023, she was in disbelief. The pages of *The Herald* prompted her to again remember what those ordinary teachers and black community members had meant to her. It prompted her to reflect on how they had helped clear a path for all that she has done for her people and the world of literature. She shared the satisfaction and gratitude such memories invoked for her in the following words.

> Wow. This is such a shock. To even see East Putnam Consolidated School and to be alive to remember being there! My father. My mother. My teachers. Everyone pulling so hard for us. Building that structure themselves, for us. On cousin Dave Henry Simmons' land that he donated to the community.
>
> Ah, it brings tears . . . they worked so hard, believed so hard. Love us.
>
> Blessed be for memories of community that thrived. Regardless. . . . And what about that "manless" wedding! If they only knew! Some of them probably did know! ;-). Ah, the innocence to youth; the subtle un-programming!

Walker's memories of East Putnam Consolidated School and the labor of the local community to build the school is substantiated in the archival record. In 1949, Georgia's black teachers described how local parents had helped erect the school building, particularly how they had organized before and after church on Sundays to continue the work. They reported, "In an effort to administer to their spiritual needs and carry out their educational obligations to themselves and their children the P. T. A. members of East Putnam Consolidated School met Sunday, March 6, at 10:00 A. M. and from the school they went to their church services. In order to keep the progress wheel rolling the ladies in this latter group adorning themselves in men's attire have put the second coat of paint on the front of their new school."[57]

While Walker recalled the subtle "un-programming" that occurred through the "Manless Wedding" staged by her teachers in 1955, we might also read the women "adorning themselves in men's attire" in 1949 to assist with painting the school structure as part of a much longer history of black women challenging conventional notions of gender, particularly when it came to leadership and labor. Such narratives prompt one to consider how such memories from the black world of Walker's youth inspired her creation of the black life worlds rendered by her imagination years later. Indeed, black novelists and poets have also played crucial roles as black memory workers, helping preserve historical truths through fictionalized accounts, especially in areas in which the historical record has been silent, even when an abundance of memories passed on by members of black communities exposes those absences and the distortions they perpetuate.

•

BLACK MEMORY WORKERS of previous generations made clear that digging up the past and organizing communities to engage the work of its preservation was a central part of the black freedom struggle, because such knowledge has, and must, continue to inform the curricular foundation of any meaningful model of liberatory education. What's more, they recognized that black memory work would continue to be an archaeological project bound up in the continued struggle of a persecuted people. They knew that their efforts to recover critical information about the black past would be tested, undermined, and at times devalued by those in positions of power, precisely because black memory has always exposed difficult truths that many people would prefer to ignore. For these reasons, black memory has often been deemed seditious and at odds with state memory; these recollections of the past have been deemed too politicized and radical, too discomforting to those in power, especially when they delve into the lives and stories of everyday black people.

As we move into the next era of Black History Month, it is important that the politics of black memory work and the labor required for its development be made more transparent. I was reminded of this while working with a group of African American high school students in an out-of-school program focused on black history, in which they said that they had never heard of an archive or what an archivist does. They told me that after listening to Micha Broadnax, the project director of the Black Teacher Archive, discussing the work she had done to collect and preserve black memories and why she felt compelled to do so. The students were intrigued; they made many connections with the process of archiving material on social media in their own lives, expressing a heightened awareness of the need to do more work to preserve black histories in their community of Long Beach, California. At the same time, they were transparent about the fact that they had never been invited to think about the behind-the-scenes labor of preserving black history. They had never had the opportunity to consider the work that enables the truths of black history, both beautiful and terrible, to have a hearing.

At a time when black history is being attacked on many fronts, we must educate communities about how power shapes the process of historical production. To develop vigilant memory workers and scholars of the black past, concerned parties must accept the responsibility of clarifying how silence has been and continues to be produced in the way historical sources are created, through the decisions made regarding which sources should be preserved, and furthermore, that this silence can influence the historical record when scholars (myself included) make decisions about where to look for answers and how historical information is presented to the world. The truth about black history is that its form emerges from the substance of black lives lived in the past as well as the decisions we make as memory workers in narrating the details of said lives. Knowing these things is critical for the development of a mature historical consciousness in both individuals and communities.

Our memories carry our truth, and our truth is cumulative. Therefore, every generation of black people bears the responsibility to cultivate memory workers who will continue to recover, rewrite, and seek new depths of understanding about the black past to be shared with themselves, first, for their own growth and empowerment, but also with the world, for the broader pursuit of freedom and justice. The cultivation of such laborers is urgent, precisely because the threat of erasure, as proven by history, is so fiercely repetitive.

PART IV

WHERE DO WE GO FROM HERE?

Creating the Future(s) of Black History

> The tendency to ignore the Negro's contributions to American life and strip him of his personhood is as old as the earliest history books and as contemporary as the morning's newspaper. To offset this cultural homicide, the Negro must rise up with an affirmation of his own Olympian manhood. Any movement for the Negro's freedom that overlooks this necessity is only waiting to be buried.... The Negro will only be truly free when he reaches down to the inner depths of his own being and signs with the pen and ink of assertive selfhood his own emancipation proclamation.
>
> —MARTIN LUTHER KING, JR., *WHERE DO WE GO FROM HERE: CHAOS OR COMMUNITY?* (1967)

ON MONDAY, FEBRUARY 19, 1934, W. E. B. Du Bois delivered a Negro History Week lecture to more than four hundred educators and students at Central Congregational Church in New Orleans. The event was hosted by the New Orleans Teacher Association, a local affiliate of the Louisiana Colored Teachers' Association. To welcome the widely celebrated black scholar, the association's president, Miss Inez Labat, introduced Du Bois, prompting the audience to greet him with "thunderous applause" as he approached the podium.[1] Du Bois's speech was based on his forthcoming book *Black Reconstruction in America, 1860–1880*, the field-shifting interpretation of the critical period following the Civil War, when African Americans gained unprecedented access to political power before it was stripped away by the emergence of Jim Crow. The book was published in 1935, quickly becoming an "imperishable" and "monumental achievement," to echo Martin Luther King, Jr.'s assessment years later.[2]

According to *The Louisiana Weekly*, "The well-informed speaker began his discussion by showing that unlike other races the heritage of the Negro has not been pictured in sculpture, friezes, pictures, widely circulated stories, magazines, newspapers, and other periodicals." However, Du Bois insisted, the issue was not only that scholars ignored critical aspects of black history and culture but that white historians twisted key aspects of the race's history and that such whitewashing of the past compromised the public's ability to conceive of historically informed visions of justice. For instance, he criticized the treatment of slavery, abolition, and Reconstruction in the dominant historical narratives in his speech in New Orleans. He stressed, according to white historians, "It looks as though slavery in the U.S. was apparently nobody's fault . . . [and] at the close of slavery, the Negro was given the vote" then "failed dismally." Yet "this story," he explained, "is entirely false in interpretation . . . and is entirely misleading." To correct such myths, he presented "conclusive facts and figures on 'The Negro and Reconstruction'" as the teachers and students sat spellbound for forty minutes.[3]

Du Bois discussed the political role of fugitive slaves in the abolitionist movement and how a tradition of black self-determination and freedom dreaming laid the groundwork for the political organizing and later campaigns waged by black leaders and their allies during Reconstruction. He delivered his talk very matter-of-factly. He spoke without moving "from a chosen spot, without any mannerisms, without any oratorical flights of fancy, without any play upon the emotions of his listeners." The facts alone kept the audience on the edge of their seats as they contemplated their history as a people and their current circumstances in Jim Crow Louisiana.[4]

Du Bois's revision to the dominant historical interpretations of Reconstruction arose from a longer tradition of black memory work among black teachers. For indeed, he was not just filling a gap in the historical record; he was applying a red pen to the narratives constructed by white historians, whose interpretations for so long had been based on the racist ideology of the period. Yet black educators had long recognized the history of Reconstruction to be critically important because it was intimately connected with the status of black citizenship and freedom. During Reconstruction the freedmen and their radical Republican allies worked to rebuild the South and create the conditions for social equality. It was the first time African Americans had significant access to the levers of power in the United States, as black men could now exercise the right to vote and held political office in sizable numbers, amounting to more than 1,500 officeholders in state legislatures, Congress, and various local positions during the era. Reconstruction and the gains made during the period would be gutted after the Compromise of 1877, especially after federal troops were removed from the South, thus removing the sole force helping to maintain order in a context where the former white masters were eager to reassert control in a manner reminiscent of the slavery era. The narrative perpetuated by white historians such as William Archibald Dunning of Columbia University—that Reconstruction had been a failure—had major political ramifications, especially because that "failure" was interpreted as evidence of black people's inferiority and inability to lead. That skewed interpretation of Reconstruction functioned as a racial myth and was used to justify why black disenfranchisement was necessary. The "failure" of Reconstruction, and of supposedly ill-prepared black political leaders, was evidence (for some) that black people were a "helpless race ... [a] child race" and could not be expected "to work out its own salvation in fierce and hostile competition with the strongest and best developed race on the globe," as explained by the president of North Carolina College of Agriculture and Mechanic Arts during an address to a meeting of the American Academy of Political and Social Science in April 1901.[5] The distorted interpretation of Reconstruction used to justify African Americans' second-class citizenship is one of the many examples of how history has been used as a weapon and demonstrates the cost of not being armed with the intellectual resources produced by black memory workers, for indeed, the myth of black people's alleged failure during Reconstruction had real material consequences.

To be clear, the black people who lived through Reconstruction and those who came to study the historical record while accounting for the perspectives and experiences of black people knew otherwise. African American teachers were especially sensitive to such a flawed historical perspective. Indeed, their social standing as a professional group resulted largely from the Reconstruction government's creation of free public schooling in the South, which is widely accepted as one of the greatest achievements of the period.

Oliver Pope, a teacher in Templeton, Virginia, was one such educator whose black memory work anticipated the corrections made by Du Bois. However, his desire to render a truthful historical account would cost him his job in 1908 when a white school superintendent overheard him challenge the official curriculum in his classroom. In his memoir, Pope recalled the administrator, who was also a former Confederate soldier, entering his classroom midlesson while Pope's back was toward the door. The teacher and his students "were discussing the reconstruction period when he entered without my knowledge," Pope wrote. "I was defending, contrary to our text, the Congressional plan: 'If the Negro had not been given the vote at that time—' A sharp 'Then what?' interrupted, and I turned, startled and confused." The superintendent had caught Pope off guard; for indeed, the educator would have never risked teaching the lesson that way in the presence of white school leaders, who, in the early twentieth century, were openly antiblack and generally used their positions of authority to keep African Americans "in their place." As opposed to walking back his comments, Pope invited the superintendent to address the class. However, the administrator refused. Pope recalled, "the red-faced old soldier turned on his heels and walked out with military dignity. And then I knew my name was Ichabod." He was fired shortly thereafter.[6]

Pope's attempt to reconstruct the black past for students in his classroom, both to fill absences and to correct racist interpretations, was not an isolated event; it was part of a persistent struggle that was always a collective endeavor. A through line exists from the actions of freedpeople waging campaigns during Reconstruction to build schools as one of their first acts following emancipation to the curricular programs of teachers such as Pope, often passed on through oral tradition, all the way to Du Bois's extensive corrections to the dominant interpretations of black life and culture in schoolbooks and scholarly literature. Nearly thirty years after Pope's classroom encounter, Du Bois undertook a similar task of historical recovery, one that became a defining project of his career.

Black teachers in New Orleans were still discussing Reconstruction following Du Bois's visit. They explored ways of incorporating the new insights they had learned from him into the academic program for the school year. In November 1934, a delegation of New Orleans teachers attended the annual meeting of the Association for the Study of Negro Life and History in Houston, Texas, where they shared plans for their lessons on Reconstruction. At the meeting, they discussed with Carter G. Woodson and other attendees the fact that the teachers in New Orleans were organizing a special float for the city's Mardi Gras Carnival that would commemorate the lives and leadership of African Americans during Reconstruction in Louisiana.[7] It is very possible that Woodson discussed the Reconstruction period with black students in New Orleans' segregated schools when he visited them on his way back to Washington, DC, from the association's meeting.

John W. Hoffman Junior High School was one of the stops Woodson made on his journey back east. A photo was taken of nearly thirty-five Hoffman students as they awaited his arrival. The students are dressed in their best attire and are shown to be studying in anticipation of meeting "the Father of Negro history," as he was often called. In the photo, students are reading from a class set of *Negro Makers of History*, the textbook Woodson had published in 1928. The book can be seen in the students' hands or on their desks. In the book, he provided an extensive treatment of the Reconstruction period, particularly in a chapter entitled "Rebuilding the Waste Places." In it, the students encountered a black perspective on the Reconstruction era. Woodson explained that "a majority of the Negro officeholders were competent in spite of statements to the contrary [referring to white historical narratives]. There was much opposition to the Negro as a voter and an officeholder, but this was founded largely on prejudice. The strongest argument against this policy was that the majority of freedmen were uneducated and did not own property."[8]

He also described how racial violence had been used to undermine the work being done by elected black officials during Reconstruction—a fact substantiated by an abundance of historical evidence, though absent in accounts by white historians. He wrote, "A hooded order, called the Ku Klux Klan, rode in robes of disguise by night and struck terror to the hearts of Negroes by beating and killing them and their leaders. Actual massacres followed at places like New Orleans, Louisiana, and Hamburg, South Carolina." What's more, he emphasized, while black people had been elected in historic numbers, they had never been in the majority of elected officials. He noted, "People became enraged against the Negroes for offenses which they never committed; for only a small portion of the offices were ever held by Negroes." Indeed, it was "interlopers from the North and native loyal whites [who] were always in the majority of the offices." Therefore, he argued, corruption in the Reconstruction government could not be explained away by the supposed ineptitude of black leaders: "If these State governments were not properly administered, if they were corrupt, then, it was the fault of the whites, not of the Negroes."[9]

Hoffman Junior High School students studying the history of the Negro, from Negro History Week pamphlet published by the Association for the Study of Negro Life and History, 1935

Conversations continued among New Orleans educators after Du Bois and Woodson visited the city and even after Du Bois's *Black Reconstruction in America, 1860–1880* was published. In 1937, two years after the book's release, Vivian Robinson, a senior at Valena C. Jones Normal and Practice School of New Orleans, wrote a short review of Du Bois's book in the school publication, *The Moving Finger*. In it, she appealed to readers, comprising other preservice teachers, to "Read the book, 'Black Reconstruction' and make all of this information part of your own!"[10]

Teachers and students in New Orleans were not alone in their studies of Du Bois's text, just as they were not alone in celebrating Negro History Week or reading Carter G. Woodson's popular textbooks. Using their networks, including Colored Teachers Associations and other black social and civic organizations, they shared strategies for carrying forward the tradition of black memory work. Knowledge about the black past, especially critical junctures in the African American freedom struggle such as Reconstruction, was of great concern to black educators and students. And Reconstruction was one of many historical topics that became major points of contention between black memory workers and mainstream white historians—for indeed, black scholars had strong criticisms of the treatment of slavery in mainstream historical narratives. White scholars overwhelmingly presented the violent system as a benevolent institution, often suggesting that the enslaved had generally been treated well and had been found happy and singing on plantations. Likewise, black scholars took issue with the racist depictions of the African continent in geography books, as well as the whitewashing of the abolitionist movement. And the list goes on.

IN APRIL 1944, a decade after Du Bois's Negro History Week speech in New Orleans and nearly forty years after Oliver Pope was fired from his teaching post in Virginia, the fifteen-year-old Martin Luther King, Jr., traveled with Miss Sarah Grace Bradley, his English teacher at Booker T. Washington High School, from Atlanta to Dublin, Georgia, to deliver a speech on "The Negro and the Constitution." In Dublin, he competed in an oratorical competition sponsored by the Elks at First Baptist Church, where his prizewinning speech interpreted the political crisis African Americans were facing as having stemmed from the nation's abandonment of the Reconstruction Amendments.

A copy of King's speech, which he wrote under the guidance of Miss Bradley, can be found in his 1944 yearbook, wedged between other student essays and photographs from the academic year.[11] I enjoy looking through old black school yearbooks. My goal in searching that historical source was to locate references to Negro History Week during King's time at the school, only to unexpectedly stumble upon a speech from his teenage years—which is perhaps stronger evidence of student engagement with black history at Booker T. Washington than a passing reference to a calendar of Negro History Week events. Yet while skimming that source, I was again reminded that all the content in the yearbook, reflecting the everyday lives of black students, was relevant to present-day studies of the black past. The lessons we learn from such sources are dependent on the questions we ask, on what we choose to notice and study. Before turning to King's speech, I'd like to take the privilege of noting one of my favorite images in the yearbook: a photo of the school newspaper's staff in which all of the students are crowded around and on top of a replica of the Booker T. Washington memorial statue in front of the school's entrance.

The original statue is on the campus of Tuskegee University, which Washington founded in 1881, the monument having been erected in 1922, just two years before Atlanta's Booker T. Washington High School was established as the city's first public high school for black students. This statue depicts Washington "lifting the veil of ignorance" from (or lowering it onto, as some students wittily joked) a kneeling, unclothed black male figure holding a book in one hand and an anvil in the other. There is an ambiguity not only in the historic statue itself, but also in the photo of the newspaper staff overall. The statue can be read either as Washington revealing "the Negro" to the world or the teacher revealing the world to the black race through education. The symbolism of the statue aside, I am mostly taken by the playfulness of the students in the photo, which mutes some of the monument's intentions. The students' poses seem to be in contrast to the monument, and the students strike me as innocent yet critical; for indeed, dressed in their formal attire as writers for the school newspaper, they were likely not interested in the model of "practical education" based on industrial and agricultural training most closely associated with the memory of Washington. They are an assembly of students frozen in a particular historical moment; but when I think about the sociality among them, near and around that statue, they also represent a gathering of black learners that transcends any particular time or place. Like the yearbook from which I recovered King's oration or the newspaper in which I learned of Du Bois's Negro History Week speech, the statue is itself a site of black memory. I am personally reminded of the dozens of other images and stories I have encountered of people—both those famous and others unknown to me—posing in front of the Booker T. Washington memorial statue at Tuskegee University, including a photo of my own family at my sister's graduation from there in 2022.

It is important to remember that the young Martin Luther King, Jr., was part of that thriving and richly textured educational community in all of its complexity; he attended a school named for Booker T. Washington but the institution was certainly not at odds with the Du Boisian tradition (despite historical narratives that often present the two in binary terms). I also think of my late college mentor, Professor Robert L. Allen, who attended the high school in the 1950s. Allen told stories of passing the statue on his way to class as a student activist of the Emmett Generation, a time when King was no longer a student at Washington but a movement leader. In the photo, I see a continuum of black historical consciousness. I am reminded of the broader intellectual and political context that informed the speech King delivered in Dublin, Georgia—indeed, a speech that extended from Du Bois's Negro History Week lecture a decade prior. While King is usually seen as exceptional, I would offer a different reading; we should think of him as someone who emerged from the social context of a community long steeped in black political struggle. Understood in the context of his community, King was perhaps more the rule than the exception; he was a young black man who learned black history from his black teachers, a man whose knowledge of the black past came to inform a life invested in liberation work. There are scores of individuals such as King who never became household names, yet who are also reflective of this tradition: those who lived out the meaning of black memory work because the seeds were sown during the years of their early development, when knowledge of the black past was a critical part of their education and their journey to becoming black political subjects, individuals shaped by a critical consciousness about racial injustice and

Staff of *The Washingtonian*, *The Cornellian*, Booker T. Washington High School yearbook, Atlanta, Georgia, 1944

who understood themselves to be partly responsible for its dismantling.

In his speech, King named the contradictory history of American slavery and American freedom to identify the predicament of black citizens in the United States. After providing a cursory view of US slavery from the colonial era through the end of the Civil War, he asserted that the country had briefly attempted to correct its wrongs: "America gave its full pledge of freedom seventy-five years ago. Slavery has been a strange paradox in a nation founded on the principles that all men are created free and equal. Finally after tumult and war, the nation in 1865 took a new stand—freedom for all people. The new order was backed by amendments to the national constitution making it the fundamental law that thenceforth there should be no discrimination anywhere in the 'land of the free' on account of race, color or previous condition of servitude." Yet that change had been short lived, he explained. "Black America still wears chains" because "the finest Negro is at the mercy of the meanest white man" and because "even winners of our highest honors face the class color bar." To illustrate his point, he turned to the example of the singer Marian Anderson. Despite her widespread international fame, she was "barred from singing in the Constitution Hall" by the Daughters of the American Revolution in 1939, and she was also denied service in many hotels and restaurants around the country, even in many northern cities, including her hometown of Philadelphia. Elaborating on the crisis of African American citizenship, the future civil rights leader surmised, "So, with their right hand they raise to high places the great who have dark skins, and with their left, they slap us down to keep us in 'our places.'"

Evoking the Reconstruction Amendments directly, he lamented that "Today thirteen million black sons and daughters of our forefathers continue the fight for the translation of the 13th, 14th, and 15th amendments from writing on the page to actuality." Those three amendments, which abolished slavery, guaranteed due process and equal protection under the law for all citizens irrespective of race, and prohibited the government from denying black people the right to vote, respectively, were part and parcel of the story of black Reconstruction. In this instance, we witness King, as a high school student, using the substance of black history as an interpretive resource for the present-day challenges faced by African Americans. It is an example of the many black students in segregated schools all around the country whose access to black history (in varying degrees, to be clear) helped them achieve a critical social analysis of race and power while inspiring them to actively seek justice. King's speech was also an example of how black history and culture were used as a resource for skill development, as the oratorical skills he honed for that competition (and surely others) would later be used in service of a broader struggle for human rights. What's more, historical knowledge became important for more personal reasons, as it could be used to make sense of the events that transpired in everyday life.

After winning a prize at the oratorical competition, King headed back to Atlanta by bus, accompanied by Miss Bradley. He would later offer the following account of an incident that occurred on the bus home that evening. "Along the way, some white passengers boarded the bus, and the white driver ordered us to get up and give the whites our seats. We didn't move quickly enough to suit him, so he began cursing us. I intended to stay right in that seat, but Mrs. Bradley urged me up, saying we had to obey the law. We stood up in the aisle for ninety miles to Atlanta. That night will never leave my memory. It was the angriest I have ever been in my life."[12]

Like Marian Anderson, King and his teacher were reminded that despite their successes, they were still second-class citizens in Jim Crow America. Like many other African American students of the past, that civil rights leader in the making came to recognize the importance of cultivating a black historical consciousness, not only to interpret the past but to make sense of the social realities of the present day and chart a path to a more liberated future. It is essential that we do not lose sight of teachers such as Miss Bradley in the frames we cast to remember, especially when it comes to the black historical tradition. Without going into much detail, I'll note that Miss Bradley was a member of Georgia's colored teachers association and on at least one occasion appears in the Black Teacher Archive as a panelist alongside King's grandfather. As the previous examples have shown, black educators have often been the first line of defense in the struggle to sustain the tradition of black memory work. As stewards of the black past, educators such as Miss Bradley and Mr. Pope played a critical role in helping future generations gain access to intellectual resources about black history. This has allowed the tradition to be passed on, refined, and expanded to meet the emergent needs of black communities amid changes in an ever-evolving world.

NEARLY TWENTY-FIVE YEARS later, on February 23, 1968, the now thirty-nine-year-old Martin Luther King, Jr., delivered a speech in New York City's Carnegie Hall to commemorate the life of W. E. B. Du Bois. The occasion marked the anniversary of Du Bois's one hundredth birthday, although the black scholar had passed away five years prior on August 28, 1963—the same morning as the historic March on Washington, where King delivered his famous "I Have a Dream" speech. At the time, Du Bois was living in exile in Ghana, having been invited there by Kwame Nkrumah, the first prime minister and president of the nation, which gained independence in 1957. While there, Du Bois would live out his last days writing an Encyclopedia Africana, a multivolume project providing an extensive treatment of the histories and cultures of black people in the African diaspora. Time did not permit him to see the project to fruition, yet its aims live on in his scholarship and activism and through the black memory work that continues to be inspired by his legacy. For as King asserted, "Dr Du Bois has left us but he has not died." He stated, "He will be remembered for his scholarly contributions and organizational attainments. These monuments are imperishable." He celebrated Du Bois's writing, recalling how he took on a "powerful structure of historical distortion and dismantled it. He virtually, before anyone else and more than anyone else, demolished the lies about Negroes in their most important and creative period of history. The truths he revealed are not yet the property of all Americans but they have been recorded and arm us for our contemporary battles."[13]

In his speech, King acknowledged Du Bois's contributions to "Negro studies," which contemporary readers might understand as Black studies or African American studies. Of Du Bois, he noted, "Long before sociology was a science he was pioneering in the field of social study of Negro life and completed works on health, education, employment, urban conditions, and religion," thus noting Du Bois's early contributions to the social sciences. And while King emphasized Du Bois's contributions across disciplines, he especially focused on Du Bois's historical scholarship, implying that history was the central basis for cultivating self-determined and critically aware black political subjects: "Dr Du Bois knew that to lose one's history is to lose one's self-understanding and with it the roots for pride. This drove him to become a historian of Negro life and the combination of his unique zeal and intellect rescued for all of us a heritage whose loss would have profoundly impoverished us."[14]

He further asserted that in the absence of the memory work

undertaken by Du Bois, black people would have been left to the whims of "white propagandists—the myth makers of Negro history."[15] Thus, Du Bois's contribution had involved more than filling in the gaps of history, because, despite the popular assertion that black people had been erased from history, he understood that exclusion was not the only method of violence employed against "the Negro" when it came to the politics of history; he was intimately aware that white scholars had much to say about black people in their history books, in their literature, and in other forms of representation.

Black memory work, as conducted by Du Bois, was just as much corrective as it was descriptive. The transformed understanding about the past of human experience that it brought, especially as it pertained to black people, was to be studied in the service of developing ways of addressing social issues and creating beautiful experiments of human life. To emphasize the prescriptive nature of Du Bois's work, King made parallels between Du Bois's scholarship and activism. He drew connections between Du Bois's sociological studies of black life and his founding of the National Association for the Advancement of Colored People, linked Du Bois's studies on black life and history in the diaspora to his planning of and participation in the Pan-African Congresses, and tied together his fierce criticism of racial capitalism with his affiliation with the Communist Party, in addition to speaking of the work he had done during his final years in Ghana.

More than anything else, King's speech focused on Du Bois's "monumental" seven-hundred-page tome *Black Reconstruction in America, 1860–1880* as a concrete example of the corrective work Du Bois had done to root out the flagrant distortions of black life and culture in prevailing academic scholarship and demonstrate why black memory work was important to the political struggles of black people.

Speaking in 1968, King was especially interested in the white propaganda pertaining to black Reconstruction leaders' supposed failure that had been used to justify the disenfranchisement of black citizens. He noted that "White historians had for a century crudely distorted the Negro's role in the Reconstruction years. It was a conscious and deliberate manipulation of history and the stakes were high. The Reconstruction was a period in which black men had a small measure of freedom of action. If, as white historians tell it, Negroes wallowed in corruption, opportunism, displayed spectacular stupidity, were wanton, evil, and ignorant, their case was made. They would have proved that freedom was dangerous in the hands of inferior beings." The now mature movement leader professed, "One generation after another of Americans were assiduously taught these falsehoods and the collective mind of America became poisoned with racism and stunted with myths."[16] King's assessments had been made by previous black thinkers, and such repetition was necessary as white supremacist attacks on the black past persisted. Readers will likely hear echoes of Oliver Pope in Virginia as well as the interpretation presented in Woodson's textbook from the 1920s in King's words. King's high school speech was evidence of such teaching, and his tribute to Du Bois was an elaboration of it.

To fortify black people's struggle to hold on to truthful accounts of the past and to achieve a new understanding of black history, Du Bois interpreted historical evidence through lyrical prose, all the while writing against the force of the powerful white historians of the period and the racist propaganda they produced. In doing so, he documented many important things achieved during Reconstruction. Noting the development of free public education in the South for blacks and free whites, he argued that "Public education for all at public expense was, in the South, a Negro idea."[17] In correcting the historical record, Du Bois also exposed the nefarious goals of those who perpetuated such myths. King stated, "[Du Bois] revealed that far from being the tragic era white historians described, [Reconstruction] was the only period in which democracy existed in the South. This stunning fact was the reason the history books had to lie because to tell the truth would have acknowledged the Negroes' capacity to govern and fitness to build a finer nation in a creative relationship with poor whites." He further noted that there was a "substantial body of legislation that was socially so useful it was retained into the twentieth century even though the Negroes who helped to write it were brutally disenfranchised and driven from political life."[18]

Yet the good that was achieved during Reconstruction would be halted and much of it undone by white revanchism and political retrenchment resulting from the alliances formed by white citizens across the class and political spectrum. Metaphorically describing such retrenchment as a major theme in black history, Du Bois offered the following in *Black Reconstruction in America*: "The slave went free; stood a brief moment in the sun; then moved back again toward slavery."[19] Reconstruction was the sun. It was a brief era of promise followed by a white backlash, during which racial progress was undone and white possessive logic once again took center stage in dictating the political future of the nation. Speaking in 1968, at the tail end of the Civil Rights Movement, King revisited Du Bois's assessment of Reconstruction and the distortions of history that followed in its wake, because he witnessed the signs of oncoming curtailment all around him. Indeed, he saw the signs of "white backlash" on the heels of a historical period that many have referred to as a kind of second Reconstruction. A long memory of black history would be essential to refusing such retrenchment and maintaining the tradition of the black freedom movement in the years ahead.

THE FRAGMENTS OF black history recalled above were all recovered from various sources of black memory—autobiographies, newspapers, school yearbooks, black archives, sculpture, and a speech memorializing the life and work of a deceased black scholar—and they collectively reinforce several themes that have appeared over the course of this book. In gathering these stories together, I hope to have demonstrated the relationship between the ordinary and the monumental, the dead and the living, as well as the political stakes of preserving and passing on the truth about black history for present and future generations of black people. Most important, all of these narratives—from Oliver Pope's classroom in 1908 to King's reflections on Du Bois's contribution to historical memory in February 1968, just months before his own assassination—reflect, for me, what is politically at stake in the ongoing struggle to research, preserve, and disseminate knowledge about the black past both during Black History Month and beyond. However, they also frame my response to a central question I'd like to address in the final pages of this book: Where do we go from here?—the same question raised by King in his final book, published the year before his speech on Du Bois.

When pondering the question of what is required to sustain the tradition of black memory work, especially during a heightened phase of political and intellectual retrenchment focused on silencing the truth about black history, I believe the story of King's own initiation into the black past is instructive. I find King's story instructive because it emphasizes that any meaningful response to the present attacks on the black past requires being youth focused and thus future oriented in our efforts to preserve and expand the tradition of black history. What's more, King's example underscores that such a focus has to do with more than simply offering young people greater access to the content of black history. It is essential that we support young people (and all learners, for that matter) in developing a critical understanding about what is at stake in the act of preserving critical perspectives on the past. It requires being more transparent about how power informs our social constructions of history and how historical consciousness informs our identities as individuals, as well as how our collective memories of the past shape our aspirations, both for our individual selves and the communities to which we belong. Our task is not only to engage black students, and other willing participants in the "what" of black history—its facts, dates, names, places, and stories. Our task also requires supporting black learners to understand how narratives of history are constructed, as well as why they are constructed in the ways they are, all of which helps to make clear why knowledge of the past is so heavily contested and thus exposes how history—and more broadly speaking, education—is always political.

Past, present, and (what will surely be) future attacks on black history threaten more than just the passing on of facts. Their impact is far greater. Attacks on black history are about disrupting the power such knowledge can have for reshaping our relationships to one another and expanding our conceptions of justice. The early movements to popularize the teaching and study of black history and culture—as evidenced by Miss Bradley, Du Bois, and Woodson, as well as the many other black memory workers discussed in this book—were always about more than people gaining encyclopedic knowledge about the black past; they were also about helping students see the capacity for achievement in all people, especially themselves, and develop an awareness of how the lies and studious omissions in our system of knowledge have been used to justify blatantly unjust societal arrangements. The central objectives of black history—as critical history—from its inception among black scholars during the time of slavery and after were to correct the lies told about black people, to replace those lies with rigorous descriptions of black life in all of its human complexity, and to use this knowledge as a tool for cultivating aspirations and actions toward more freedom and justice in our communities. What's more, beyond responding to external attacks, black memory work was about sitting with the particular offerings black histories provide for advancing the greater good, for the inspiration it provides for those seeking to create and sustain meaningful lives steeped in a cultural legacy shaped by freedom dreams and a commitment to collective human flourishing.

In the hundred years since the first Negro History Week was observed in African American communities and the fifty years since Black History Month was recognized by President Gerald Ford as a national observance, the attacks on the black past have not ended, precisely because the knowledge of it remains a powerful tool for political organizing and force for liberation. Indeed, black history has the power to help win more than just symbolic victories; it has the power to help win the moral war that is always at stake in our interpretations of the past, shedding a light on past injustices so that present and future political actors will make decisions about what is right and wrong, what is just and unjust, based on what we understand to be true about the world we have inherited. This is the power of the past, and this is why we must continue to be vigilant of the stories we construct and pass on.

Responding to the political moment in which "Black Power" was the rallying cry of African American communities across the country, King asserted that knowledge of the black past is "positive and necessary power for black people."[20] While he had always believed that to be true, his assertion of the claim in the late 1960s was motivated by the challenges he began to observe in the new racial regime taking shape amid the changing political landscape. For instance, as the father of children who braved their way through newly desegregated schools, he became increasingly sensitive to the politics of historical memory in the contested territory of US education, as white supremacist curricula continued to go unchecked despite demographic and structural shifts in the social landscape of US schools. In fact, a great deal of the backlash occurring during the time of King's writing occurred in response to educational developments as African Americans gained access to new opportunities in higher education and K–12 schools resulting from litigation brought by civil rights activists, lawyers, educators, and communities. Indeed, by the late 1960s, black students desegregated historically white colleges at record numbers, and desegregation efforts were making waves in school districts across the country.

I was surprised to learn that my own introduction to Black History Month had much to do with this piece of educational history. For according to my preschool teacher, Miss Butterfield, King's participation in the struggle to desegregate schools in her hometown had been part of her motivation for teaching my classmates and me excerpts of his "mountaintop" speech to perform for our first Black History Month program in 1993.

During our conversation in 2019, Miss Butterfield casually mentioned, "You know, Dr. Martin Luther King came to Grenada." She described how a few years after she had moved to California, King had gone "marching through Grenada" with black elementary school students seeking to enroll in a previously all-white school. On September 12, 1966, twelve years after the *Brown v. Board of Education* decision, 250 black students arrived to begin their first day at a desegregated school in Grenada. Instead of being welcomed, they were met by angry white mobs carrying pipes, chains, and other items they planned to use as weapons. Most of the students were turned away by the mob, but some managed to enter the building. When they left for lunch, they were harassed and physically assaulted. Some of them were hospitalized and even suffered broken bones. The attacks on black children by mobs took place over the course of several days before law enforcement officials intervened.

Hearing Miss Butterfield talk about King marching with students to desegregate the schools in her hometown put my early encounter with Black History Month into a new perspective. It made me understand that King was not a distant, monumental figure to her; he was someone connected to the history of the community from whence she had come, a relationship that many black people whose lives were close to the era of the Black Freedom Movement associate with the names of people and events from the period. More than this, the story of King and the desegregation struggles helped me appreciate one of the tragic developments in black history: the way some victories of the past require new interpretations as time evolves and as new analyses emerge that require us to see history with new levels of political clarity gained through the distance of time and deep study. Indeed, even as King worked to desegregate schools around the country, he began to witness some of the immediate costs and limitations of that political strategy for black youths and communities.

Eva Grace Lemon (age seven), Martin Luther King, Jr., and Aretha Willis (age seven) march to integrate schools in Grenada, Mississippi, 1966

The Bob Fitch Photography Archive, Stanford University, Libraries, Department of Special Collections

In the newly desegregated schools, which lacked African American teachers, who had been fired in great quantities across the South, black students rarely had access to teachers such as Mr. Pope, Miss Bradley, and

Miss Butterfield, who had prioritized teaching critical perspectives on black life and culture and who had possessed the courage to correct official curricula that occluded such knowledge. King observed that particular challenge in the education of his own children, when his son Martin and daughter Yolanda became part of the first wave of black children to desegregate schools in Atlanta.

In *Where Do We Go from Here: Chaos or Community?*, King spoke to the broader erasure of black history in the United States before describing how it manifested in the new racial regime taking shape in the late 1960s. For instance, in the following passage, he speaks to the legacy of historical erasure while also pointing out the importance of black memory work in combating distortions of the past and insisting that black people's recovery and study of black history are just as important as, if not more important than, policies enacted by government officials to root out and mitigate antiblack oppression.

> The tendency to ignore the Negro's contributions to American life and strip him of his personhood is as old as the earliest history books and as contemporary as the morning's newspaper. To offset this cultural homicide, the Negro must rise up with an affirmation of his own Olympian manhood. Any movement for the Negro's freedom that overlooks this necessity is only waiting to be buried. As long as the mind is enslaved the body can never be free. Psychological freedom, a firm sense of self-esteem, is the most powerful weapon against the long night of physical slavery. No Lincolnian Emancipation Proclamation or Kennedyan or Johnsonian civil rights bill can totally bring this kind of freedom. The Negro will only be truly free when he reaches down to the inner depths

of his own being and signs with the pen and ink of assertive selfhood his own emancipation proclamation.[21]

King articulated a vision of black history as an expression of black self-determination essential to any vision of freedom for African Americans. Indeed, he saw black history as a form of black power. He believed that "The history books, which have almost completely ignored the contributions of the Negro in American history, have only served to intensify the Negroes' sense of worthlessness and to augment the anachronistic doctrine of white supremacy." Unfortunately, this form of curricular violence would continue in the context of newly desegregated schools. Black students continued to be subjected to such violent erasure. Yet in these new contexts, they had fewer advocates and resources to help them challenge the distortions and mitigate the damage they caused. King would come to recognize this phenomenon firsthand.

A few months after his children started at an integrated school in Atlanta, he and his wife, Coretta Scott King, had been invited to a school program entitled "Music That Has Made America Great." In attending the event, the couple expected black people's contributions to American music—of all things—would surely be acknowledged in some way. They were sadly mistaken. King recalled, "As the evening unfolded, we listened to the folk songs and melodies of the various immigrant groups. We were certain that the program would end with the most original of all American music, the Negro spiritual. But we were mistaken. Instead, all the students, including our children, ended the program by singing 'Dixie.'"[22]

Martin and Coretta left the event feeling a combination of "indignation and amazement." That had been no minor oversight but a flagrant distortion of American musical history—a subject

Coretta Scott King knew all too well, having come from a musically inclined family in Alabama and having formally studied music at Antioch College in Ohio as well as the New England Conservatory of Music in Boston. King wrote that everyone in attendance "had been victimized by just another expression of America's penchant for ignoring the Negro, making him invisible and making his contributions insignificant."

To see the promise of integration undermined in such a way made him wary of the road ahead. He related, "I wept within that night. I wept for my children and all black children who have been denied a knowledge of their heritage; I wept for white children, who, through daily miseducation, are taught that the Negro is an irrelevant entity in American society."[23] He recognized the late 1960s to be yet another period of retrenchment, and what he saw happening in the newly desegregated schools was evidence of the backward steps being taken. The original intent of school integration, at least in the minds of political activists such as King, as well as the many black teachers who had helped pave the road to *Brown v. Board of Education* in 1954, was a vision centered on transforming the constitution of education in the US social order, not merely about including black people in racially hostile white schools. Despite the hope he continued to maintain for the future of black people and for the nation—because their fates were intertwined—he witnessed the shattering of the dream right before his eyes.

African Americans' desire for full integration included the removal of barriers that would allow students to attend schools with peers from other racial backgrounds, with racially mixed faculties and transformed curricula that would be responsive to the needs of all students. It was a vision of education that would ensure full access to opportunity and affirmative learning environments that would model the best version of what a multiracial democracy could be; that would require an explicit commitment to racial justice, given the nation's history and present social realities. Yet the model of integration that transpired was no real integration; it was ultimately a second-class integration, one in which the first cohorts of black students to desegregate schools found themselves in hostile territory with fewer advocates than they'd had before, in schools where the curricula reinforced the status quo of white supremacy and provided fewer paths toward more enlightened forms of knowledge.[24] In such contexts, black students, such as the children in Miss Butterfield's hometown, had to endure physical injuries by their classmates and face angry white mobs. They also accumulated less visible injuries, harms that left marks beneath the surface—psychic and emotional wounds that have only recently come to light with new historical and sociological scholarship.[25]

As we settle into the semi-quincentennial of America's founding, when historical reflections on the nation's 250 years of independence are sure to abound, and as the hundredth anniversary of the nation's commemoration of black history is observed in February 2026, a new era of retrenchment has emerged. This period of political backlash is especially obvious in the war being waged in the realm of black historical memory, a response to the unprecedented gains since the late twentieth century as the enterprise of black historical knowledge production became influenced by groups who were previously kept out or contained in very limited roles in the American academy. The irony is that such intellectual development, largely in higher education, occurred alongside major underdevelopment of opportunities for deep engagement with black history in schools for African American students, as black teachers were fired by the thousands and the institutions they had developed to support their liberatory work in schools were integrated out of existence.[26]

Since the late 1960s, key areas of critical scholarship in the realms of racial oppression, patriarchy, and capitalism have made waves in the landscape of the American academy, as historically oppressed communities sought to resist and transcend the epistemic violence waged against them. Most impactful in these bodies of work has been scholarship that privileges the perspectives of marginalized communities, including African Americans—experiences that were previously ignored or interpreted primarily through the biased lenses of white scholars. As a result of the student movements that ushered in black studies, ethnic studies, and women, gender, and sexuality studies, these fields made significant progress in exposing silences in history and correcting distortions in knowledge about the past. Without question, these educational movements, though imperfect, have allowed truths about the experiences of marginalized communities to come to light before broader audiences in unprecedented ways.

Those gains have been met with skepticism. From the very beginning, attacks were waged against black studies by university administrators and especially by scholars committed to the norms of traditional disciplines: history, sociology, English, economics, and so on. While administrators gave in to demands by student organizers for "relevant education" in colleges and even some high schools, many of the efforts to include the curricular changes students asked for were done in a manner that intentionally restricted their more radical aspects. Skepticism can also be seen in the late-twentieth-century critiques of multicultural education in K–12 schools, where some critics insisted that multicultural curricular reforms politicized education and compromised rigor—that they were focusing too much on students' identities and instilling pride as opposed to providing strong training in fundamental academic skills and critical thinking, as though such aims were antithetical and could not be pursued in complementary fashion. Yet despite such assessments, progress continued to be made.

The current wave of conservative efforts to restrict what can be taught in American schools cannot be understood apart from the longer political struggles in knowledge recalled above and over the course of this book. For indeed, what we are experiencing in this moment is yet another instance of retrenchment in the black freedom struggle; and black history is again a vital weapon that must be preserved and refined to support new generations of young people as they prepare for the ongoing battle to build meaningful lives. To cede the territory gained in the fight to preserve and disseminate critical knowledge about the black past would be a great mistake, a great loss to future generations, and especially for black youths. For indeed, "Any oppressed people who abandon the knowledge of their own protest history, or who fail to analyze its lessons, will only perpetuate their domination by others," to quote the late historian Manning Marable.[27] To be clear, the story of black memory workers is an essential part of African Americans' protest history—as black people have long identified historical memory as a primary battleground in their struggle for freedom. Such is the case for black people and indeed for all of humanity.

As a people of dreams, African Americans are well practiced at being future oriented. In more ways than one, our people have had to construct paths forward where bridges had intentionally been destroyed to prevent their crossing. Due to delayed freedoms, African Americans have had to create, amid the rubble, new roads for meaningful education and better tomorrows. The story of Black History Month's journey from Negro History Week and early black historical traditions even before the twentieth century is an example of this; and there are many forces today that continue to sustain this tradition.

While mainstream observances of Black History Month have been overtaken by corporate interests, there are many cases of students and communities engaging in reflection on the black past that mirrors the aims of black memory work. I have been reminded of this over the last two years by a group of high school students who are engaging in ongoing study of the black past. From what I have observed of their work, these young people are working to ensure that the future of black history will be even stronger and accountable to the best of the tradition.

Since 2023, I have been working with African American students in the high schools of Long Beach, California, who formed a Black Literary Society (or "BlackLit," as it is commonly referred to by the students) focused on studying black history and literature, building community across school sites, and supporting the students' collective academic development. Most important, this group has become one of the only sustained spaces in which students can process their experiences as African American learners in a district with documented patterns of underserving this community. I became connected with the students through Dr. Pamela Lovett, who helped initiate and centralize the Black Literary Society in response to student and parent feedback in Long Beach. In 2023, Dr. Lovett informed me that the Black Literary Society would be using my book *School Clothes: A Collective Memoir of Black Student Witness*, a history of black student life in the United States, and she invited me to partner with the BlackLit students and their faculty sponsors.

The students convene at their respective school sites and occasionally come together for districtwide events. When visiting some of the events, I have benefited from listening to students' reflections on the history of African American education and its meaning in their lives. It has also been eye opening to hear students make direct connections to the challenges they face in a city with a shrinking black student population where they continue to experience various forms of social alienation. They describe the absence of critical conversations about black history and culture in their classrooms, and they have discussed comments made by other members of their school communities that imply that black students and their communities are unworthy of being treated with dignity and respect.

In some ways, these students and I have become intellectual partners. While they are learning details about black history through their engagement with me, I have learned a great deal, through their reflections, about the uses of black history for the developmental needs of black students and the training of future black memory workers. Through our dialogues, we have worked to make sense of the various purposes black history can serve both in the present moment and in the future as we witness the merits of such work being constantly debated, and its meaning flattened, in the American public sphere. Our interactions remind me of the immense potential of young people and their vast capacity to grapple with complicated historical narratives when given the proper support tools and a caring environment committed to their collective success. My conversations with these students have also taught me some important lessons about how we can strengthen black memory work to be more responsive to the present and to address oversights in our methods, both during Black History Month and year-round.

In an era of unprecedented access to information through technology and widespread competition for young people's attention, there is a continued need for tailored and immersive engagement in black memory work. In particular, there is an urgent need to demystify the process of historical production and the role that power plays in it. Failing to do so runs the risk of encouraging future generations to be passive consumers of historical knowledge while missing the opportunity to explore creative ways of expanding the tradition using the possibilities of emergent technology. For indeed, there are things than can be done in digging up and preserving the black past today that simply could not be done fifty or even ten years ago. Engaging students in critical studies about the black past earlier will ensure that they have more opportunities to expand and build on this work in meaningful ways, as opposed to belatedly coming into a critical consciousness about black history later in life. Such delayed engagement, I would argue, stunts the development and growth of this worthy tradition.

One of the biggest lessons I have learned from the BlackLit students is that there is a need to make explicit that black history is not only about the details of the past. The politics of black memory work is also about clarifying how history has been and must continue to be used as a resource for sustaining ongoing struggles for social justice. That is to say, students must be presented with opportunities to understand how history functions in our lives. For instance, when black students in Long Beach express concern about racial slurs being used by classmates of other races or the fact that some teachers have low expectations of them, they should not be left to experience these social phenomena as isolated incidents with no relation to the past. Learning that black students before them also navigated such situations and left behind lessons for how they triumphed over such encounters with antiblackness is important. If for nothing else, doing so is a reminder to young people that they are not alone in their struggles.

The BlackLit students also help clarify that our work during Black History Month and in teaching black history year-round must include making sure that those who will carry on black memory work in the future have the skills to be good stewards of the tradition. This is not a new observation; it is a reminder of the original intent of Negro History Week and Black History Month. The persistence of the black historical tradition is made possible only when there is a changing of the guard, thus requiring the intentional cultivation of the future of black history, which will be ensured only by a significant investment in the young people who will become the future "watchmen on the wall," to borrow from Carter G. Woodson.

I have also learned that students need more access to richly textured narratives of black history, especially those about ordinary people, that move beyond the stories that are the easiest to tell and most familiar; this need extends to historical figures and events that have become obscure over time. The students stressed that early black historical figures rarely appear in their classes, giving the illusion that the important aspects of black history did not begin until the mid–twentieth century. Thus it is necessary to recover stories and people prior to the Civil Rights Movement that are relatable to the lives of people today.

For the past two years, Dr. Lovett has coordinated an East Coast college tour and place-based learning experience for approximately thirty leaders of the Black Literary Society. During those trips, the students visited HBCUs in the DC region, including Howard University, Virginia State University, and Hampton University, and toured the National Museum of African American History and Culture. While traveling, they completed assignments related to their reading of *School Clothes* while drawing connections between the historical narratives in the book and the black historic sites they visited. They also reflected on the relationships among the text, the historic sites, and their own identities, as well as connections to present-day issues observed in their communities and current events. The trips ended in Boston, Massachusetts, where BlackLit students visited more universities and historic sites such as the Royall House and Slave Quarters, a site of slavery dating from the seventeenth century, as well as the Abiel Smith School, a segregated school for black Bostonians opened in 1835. The Smith School is connected to the African Meeting House, a chapel where black abolitionists such as Frederick Douglass,

David Walker, William Cooper Nell, and Maria Stewart met and delivered speeches during the antebellum era.

It was powerful to hear BlackLit students' reflections on their experiences, as a counterweight to the media noise about whether such history is "divisive" or causes "discomfort." "Until then, I don't think I had ever visited a black historical site, at least not that I was aware of," said Kysean Ferreira, who emphasized how inspired he was to learn that some of the nineteenth-century black students he had read about in *School Clothes* had gathered in the very structure he sat in. He declared, "I stood in the exact spot as Black abolitionists"; for him, it was a learning experience that caused him to feel empowered and part of an important historical legacy.

The students identified their visits to sites in Boston as particularly eye opening because, as one student explained, "We never hear about racism and things that happened to black people up here." They arrived at a critique shared by many historians of the black past: that histories of racial violence and slavery typically focus on the South, when in reality the story was—and has always been—national in scope. The exercise forced them to remap their conceptual terrain of the nation's past struggles with racial justice. Their reflections drove home the point that despite their unprecedented access to technology and information, deep knowledge gaps persist and that in a time in which there is fierce competition for everyone's attention, focused and sustained study of the black past is critically important.

Some of the students were amazed at the parallels they immediately began to identify between their experiences in Long Beach, California, in the present day and the experiences of students such as Charlotte Forten, who in the 1850s attended a racially mixed school in Salem, Massachusetts. Many of the students reflected on the things Forten wrote about in her diary, such as the degrading comments made by her white teachers and classmates, as well as her experiences witnessing racial injustice at the hands of police seeking to capture fugitive slaves.

At the end of the trip, I held a seminar on Harvard's campus with BlackLit students and their teachers, where we discussed their learning over the course of the year. The seminar included a short lecture about my approach to researching black educational history, a whole-group discussion, some small-group activities, and designated time for individual writing. In our discussions, the students unpacked some of the core themes in my book and the kinds of sources used to find the voices of black students in the past, and space was provided for them to express how they felt about encountering those voices in the historical sources. It was eye opening to hear them express, in a very vulnerable way, that they had never had a conversation about how history was made. Never had they been invited to think about power and the production of historical knowledge. That seemed to me a major oversight, given how the tradition of black memory work and Black History Month had emerged to begin with.

After a presentation by a black archivist in our seminar in April

Black Literary Society students after book review panel in Long Beach, California, May 3, 2025

2024, I recall the students saying that they had never heard of an archive or the work of an archivist in their education thus far. That signaled several things for me. It clarified that many of our young people are being encouraged to be passive consumers of historical knowledge as opposed to critical thinkers with a mature historical consciousness. The distinction in the latter case is that they learn about not only stories from the past but also how we come to know those stories. They are taught to understand how power shapes the creation of historical sources, which historical sources are preserved, and how narrators of history go about studying the past to preserve and represent its lessons for present and future communities. Indeed, the legacy of the black historical tradition is critical, as there is much to be learned about power from the ways black people have asserted their agency to disrupt the kinds of violence enacted through historical erasure, silencing, and racist distortions. This revelation through the dialogue with BlackLit students suggested that those who are to be the future leaders of black memory work are rarely given opportunities to develop the critical lens for viewing the past that will support them in carrying forward this work in the years to come. Despite the decades of scholarship in black historical studies that have detailed these dynamics, this knowledge is being kept from those who are the future of the tradition. Allowing such a trend to persist comes at a tremendous cost.

What might it mean for young people to learn about the ongoing struggle for black history and develop an understanding of its stakes well before they arrive in a college classroom or (more likely) a graduate seminar? It seems to me that these are the kinds of goals we ought to prioritize in future Black History Month observances as an effort to cultivate the development of future black memory workers. What if Black History Month were not just about observing and recognizing the black past but also focused on reinvigorating and celebrating the labor that makes such knowledge possible and ensures its continuity? How much better might the future of the tradition be if Black History Month was not just a time to tell good stories about black people and to admire good black music, films, and art but equally a time of collective investment in the skills, institutions, and people who make our knowledge about those things possible throughout the calendar year? What if Black History Month and black memory work throughout the year could be refocused on their original mission of liberatory education infused with the political clarity of black people who have discerned the relationship between critical historical knowledge and the present and future struggles for freedom and justice?

AS I REFLECT on the hundred-year journey of Black History Month, I am left to wonder what the present generation's contribution will be to this tradition in the next half century and beyond. Our answers to the question "Where do we go from here?" must certainly account for the current backlash; however, responding to external hostilities cannot be the only concern. We must also focus on what it means to grow and evolve the tradition of black memory work in a way that honors the work done by those who came before us and that will meet present and future needs. This means not merely sustaining the tradition but also engaging in meaningful criticism and revision, striving to make the work that we know to be meaningful and necessary even sturdier and more responsive to the needs of evolving black communities and our ever-changing world. For at its best, black history is critical history, and it must continue to be so if it is to persist.

While we support the development of the black memory workers of tomorrow, we must keep in mind a few things that I hope to have made clear over the course of *I'll Make Me a World*. First, it is essential that we study the origins of the tradition, because the details of Black History Month's creation provide political clarity about what is at stake in black memory work. This tradition, as a critical approach to history, is one that emerged as a disruption of hierarchies of race and power in which the dominant historical narrative privileged the few at the expense of the many. Thus, a deep understanding of this origin story is instructive in guiding the work of digging up the past, how we study it to extract meaningful lessons, and how we commemorate it to ensure that such lessons are carried forward.

Second, we must remember that the black historical tradition emerged from the countermemories of enslaved people and their progeny, a people of both great achievement and ordinary lives. Black history is nothing if not a story of the resilient communities that emerged and adapted as a matter of political necessity, as well as discrete stories of individual achievements attained as a result of collective struggle. Our awareness of this fact should shape our disposition as memory workers of today and tomorrow, which we must actively cultivate lest we be taken in by the allure of celebrity culture, hyperindividualism, and great men's narratives that the culture of power encourages and celebrates. To give in to this would be an abandonment of the best in our tradition; indeed, a tradition that was created by enslaved people who insisted that they, too, were subjects of history and expanded by generations of black memory workers who continued to look to history as a tool for liberatory struggle. Finally, we should remember that the struggle for knowledge about the black past, like the black freedom struggle more broadly, has never been confined to any particular national context, even if most of our work takes place in the United States. The struggle for black history has always been international in scope, as exemplified by the case of Du Bois recalled a few pages ago, by the story of Nannie Helen Burroughs's diasporic consciousness described in part III, and by the actions of the enslaved African woman aboard the *Hudibras* as they asserted their memory of the past and their relations to one another in the face of unspeakable acts of violence committed while they were suspended on the waters of the Atlantic Ocean.

It should come as no surprise that Black History Month is celebrated in countries around the world at various times of the year, including the Netherlands, the United Kingdom, Colombia, Ecuador, and more. Across these countries, one can trace similar patterns of black social movements and context-specific black intellectual struggles as having led to these annual observances of the black past, even as these monthlong celebrations may have drawn inspiration from the African American example. Gaining knowledge about the black past has been a contested activity for black people everywhere, just as antiblackness has been a defining phenomenon across national boundaries.

Across such geographic and linguistic diversity, black history has been a political force for liberatory struggle. This can be found in the Black Supplementary School Movement in Great Britain, for instance, which began in the 1960s when black education activists formed out-of-school learning spaces to counter the antiblack ideas expressed in the British school curriculum and policies. Indeed, to that end, the Grenadian black educator and political activist Bernard Coard published a widely circulated book, *How the West Indian Child Is Made Educationally Subnormal in the British School System: The Scandal of the Black Child in Schools in Britain*, in 1971.[28]

The tradition of black memory work in the African diaspora and as part of the formation of diasporic consciousness can also be traced though the formation of independent institutions such as the Black Europe Summer School in Amsterdam, founded in 2007 by Kwame Nimako, a scholar of Ghanaian origin who studies the history of Dutch slavery. In this two-week summer program, scholars from around the world gather to learn about the black presence in Europe in the past and how it continues to shape black European experiences today. The summer school is led by scholars from around the world who study topics related to black Europe, and many scholars enroll because they have limited opportunities to study these topics elsewhere. Nimako and his colleagues began the program after experiencing ongoing hostility to and a lack of support for research on black history and culture in European universities.

When I attended the Black Europe Summer School in 2015, I had the opportunity to attend the celebration of Keti Koti, the annual commemoration of the abolition of slavery in the Dutch colony of Suriname on July 1, 1863. Keti Koti translates to "broken chains" in the Surinamese language, and the meaning of the celebration is similar to that of Juneteenth in the United States. The Black Europe Summer School is intentionally hosted during the period of Keti Koti, as the public history observance aligns with the mission of the summer school: to study the black presence—then and now—in various European contexts and to connect such knowledge to ongoing struggles to address the legacies of slavery and colonialism. Participating in the observance while a graduate student in African diaspora studies became a place-based learning experience for me as an education scholar, where I experienced one of the many ways black people around the world have used black commemorative practices not only to hold the public accountable for remembering black history but also as a source for sustaining a liberatory educational tradition rooted in black memory work.

Recognizing the attacks on black history to be a global phenomenon, black people have waged intellectual warfare through historical study and preservation, often forming connections across their differences while partnering in this struggle. Hearing

Afro-Dutch political organizers say the names of various black freedom fighters in a political protest staged during Keti Koti helped reinforce those lessons. While I couldn't make out the words they spoke in Dutch, I could understand their references to Martin Luther King, Jr., Malcolm X, Marcus Garvey, and Angela Davis as they protested a recent incident in which Dutch police officers had beat a man in public for wearing a T-shirt that said "Zwarte Piet Is Racist." Their protest was not only a rebuttal of the tradition of Europeans dressing up in blackface to imitate the character of Zwarte Piet (Black Pete) during Christmastime but also an effort to challenge centuries of historical distortions that associated black people with the racist ideas embodied by this holiday tradition.

The Black Europe Summer School and Keti Koti, as well as the Black Supplementary Schools in Great Britain, are among many examples of the international traditions of black memory work. There is much to be gained from studying and exchanging traditions across diasporic contexts in the years ahead, not only as a means of retooling Black History Month celebrations but also to refine organizing strategies amid current attacks that, to be sure, exceed those in the United States.

Afro-Dutch protesters against Zwarte Piet (Black Pete) and recent incidents of antiblack police violence at Keti Koti ceremony in Oosterpark, Amsterdam, the Netherlands, July 2015

•

THE THREATS POSED to black history in 2026 are reminiscent of the context in which Carter G. Woodson founded Negro History Week in 1926. He, too, was operating in a hostile intellectual environment; such threats ebbed and flowed throughout the expansion to Black History Month in 1976 and have reemerged in the high tides of the present day. Woodson's white professors at the University of Chicago and Harvard—and historians more generally—blatantly declared that black people had no history and culture, or at least none worthy of respect. Yet Woodson came from ordinary black people who had formerly been enslaved, and it was the knowledge he had gained from them that inspired his opposition. He knew them to be a storied people. In their everyday striving, he saw living, breathing proof that such claims were false.

The inspiration that led to the development of Black History Month did not begin with Woodson looking exclusively to the most famous African Americans or to precolonial African kings and queens—though he certainly had an appreciation of such histories and admired these monuments of achievement. His most enduring motivation came from the lives and lessons of illiterate African American men alongside whom he worked in the coal mines of West Virginia; from the stories of his formerly enslaved mother and the lessons he learned from her brothers, who were Woodson's first teachers in a one-room schoolhouse. Woodson's labor to preserve, study, and cultivate a public appetite for black history was inspired and sustained by women such as Nannie Helen Burroughs, who founded a school that cultivated the dreams of working-class black girls. He was inspired by those whom he referred to as "the workadays" and "undistinguished

Negroes" even as he celebrated the lives of Douglass and Tubman. He saw value in their lives and their labor, and he knew that their contributions to human civilization are worthy of study and celebration. He placed them alongside "African Heroes and Heroines" and the great statesmen of the Reconstruction era, crafting a memory of the black past that was expansive, diverse, and richly textured.

I find it urgent that more attention be given to everyday histories of black life and culture in the years ahead. I emphasize this point not only for ethical reasons but also for more pragmatic ones. It is essential that we do not lose sight of the ordinary aspects of black life because it is everyday people that built this tradition of black memory work. What's more, it is the ordinary black people of today—and of the future—who will sustain it. This lesson has been taken up by the Black Literary Society students, and I think we would all do well to remember and relearn it.

As I worked to close this book, a colleague sent me an unprompted message after attending an event in Southern California featuring students from the Black Literary Society. Their text included a short video of six students onstage discussing their recent studies of black educational history and why the information had become so important to them. I recognized all of the students, having met them on several occasions in Long Beach and during their trips to Boston. One of them, Christian Hoke, expressed their new commitment to practicing what he referred to as a "communal literacy" of black history, stressing that he and his peers have "gained a new passion for speaking up and sharing these oftentimes overlooked and unheard-of black histories" not only with their families but also with other students in their school and even their teachers, by advocating for new books to be included in their classes. Christian's comments are a reminder that deep study of black history involves being initiated into a knowledge system about the past informed by black consciousness—a consciousness formed through a critical awareness of the clash between mainstream American memory, which privileges white perspectives in historical interpretations, and the long tradition of black memory work focused on reclaiming the truth about the black past and creating more opportunities for it to be heard.

One of Christian's copanelists, Soraya Whaley, elaborated on the importance of studying overlooked black histories, especially stories that connect to the present-day experiences of black students. To emphasize the point, she read a passage about the Little Rock Nine, then elaborated on why the story resonated so deeply with her. The passage included a quote from Carlotta Walls LaNier, the youngest of the nine students, who reflected on her motivations for desegregating Central High School in Little Rock, Arkansas, in 1957. She connected her participation in that important black historical event to her studies of the black past under the tutelage of African American teachers in the segregated elementary and junior high schools of Little Rock before she braved her way through the white mobs seeking to keep her and her fellow student activists from entering the all-white public high school paid for by taxpayer dollars.

Soraya read LaNier's words aloud: "We were standing on the shoulders of others. . . . We had Negro History Week in the segregated black schools. And I was always proud to read more and hear about what African Americans or Negroes or Coloreds did for this country. . . . I knew I was standing on their shoulders." She then explained why LaNier's words had stuck with her: "I connected with Carlotta's words because, like her, I know what it means to step into an academic space as a black student, carrying not only the hopes but also the sacrifices of those who came before me. It means knowing that every classroom I step into, every book I study, and every dream I chase is a continuation of a larger story.

Her story reminded me that black excellence is never a solo journey; it's deeply rooted in the strength of our families, the resilience of our communities, and the transformative power of education. Her choice to walk into school with her head held high every day was not only for herself but for the generations that came before her to fight for that right and the generations that would follow and inherit that path that she paved."

In that high school student's words, we witness the tradition of black memory work at its best. While LaNier's story is one of past racial harms, it is also a story of African American agency and the collective struggle to resist antiblack violence, one in which individual black achievement is understood in relationship to past and present generations. Soraya models a budding and critical disposition toward the black past, one that is unafraid to face the difficult elements of history, in which harm and violence occurred, while also being mindful to notice the voices of black people having such experiences, elevating what they had to say about it, how they felt, and what they chose to do. She was careful, even in bearing witness to the harm, not to negate their humanity; she does not reduce the black people of the past to the details of their suffering.

By making the text-to-self connection between black students of the past and her reality as a black student in the present, Soraya also emphasized how black memory work is about treating the details of history critically while also using this historical knowledge as a resource for making sense of the world today and charting paths to a better future. For indeed, "as the gap between the past, present, and future diminishes, individuals can acquire a greater sense of becoming the 'makers' of their own history," to quote Manning Marable's characterization of "authentic histories of black people": narratives in which black people are the primary actors and the stories are spelled out in a way that accounts for their own perspectives. Soraya modeled a way of using the black past as it was intended by the many educators, scholars, and memory workers who have created and maintained the tradition over the generations; for these laborers, and for oppressed communities more broadly, "the act of reconstructing history is inextricably linked to the political practices, or praxis, of transforming the present and future."[29]

When I heard Soraya's words and those of her Black Literary Society peers, I saw the future(s) of black history in the making. The scene of those students onstage as they made meaning of the past and its relationship to their present, while particular to a specific time and place, also exceeds them, reflecting a more general pattern in the tradition. What could have been an anonymous moment in black history—a gathering of students discussing their study of a particular text—is now a permanent scene in the story of the black past, one in which the memory work done by previous generations persists. I trace a through line between the reflections of students such as Soraya, Christian, and Kysean and the black students of the past, including Alice Walker as a student participating in local academic competitions in the rural schools of Georgia, as well as the words prepared by the fifteen-year-old Martin Luther King, Jr., for his high school speech "The Negro and the Constitution." I see a resonance between those stories, where the tradition was passed on, and my first encounter with Black History Month in 1993, when I performed words lined out for my classmates and me by Miss Butterfield, words that carried memories and feelings that were just as important as the names of the people and places we learned about. These stories are a reminder that part of the work of training the next cohorts of black memory workers requires, first, believing that they have the capacity to carry the work forward and, second, that they have the ability to grasp the deeper meaning of history, that they have unique resources as emerging scholars to interpret the black past in ways that speak powerfully to the present moment, as a new generation of thinkers, while also serving as a bridge to those who will come after them.

The only sure way of rescuing the future(s) of black history amid persistent attacks is for ordinary black people to be equipped with the power of a historical consciousness accrued from the collective memory of those who came before. The persistence of this tradition requires work, and sometimes the labor is thankless and unglamorous: the digging up, the preserving, the constant rebuilding and remembering in the face of external forces of destruction, then the documenting of such events of destruction and rebuilding, only to do more recovering, writing, and teaching to bring new generations along in work that has been repeated over the centuries in one form or another. There is no magic solution that will end the onslaught of recurring, organized efforts that seek to erase and silence knowledge about the black past and the calls for justice it incites. The only sure method is a commitment to black study and black struggle and the use of them to shape our world-making practices today and tomorrow. This is the way black people can continue to bring truth and beauty to themselves and to the world, even when the world is undeserving of our gifts.

ACKNOWLEDGMENTS

I initially planned to write this book as a collection of letters to my former teachers. I wanted to acknowledge them for introducing me to the tradition of black memory work that informed the creation of Black History Month. While the book took on a different form, I would still like to express gratitude to the amazing teachers I had over the course of my life, because it was their spirit and my memory of them that stimulated the writing of *I'll Make Me a World*.

The idea for this book developed over a series of conversations with several friends and colleagues as I prepared for my sabbatical year in 2025 as a Leverhulme Visiting Professor at University College London's Institute of the Americas. As with my prior work, the writing of this book benefited greatly from ongoing conversations with those who are friends to my mind; therefore, I would like to thank Joshua Bennett, Micha Broadnax, DeRay Mckesson, Roshad Meeks, Ernest Mitchell, Traci Parker, Tim Pantoja, Imani Perry, Jermaine Thibodeaux, Brandon Terry, and Rhaisa Williams, for their feedback and encouragement along the way. Their support came in various forms, from phone and Zoom conversations where we discussed my thinking about key arguments and historical narratives to them recommending relevant texts to read or providing generative feedback on the manuscript as I drafted it. I must also express gratitude for my colleagues at the Institute of the Americas, especially Nick Witham, for providing me with the space and time to complete this project.

I am grateful for my agent, Nate Muscato, my editor, Adenike Olanrewaju, as well as her team at Harper, and Liz Velez, in particular, for supporting me in completing this project. It has been a joy working together on such a timely and meaningful book. I am also thankful to my faculty coordinator, Anne Korte, at the Harvard Graduate School of Education for assisting me with the many administrative tasks that go into preparing a book manuscript for publication. I feel very privileged to have such a capable and committed community of support around me.

Finally, I am deeply appreciative to several African American history scholars who have directly mentored me as well as a few who have made lasting impressions on my thinking indirectly, through their scholarship. The first among them is Professor Ula Taylor, whose mentorship and teaching are most responsible for my becoming a professor and scholar of black history. Her commitment to deep archival research, to beautiful and clarifying writing about black life, and to generously mentoring younger scholars continues to inspire me. I also feel deeply indebted to James D. Anderson, Vincent Brown, Pero Dagbovie, LaShawn Harris, Robert L. Harris, Jr., Saidiya Hartman, Darlene Clark Hine, Evelyn Brooks Higginbotham, Gerald Horne, Tera Hunter, Robin D. G. Kelley, and Vanessa Siddle Walker. Each of these historians, either through their scholarship or field leadership, has had some personal impact on my intellectual development and journey to writing this book. I am grateful for these stellar models of black memory workers from whom I continue to draw inspiration, and especially so in such dispiriting times as the present.

NOTES

INTRODUCTION: FOR MY PEOPLE

1. George Washington Williams, *History of the Negro Race in America from 1619 to 1880. Negroes as Slaves, as Soldiers, and as Citizens; Together with a Preliminary Consideration of the Unity of the Human Family, an Historical Sketch of Africa, and an Account of the Negro Governments of Sierra Leone and Liberia* (G. P. Putnam's Sons, 1885), 91.
2. Tonia Sutherland and Zakiya Collier, "Introduction: The Promise and Possibility of Black Archival Practice," *Black Scholar* 52, no. 2 (2022): 1–6, https://doi.org/10.1080/00064246.2022.2043722; Chaitra Powell et al., "This [Black] Woman's Work: Exploring Archival Projects That Embrace the Identity of the Memory Worker," *KULA* 2, no. 1 (2018): 1–8, https://doi.org/10.5334/kula.25.
3. My broad engagement with the "historical enterprise" is informed by the following work: Robert B. Townsend, *History's Babel: Scholarship, Professionalization, and the Historical Enterprise in the United States, 1880–1940* (University of Chicago Press, 2013), 4: "I use the term *historical enterprise* here to denote the broad range of activities where knowledge about the past is produced and used in an organized and systematic way."
4. Brandon R. Byrd, *The Black Republic: African Americans and the Fate of Haiti* (University of Pennsylvania Press, 2020).
5. This notion of authentic black history is informed by the following text: Manning Marable, *Living Black History: How Reimagining the African-American Past Can Remake America's Racial Future* (Civitas Books, 2006).
6. Vincent Brown, *Tacky's Revolt: The Story of an Atlantic Slave War* (Belknap Press, 2020), 242.
7. Imani Perry, "Racism Is Terrible. Blackness Is Not," *The Atlantic*, June 15, 2020, https://www.theatlantic.com/ideas/archive/2020/06/racism-terrible-blackness-not/613039.
8. J. Rupert Picott, "Editorial Comments," *Negro History Bulletin* 38, no. 8 (December 1, 1975): 473.
9. Thelma D. Perry, "Black Power, Circa 1971," *Negro History Bulletin* 48, no. 4 (1985): 59–60.
10. J. Rupert Picott, "Editorial Comments," *Negro History Bulletin* 37, no. 2 (1974): 209.
11. Phil Tomsovic and Thomas Preston, "President Ford, the ASALH, and the Political Origins of Black History Month," *Presidential Studies Quarterly* 53, no. 1 (2023): 4–18, https://doi.org/10.1111/psq.12802.
12. Gerald R. Ford, "Presidential Message for National Black History Month, 1976," Eliska Hasek Files, White House Office Collection, Box 1, folder "National Black History Month Message, 1976," Gerald R. Ford Presidential Library, Ann Arbor, MI.
13. Robert Allen, *Black Awakening in Capitalist America: An Analytic History* (Africa World Pr, 1969).

14. John Hope Franklin et al., "Black History Month: Serious Truth Telling or a Triumph in Tokenism?," *Journal of Blacks in Higher Education*, no. 18 (1997): 88.
15. Franklin et al., "Black History Month," 87.
16. Lerone Bennett, "Remarks at ASALH 60th Annual Meeting," *Negro History Bulletin* 39, no. 2 (1976): 524.
17. Traci Parker, *Department Stores and the Black Freedom Movement: Workers, Consumers, and Civil Rights from the 1930s to the 1980s*, John Hope Franklin Series in African American History and Culture (University of North Carolina Press, 2019), 12, 11, 5; cases of department stores observing Negro History Week were shared with me by Parker through correspondence, though such examples do not appear in her book.
18. Julieanna Richardson, interview with Lerone Bennett, The HistoryMakers Digital Archive, August 29, 2002, session 1, tape 1, story 8.
19. Franklin et al., "Black History Month," 91.
20. Tera W. Hunter, "If 'Woke' Dies, Our Nation's Truths Die with It," *Hammer & Hope* 2 (Summer 2023), https://hammerandhope.org/article/florida-history-slavery-ron-desantis-woke.
21. The historian Charles H. Wesley, for instance, used the term *heroic* to describe African Americans' reclamation of enslaved people who led insurrections as folk heroes, because they chose to interpret the lives of those political actors who were written off as "demented and deluded" by white historians, if acknowledged at all, on new terms that accounted for the perspectives of black people and their material conditions. Charles H. Wesley, "Creating and Maintaining an Historical Tradition," *Journal of Negro History* 49, no. 1 (1964): 13–33, https://doi.org/10.2307/2716474.

PART I: THE CREATION

1. Daphne A. Brooks, *Liner Notes for the Revolution: The Intellectual Life of Black Feminist Sound* (Harvard University Press, 2021), 156.
2. Colin Kaepernick, Robin D. G. Kelley, and Keeanga-Yamahtta Taylor, eds., *Our History Has Always Been Contraband: In Defense of Black Studies* (Haymarket Books, 2023).
3. George T. Winston, "The Relation of the Whites to the Negroes," *Annals of the American Academy of Political and Social Science* 18 (1901): 105–18.
4. C. G. Woodson, "Negro History Week," *Journal of Negro History* 11, no. 2 (1926): 240, https://www.journals.uchicago.edu/doi/epdf/10.2307/2714171.
5. Woodson, "Negro History Week," 241, 238.
6. Thomas L. Dabney, "The Study of the Negro," *Journal of Negro History* 19, no. 3 (1934): 266–307, https://doi.org/10.2307/2714215.
7. W. E. B. Du Bois, *Darkwater: Voices from Within the Veil* (Washington Square Press, 2004).
8. James Baldwin, "The White Man's Guilt," in *James Baldwin: Collected Essays*, ed. Toni Morrison (Library of America, 1998), 722–23.
9. W. E. B. Du Bois, *Black Reconstruction in America, 1860–1880* (Free Press, 1998), 20.
10. Cheryl I. Harris, "Whiteness as Property," *Harvard Law Review* 106, no. 8 (1993): 1707–91; Aileen Moreton-Robinson, *The White Possessive: Property, Power, and*

Indigenous Sovereignty (University of Minnesota Press, 2015); Stephanie E. Jones-Rogers, *They Were Her Property: White Women as Slave Owners in the American South*, illustrated ed. (Yale University Press, 2020).

11. James W. C. Pennington, *The Fugitive Blacksmith; or, Events in the History of James W. C. Pennington*, 2nd ed. (Charles Gilpin, 1849), iv–v.
12. Pennington, *The Fugitive Blacksmith*, xii.
13. Thavolia Glymph, "Paper Tracings in the Spectacularly Boisterous Archive of Slavery," *American Historical Review* 130, no. 1 (2025): 1–18, https://doi.org/10.1093/ahr/rhaf003; Emily Owens, "Enslaved Women, Violence, and the Archive: An Interview with Marisa Fuentes," *Black Perspectives*, October 4, 2016, https://www.aaihs.org/enslaved-women-violence-and-the-archive-an-interview-with-marisa-fuentes; Michel-Rolph Trouillot, *Silencing the Past: Power and the Production of History* (Beacon Press, 1995); Saidiya Hartman, "Venus in Two Acts," *Small Axe* 12, no. 2 (2008): 1–14.
14. George Washington Williams, *History of the Negro Race in America from 1619 to 1880. Negroes as Slaves, as Soldiers, and as Citizens; Together with a Preliminary Consideration of the Unity of the Human Family, an Historical Sketch of Africa, and an Account of the Negro Governments of Sierra Leone and Liberia* (G. P. Putnam's Sons, 1885), 1.
15. Mary Church Terrell, "Proof That Terrell Established Douglass Day," n.d., Mary Church Terrell Papers: Speeches and Writings, 1866–1953, Library of Congress, box 33.
16. Terrell, "Proof That Terrell Established Douglass Day"; see also "A Douglass Day Established for the Colored Schools," *Evening Star*, January 13, 1897, 5.
17. "Frederick Douglass, Anniversary of His Birth Observed in the Colored Schools. High Tribute to the Man, Presentation of a Portrait and an Eloquent Reply. King Among Men," *Evening Star*, February 12, 1897, 12.
18. Donald Yacovone, *Teaching White Supremacy: America's Democratic Ordeal and the Forging of Our National Identity* (Pantheon, 2022); for the reference to Douglass in the endnotes, see Albert Bushnell Hart, *Essentials in American History: From the Discovery to the Present Day* (American Book Company, 1905), chap. 22 and p. 352.
19. "Douglass Day Celebration," *Washington Post*, February 14, 1897, 13.
20. Alison M. Parker, *Unceasing Militant: The Life of Mary Church Terrell*, John Hope Franklin Series in African American History and Culture (The University of North Carolina Press, 2021), 50.
21. Jarvis R. Givens, "Teaching to 'Undo Their Narratively Condemned Status': Black Educators and the Problem of Curricular Violence," in *Schooling the Movement*, ed. Jon N. Hale, Derrick P. Alridge, and Tondra L. Loder-Jackson (University of South Carolina Press, 2023).
22. Mary Church Terrell, review of *The Education of the Negro Prior to 1861* by C. G. Woodson, *Journal of Negro History* 1, no. 1 (1916): 96–97, https://doi.org/10.2307/2713521; Mary Church Terrell, "History of the High School for Negroes in Washington," *Journal of Negro History* 2, no. 3 (July 1917): 252–66.
23. Parker, *Unceasing Militant*, 50.
24. Herman Dreer, *The History of Omega Psi Phi Fraternity: A Brotherhood of Negro*

College Men, 1911 to 1939 (The Fraternity, 1940), 153, 152–53, 154–56; William Nelson, "The Campaign for the Study of Negro Literature and History," *The Oracle: Semi-Annual Publication of the Grand Chapter of the Omega Psi Phi Fraternity*, August 1921, 31–33.
25. *The Oracle: Semi-Annual Publication of the Grand Chapter of the Omega Psi Phi Fraternity*, February 1922, 19.
26. "Omega Psi Phi Holds Conclave: Colored Fraternity to Foster Negro History," *New York Amsterdam News*, January 10, 1923, 7.
27. "School News: Negro History Week," *Washington Tribune*, February 5, 1926, 2.
28. W. E. B. Du Bois, "Does the Negro Need Separate Schools?," *Journal of Negro Education* 4, no. 3 (1935): 333.
29. Carter G. Woodson, "Fifth of March as Crispus Attucks Day," *Negro History Bulletin* 10, no. 6 (1947): 136.
30. Woodson, "Fifth of March as Crispus Attucks Day," 131.
31. "(1862) William C. Nell Speaks at the Crispus Attucks Commemoration, Boston," BlackPast, January 28, 2007, https://www.blackpast.org/african-american-history/1862-william-c-nell-speaks-crispus-attucks-commemoration-boston.
32. Mitch Kachun, "Antebellum African Americans, Public Commemoration, and the Haitian Revolution: A Problem of Historical Mythmaking," *Journal of the Early Republic* 26, no. 2 (2006): 253.
33. James McCune Smith, introduction to *A Memorial Discourse; by Rev. Henry Highland Garnet, Delivered in the Hall of the House of Representatives, Washington City, D.C. on Sabbath, February 12, 1865* (Joseph M. Wilson, 1865), 24.
34. Annette Gordon-Reed, *On Juneteenth* (Liveright, 2021).
35. D. A. Scott, "Emancipation Proclamation for the Baptist of Texas Sunday, June 19th 1892," *Sunday School Herald*, May 12, 1892.
36. Robert Farris Thompson, *Flash of the Spirit: African and Afro-American Art and Philosophy* (Vintage Books, 1984).
37. Zora Neale Hurston, *The Sanctified Church: The Folklore Writings of Zora Neale Hurston* (Turtle Island, 1981), 91.
38. Nick Estes, "The World of Paper, Restoring Relations, and the Lower Brule Sioux Tribe," in *Allotment Stories: Indigenous Land Relations under Settler Siege*, ed. Jean M. O'Brien and Daniel Heath Justice (University of Minnesota Press, 2022).
39. Carter G. Woodson and Jarvis R. Givens, *The Mis-Education of the Negro*, ed. Henry Louis Gates (Penguin Classics, 2023).
40. Carter G. Woodson, "Association on Guard," *Norfolk Journal and Guide*, October 17, 1936.

PART II: THE NEGRO DIGS UP HIS PAST

1. Saidiya Hartman, *Lose Your Mother: A Journey Along the Atlantic Slave Route* (Farrar, Straus and Giroux, 2008), 17–18.
2. Mary Ross Jones, letter, in "Our Rural Program: Materials and Activities for Mississippi 1948–1949," H. T. Sampson Library, Jackson State University, Jackson, Mississippi, 83.
3. Karla F. C. Holloway, *Passed On: African American Mourning Stories: A Memorial Collection* (Duke University Press, 2002), 139.
4. Walter Rodney, *The Groundings with My Brothers* (Verso, 2019), chap. 5.

5. E. A. Johnson, *A School History of the Negro Race in America from 1619 to 1890: With a Short Introduction as to the Origin of the Race: Also a Short Sketch of Liberia* (Edwards & Broughton, Printers, 1890), 82–83.
6. Mary McLeod Bethune, "The Association for the Study of Negro Life and History: Its Contribution to Our Modern Life," *Journal of Negro History* 20, no. 4 (1935): 407–08.
7. Carter G. Woodson, "My Recollections of Veterans of the Civil War," *Negro History Bulletin*, February 1944; Carter G. Woodson, "The Negro Washerwoman, A Vanishing Figure," *Journal of Negro History* 25, no. 3 (1930): 269–77; "Some Undistinguished Negroes," *Journal of Negro History* 3, no. 1 (1918): 90–91; Carter Godwin Woodson, *The Rural Negro* (Association for the Study of Negro Life and History, 1930).
8. Some excellent models of historical scholarship that have helped widen the aperture for thinking about the black past include Robin D. G. Kelley, *Race Rebels: Culture, Politics, and the Black Working Class* (Free Press, 1996); Saidiya Hartman, *Wayward Lives, Beautiful Experiments: Intimate Histories of Social Upheaval* (W. W. Norton & Company, 2019); LaShawn Harris, *Sex Workers, Psychics, and Numbers Runners: Black Women in New York City's Underground Economy* (University of Illinois Press, 2016); Orisanmi Burton, *Tip of the Spear: Black Radicalism, Prison Repression, and the Long Attica Revolt* (University of California Press, 2023).
9. Holloway, *Passed On*, 6, 60–61.
10. Saidiya Hartman, "The Dead Book Revisited," *History of the Present* 6, no. 2 (2016): 214.
11. Lawrence W. Levine, *Black Culture and Black Consciousness: Afro-American Folk Thought from Slavery to Freedom* (Oxford University Press, 1978), 161.
12. Thomas W. Laqueur, *The Work of the Dead: A Cultural History of Mortal Remains* (Princeton University Press, 2015); Robert Pogue Harrison, *The Dominion of the Dead* (University of Chicago Press, 2003).
13. Harrison, *The Dominion of the Dead*, xi.
14. Vincent Brown, *The Reaper's Garden: Death and Power in the World of Atlantic Slavery* (Harvard University Press, 2008), 5–6: "I call such activity *mortuary politics*, employing a capacious general definition of politics as concerted action toward specific goals. Alongside more conventional political practices like policymaking and institution building, this broad definition allows me to consider how people justify actions, claim and dispute authority, or create and use the cultural categories that mediate social life. Mortuary practices may reflect historic changes, as intense disputes about custom, authority, and religion play out within final rites of passage. More significantly, relations between the living and the dead also generate historic changes when those relations emerge as the source of struggle."
15. Daina Ramey Berry, *The Price for Their Pound of Flesh: The Value of the Enslaved, from Womb to Grave, in the Building of a Nation* (Beacon Press, 2017).
16. Alice Walker, *In Search of Our Mothers' Gardens: Womanist Prose* (Harcourt Brace Jovanovich, 1983).
17. Hartman, *Lose Your Mother*, 17–18.
18. Sylvia Wynter, "No Humans Involved: An Open Letter to My Colleagues," *Forum*

N.H.I.: Knowledge for the 21st Century 1, no. 1 (1994): 42–73, https://dcal.dartmouth.edu/sites/dcal.prod/files/center_for_advancement_learning/wysiwyg/no_humans_involved_-_an_open_letter_to_my_colleagues_-_sylvia_wynter.pdf; Jarvis R Givens, "Teaching to 'Undo Their Narratively Condemned Status': Black Educators and the Problem of Curricular Violence," in *Schooling the Movement*, ed. Jon N. Hale, Derrick P. Alridge, and Tondra Loder Jackson (University of South Carolina Press, 2023).

19. For "afterlife of slavery" see Hartman, *Lose Your Mother*, 6; Christina Sharpe, *In the Wake: On Blackness and Being* (Duke University Press, 2016).
20. Arturo Alfonso Schomburg, "The Negro Digs Up His Past (1925)," in *The New Negro: Voices of the Harlem Renaissance*, ed. Alain Locke (Touchstone, 1997), 231.
21. Laura Helton, *Scattered and Fugitive Things: How Black Collectors Created Archives and Remade History* (Columbia University Press, 2024), 32.
22. William Butterworth, *Three Years Adventures of a Minor in England, Africa, the West Indies, South Carolina and Georgia* (Leeds, Thomas Inchbold, 1831), 93-96.
23. Butterworth, *Three Years Adventures*, 93-96.
24. Berry, *The Price for Their Pound of Flesh*.
25. Marcus Rediker, *The Slave Ship: A Human History* (Penguin Books, 2008).
26. Hartman, *Lose Your Mother*, 31.
27. Zora Neale Hurston, letter to W. E. B. Du Bois, June 11, 1945, MS 312, Special Collections and University Archives, University of Massachusetts Amherst Libraries.
28. Eloise Greenfield, "Harriet Tubman," Academy of American Poets, accessed April 10, 2025, https://poets.org/poem/harriet-tubman.
29. George Washington Williams, *History of the Negro Race in America from 1619 to 1880. Negroes as Slaves, as Soldiers, and as Citizens; Together with a Preliminary Consideration of the Unity of the Human Family, an Historical Sketch of Africa, and an Account of the Negro Governments of Sierra Leone and Liberia* (G. P. Putnam's Sons, 1885), 91.
30. Jarvis R. Givens, "'He Was, Undoubtedly, a Wonderful Character': Black Teachers' Representations of Nat Turner During Jim Crow," *Souls* 18, nos. 2–4 (2016): 215–34.
31. John W. Cromwell, "The Aftermath of Nat Turner's Insurrection," *Journal of Negro History* 5 (1920): 208–34.
32. Zora Neale Hurston, letter to W. E. B. Du Bois, June 11, 1945.
33. Alice Walker, "In Search of Zora Neale Hurston," *Ms.*, March 1975, 74–79, 85–89.
34. Zora Neale Hurston, "'Court Order Can't Make the Races Mix,'" LewRockwell.com, September 13, 2003, https://www.lewrockwell.com/1970/01/zora-neale-hurston/court-order-cant-make-the-races-mix.
35. Greenfield, "Harriet Tubman."
36. Elizabeth Alexander, *The Trayvon Generation* (Grand Central Publishing, 2022).
37. Robert L. Allen, "Robert Allen: From Segregated Atlanta to UC Berkeley, a Life of Activism and African American Scholarship," interview conducted by Todd Holmes in 2019, Oral History Center, Bancroft Library, University of California, Berkeley, 2020, 145.
38. Jay Winston Driskell, *Schooling Jim Crow: The Fight for Atlanta's Booker T. Washington High School and the Roots of Black Protest Politics* (University of Virginia Press, 2014); on black southern high schools during Jim Crow, see James Anderson, *The Education of Blacks in the South, 1860–1935* (University of North Carolina Press, 1988), 145, 188.

39. Robert Allen, *Black Awakening in Capitalist America: An Analytic History* (Africa World Press, 1969).
40. Research for Benjamin Elijah Mays, 1968, carton 1, folders 19–20, Dr. Robert L. Allen Papers, BANC MSS 2017/193, Bancroft Library, University of California, Berkeley.
41. "Black History Week: Allen Recalls Malcom X's Murder," *Michigan Daily*, February 11, 1974, 1–2.
42. Holloway, *Passed On*, 7.

PART III: WHEN TRUTH GETS A HEARING

1. Nannie Helen Burroughs, "When Truth Gets a Hearing, Pageant, 1916–1920," n.d., box 47, Nannie Helen Burroughs Papers, 1900–1963, Manuscript Division, Library of Congress, Washington, DC.
2. Evelyn Brooks Barnett, "Nannie Burroughs and the Education of Black Women," in *The Afro-American Woman: Struggles and Images*, ed. Sharon Harley and Rosalyn Terborg-Penn (Kennikat Press, 1978), 100.
3. For more on Nannie Helen Burroughs and her contributions to black educational thought and curriculum studies, see Shantina Shannell Jackson, "'To Struggle and Battle and Overcome': The Educational Thought of Nannie Helen Burroughs, 1875–1961," PhD diss., University of California, Berkeley, 2015, https://www.proquest.com/docview/1873854053?pq-origsite=primo; Alana D. Murray, *The Development of the Alternative Black Curriculum, 1890–1940: Countering the Master Narrative* (Springer International Publishing, 2018).
4. A list of schools using the textbook appears in "The Negro in Our History 4th Edition Advertisement," n.d., box 1, folder 1, CGW Papers, Emory University.
5. Floyd J. Calvin, "Pointing the Way to Better Womanhood: That's Nannie Burroughs' Job, and She Does It: Notional Training School for Women and Girls Is Monument to Negro Womanhood," *Pittsburgh Courier*, June 8, 1929.
6. "How We Have Been Helped by the Study of Negro History" and "January," Student Yearbook, 1929, box 312, Nannie Helen Burroughs Papers, Manuscript Division, Library of Congress, Washington, DC.
7. Barnett, "Nannie Burroughs and the Education of Black Women," 106.
8. "Memory of Douglass," *Evening Star*, March 6, 1895, 8: "At a recent meeting of the colored teachers of the public schools of the District resolutions of regret were adopted: The meeting decided to request the superintendent and trustees to designate a 'Douglass Day,' to be observed by appropriate exercises in the schools."
9. Barnett, "Nannie Burroughs and the Education of Black Women," 107.
10. Barnett, "Nannie Burroughs and the Education of Black Women," 107.
11. Barnett, "Nannie Burroughs and the Education of Black Women," 107.
12. Sara Pelham Speaks, "Nannie H. Burroughs Stages Pageant, History Association Audience of 1,000 Applauds Allegory Monday Night," *Afro-American*, November 2, 1929.
13. Speaks, "Nannie H. Burroughs Stages Pageant, History Association Audience of 1,000 Applauds Allegory Monday Night."
14. Speaks, "Nannie H. Burroughs Stages Pageant, History Association Audience of 1,000 Applauds Allegory Monday Night."

15. "Incorporated Baptists Celebrate Golden Jubilee at Chicago Meeting," *New York Age*, September 6, 1930, 5.
16. Robert B. Townsend, *History's Babel: Scholarship, Professionalization, and the Historical Enterprise in the United States, 1880–1940* (University of Chicago Press, 2013), 4: "I use the term *historical enterprise* here to denote the broad range of activities where knowledge about the past is produced and used in an organized and systematic way."
17. Tonia Sutherland and Zakiya Collier, "Introduction: The Promise and Possibility of Black Archival Practice," *Black Scholar* 52, no. 2 (April 3, 2022): 1–6, https://doi.org/10.1080/00064246.2022.2043722; Chaitra Powell et al., "This [Black] Woman's Work: Exploring Archival Projects That Embrace the Identity of the Memory Worker," *KULA* 2, no. 1 (2018): 1–8, https://doi.org/10.5334/kula.25.
18. Laura Helton, *Scattered and Fugitive Things: How Black Collectors Created Archives and Remade History* (Columbia University Press, 2024); Adalaine Holton, "Decolonizing History: Arthur Schomburg's Afrodiasporic Archive," *Journal of African American History* 92, no. 2 (2007): 218–38; Melanie Chambliss, "A Vital Factor in the Community: Recovering the Life and Legacy of Chicago Public Librarian Vivian G. Harsh," *Journal of African American History* 106, no. 3 (2021): 411–38, https://doi.org/10.1086/714085; Kara Bledsoe, "What Dorothy Porter's Life Meant for Black Studies," JSTOR Daily, August 22, 2018, https://daily.jstor.org/what-dorothy-porters-life-meant-for-black-studies.
19. Michael Hanchard, "Black Memory Versus State Memory: Notes Toward a Method," *Small Axe* 12, no. 2 (2008): 48.
20. John Hope Franklin, "Pioneer Negro Historians," *Negro Digest*, February 1966, 5.
21. Evelyn Brooks Higginbotham, "In the Fertile Field of Black Women's History," unpublished essay, July 1, 2013, papers of Evelyn Brooks Higginbotham, personal collection of Evelyn Brooks Higginbotham.
22. Higginbotham, "In the Fertile Field of Black Women's History."
23. Larry Crowe, interview with Evelyn Brooks Higginbotham, HistoryMakers Digital Archive, April 25, 2013, session 1, tape 2, story 7.
24. Higginbotham, "In the Fertile Field of Black Women's History."
25. Evelyn Brooks, "The Women's Movement in the Black Baptist Church, 1880–1920," PhD diss., University of Rochester, 1984, iv.
26. Franklin, "Pioneer Negro Historians," 5.
27. Michel-Rolph Trouillot, *Silencing the Past: Power and the Production of History* (Beacon Press, 1995), 26.
28. Sandy Rufus Youngblood, "Autobiography—S. R. Youngblood," in Record of the Estate of J. C. Dickson, September 2, 1914, box 2, S. Rufus Youngblood Papers, Stuart A. Rose Manuscript, Archives, and Rare Book Library, Emory University (hereafter referred to as Youngblood Papers, Emory University); Bureau of the Census and Sandy Rufus Youngblood, 1870 United States Federal Census, Verdier, Colleton, South Carolina, National Archives and Records Administration, Washington, DC, 1870, via Ancestry.com; Thirteenth Census of the United States, 1910, Orangeburg Ward 5, Orangeburg, South Carolina, National Archives, Washington, DC, 1910, via Ancestry.com.
29. V. P. Franklin and Mary Frances Berry, *Black Self-Determination: A Cultural History of African-American Resistance*, 2nd ed. (Lawrence Hill Books, 1992); Heather

Williams, *Self-Taught: African American Education in Slavery and Freedom* (University of North Carolina Press, 2007); James Anderson, *The Education of Blacks in the South, 1860–1935* (University of North Carolina Press, 1988); Jarvis R. Givens, "Black Education as the General Strike: The Radical Origins of African American Teaching and Learning," *Journal of African American History* 109, no. 2 (2024): 231–59, https://doi.org/10.1086/726901.
30. Youngblood, "Autobiography—S. R. Youngblood."
31. Sandy Rufus Youngblood, Teacher's Graded Certificate, January 8, 1886, Youngblood Papers, Emory University; Claflin University, in *Catalogue of Claflin University, 1891–1892, Orangeburg, S.C.* (Hunt & Eaton, 1891), 11, 31; Claflin University, *Annual Catalogue, Claflin University, 1907–1908* (Claflin Electric Press, 1908), 7.
32. R. H. Wilson (president, State Board of Education), letter to S. R. Youngblood, June 1, 1910, box 1, folder "Letters," Youngblood Papers, Emory University; S. R. Youngblood, letter to president of Langston University, August 1, 1910, box 1, folder "Letters," Youngblood Papers, Emory University.
33. Sandy Rufus Youngblood, "In a Government like This . . ." (speech), ca. 1901, box 1, folder "Speeches," Youngblood Papers, Emory University; Sandy Rufus Youngblood, "Speech Given at Brothers of Zion Association Meeting," Orangeburg, South Carolina, prior to 1910, 7, box 1, folder "Speeches," Youngblood Papers, Emory University.
34. Robin Bernstein, *Racial Innocence: Performing American Childhood from Slavery to Civil Rights* (NYU Press, 2011), 11–12: "The method of reading material things as scriptive aims to discover not what any individual actually did but rather what a thing invited its user to do. This act of scripting, this issuing of a culturally specific invitation, is itself a historical event—one that can be recovered and then analyzed as a fresh source of evidence."
35. Caitlin Rosenthal, *Accounting for Slavery: Masters and Management* (Harvard University Press, 2018), 72.
36. Smallwood, *Saltwater Slavery: A Middle Passage from Africa to American Diaspora* (Harvard University Press, 2008), xx, 4.
37. Smallwood, *Saltwater Slavery*, 4.
38. Saidiya Hartman, *Lose Your Mother: A Journey Along the Atlantic Slave Route* (Farrar, Straus and Giroux, 2008), 12.
39. Hortense J. Spillers, "Mama's Baby, Papa's Maybe: An American Grammar Book," *Diacritics* 17, no. 2 (1987): 72.
40. James W. C. Pennington, *The Fugitive Blacksmith; or, Events in the History of James W. C. Pennington*, 2nd ed. (Charles Gilpin, 1849), xii.
41. Youngblood, "Speech Given at Brothers of Zion Association Meeting," 13.
42. Michael Fultz, "Caught Between a Rock and a Hard Place: The Dissolution of Black State Teachers Associations, 1954–1970," in *The SAGE Handbook of African American Education*, ed. Linda C. Tillman (Sage Publications, 2008), 67–82; Vanessa Siddle Walker, *The Lost Education of Horace Tate: Uncovering the Hidden Heroes Who Fought for Justice in Schools* (New Press, 2018).
43. Fultz, "Caught Between a Rock and a Hard Place"; Walker, *The Lost Education of Horace Tate*; Leslie T. Fenwick and H. Richard Milner IV, *Jim Crow's Pink Slip: The Untold Story of Black Principal and Teacher Leadership* (Harvard Education Press, 2022).

44. "Negro History Week," *Bulletin of the West Virginia Teachers' Association* 6, no. 2 (1935): 14.
45. "Wandering: O'er Hill and Through Dale," *Bulletin of the West Virginia Teachers' Association* 20, no. 2 (1953): 26.
46. Troas Lewis Latimer, "Reflections on Negro History Week," *Herald: Official Journal of the Georgia Teachers and Educational Association* 13, no. 1 (1946): 23.
47. "Let Us Have National Peace and Racial Unity," *North Carolina Teachers Record* 18, no. 1 (1947): 10.
48. Marguerite F. Christian, "Improve Communicative Skills," *Virginia Education Bulletin* 32, no. 8 (1953): 151.
49. "Lamar Elementary School Observes Negro History Week," *Texas Standard* 37, no. 5 (1964): 16.
50. "Negro History Week," *Texas Standard* 37, no. 6 (1964): 17.
51. *Spring Bulletin of the N.J.O.T.C.C.* 3, nos. 1–2 (1942).
52. A list of schools using the textbook appears in "The Negro in Our History 4th Edition Advertisement," n.d., box 1, folder 1, CGW Papers, Emory University.
53. *Mississippi Educational Journal* 10, no. 5 (1934): 6.
54. "Notes from the Field: Putnam County Activities," *Herald: Official Journal of the Georgia Teachers and Education Association* 22, no. 4 (1955): 36–37.
55. Alice Walker, *Gathering Blossoms Under Fire: The Journals of Alice Walker, 1965–2000*, ed. Valerie Boyd (Simon & Schuster, 2022), 391–92; Campbell F. Scribner, "Surveying the Destruction of African American Schoolhouses in the South, 1864–1876," *Journal of the Civil War Era* 10, no. 4 (2020): 469–94.
56. Alice Walker, *In Search of Our Mothers' Gardens* (W&N, 2005).
57. *Herald*, October 1949, 34.

PART IV: WHERE DO WE GO FROM HERE?

1. E. Belfield Spriggins, "Dr. Du Bois Holds Audience Spellbound on 'Negro and Reconstruction,'" *Louisiana Weekly*, February 24, 1934.
2. Martin Luther King, Jr., "Honoring Dr Du Bois," Jacobin, February 23, 1968, https://jacobin.com/2019/01/web-du-bois-martin-luther-king-speech.
3. Spriggins, "Dr. Du Bois Holds Audience Spellbound on 'Negro and Reconstruction.'"
4. Spriggins, "Dr. Du Bois Holds Audience Spellbound on 'Negro and Reconstruction.'"
5. George T. Winston, "The Relation of the Whites to the Negroes," *Annals of the American Academy of Political and Social Science* 18 (1901): 116, https://www.jstor.org/stable/1009885?seq=12.
6. Oliver R. Pope, *Chalk Dust* (Pageant Press, 1967), 4.
7. Albert White, "Historians Hold Session," *Louisiana Weekly*, November 17, 1934.
8. Carter G. Woodson, *Negro Makers of History* (Associated Publishers, 1928), 271.
9. Woodson, *Negro Makers of History*, 271.
10. Vivian Robinson, "Book Review: Black Reconstruction, W. E. B. DuBois," *Moving Finger*, 1937.
11. Martin Luther King, Jr., "The Negro and the Constitution," in *The Cornellian*, B. T. Washington High School yearbook, 1944, 54.
12. Martin Luther King, Jr., *The Autobiography of Martin Luther King, Jr.* (Warner Books, 1998), chap. 1.
13. King, "Honoring Dr Du Bois."

14. King, "Honoring Dr Du Bois."
15. King, "Honoring Dr Du Bois."
16. King, "Honoring Dr Du Bois."
17. W. E. B. Du Bois, *Black Reconstruction in America, 1860–1880* (Free Press, 1998).
18. King, "Honoring Dr Du Bois."
19. Du Bois, *Black Reconstruction in America, 1860–1880*.
20. Martin Luther King, Jr., Vincent Harding, and Coretta Scott King, *Where Do We Go from Here: Chaos or Community?* (Beacon Press, 2010), 45.
21. King et al., *Where Do We Go from Here*, 44.
22. King et al., *Where Do We Go from Here*, 43.
23. King et al., *Where Do We Go from Here*, 43–44.
24. Vanessa Siddle Walker, "Second-Class Integration: A Historical Perspective for a Contemporary Agenda," *Harvard Educational Review* 79, no. 2 (2009): 269–84, https://doi.org/10.17763/haer.79.2.b1637p4u4093484m.
25. Karida L. Brown, "The 'Hidden Injuries' of School Desegregation: Cultural Trauma and Transforming African American Identities," *American Journal of Cultural Sociology* 4, no. 2 (2016): 196–220, https://doi.org/10.1057/ajcs.2016.4; Leslie T. Fenwick, *Jim Crow's Pink Slip: The Untold Story of Black Principal and Teacher Leadership* (Harvard Education Press, 2022); Amy Stuart Wells, *Both Sides Now: The Story of School Desegregation's Graduates* (Berkeley: University of California Press, 2009).
26. Michael Fultz, "The Displacement of Black Educators Post-*Brown*: An Overview and Analysis," *History of Education Quarterly* 44, no. 1 (2004): 11–45, https://doi.org/10.1111/j.1748-5959.2004.tb00144.x; Michael Fultz, "Caught Between a Rock and a Hard Place: The Dissolution of Black State Teachers Associations, 1954–1970," in *The SAGE Handbook of African American Education*, ed. Linda C. Tillman (Sage Publications, 2008), 67–82; Jacqueline Jordan Irvine, "An Analysis of the Problem of Disappearing Black Educators," *Elementary School Journal* 88, no. 5 (1988): 503–13; Fenwick, *Jim Crow's Pink Slip*; Vanessa Siddle Walker, *The Lost Education of Horace Tate: Uncovering the Hidden Heroes Who Fought for Justice in Schools* (New Press, 2018).
27. Manning Marable, *Race, Reform, and Rebellion: The Second Reconstruction and Beyond in Black America, 1945–2006*, 3rd ed. (University Press of Mississippi, 2007).
28. Kehinde Andrews, *Resisting Racism: Race, Inequality and the Black Supplementary School Movement* (Trentham Books, 2013); Bernard Coard, *How the West Indian Child Is Made Educationally Subnormal in the British School System: The Scandal of the Black Child in Schools in Britain* (New Beacon for the Caribbean Education and Community Workers' Association, 1971).
29. Manning Marable, *Living Black History: How Reimagining the African-American Past Can Remake America's Racial Future* (Civitas Books, 2006).

INDEX

Abiel Smith School, 203
abolitionist movement, 53, 60–61, 81, 173, 178, 204
Abrams, Annie Mable McDaniel, 151, 152
academic freedom, 39
academics, 3
Advanced Placement African American studies, 23, 40
Africa
    diaspora, 41, 123–24, 185, 209–10
    European colonialism, 123
    "known" to be without history and culture, 40–41
    precolonial civilizations, 74
    racist depictions of, 178
African American History Standards, 23
African Americans
    access to power during Reconstruction period, 173, 177
    ancestors of, 74, 80
    as a colonized people, 107
    creation of black history by, 44–45
    death and cultural practices, 77, 82
    denigration of deceased predecessors, 79–80
    diasporic consciousness, 4, 123–24, 209–10
    future orientation of, 199
    "heroic tradition" of remembering history, 46
    historical commemoration by, 51
    racialization of, 4
    second-class citizenship, 174, 182
    value of as consumers, 19
    Williams's history of, 50–51
African American studies, 39, 42, 148, 185

African Free School, 48
African Meeting House, 203
Afro-American (newspaper), 125
The Afro-American Woman (Harley and Terborg-Penn, eds.), 133
Albany State, 155
Alexander, Elizabeth, 103–4
Allen, Robert, L., 102, 104–11, 181
American exceptionalism, 11
ancestors, 74, 80
Anderson, Marian, 182, 183
Anheuser-Busch, 18
antiblackness
    biases in historical professions, 128
    black history as a response to, 8
    colonialism, 4
    in curricula, 158, 192
    historical myths, 4, 74
    ledgers as a tool of, 146
    school systems and, 162
    slavery and, 84
    violence and, 41, 43, 72, 123
"anti-CRT" campaigns, 99
"anti-DEI" campaigns, 99
antislavery movement, 62
"antiwoke" legislation, 42, 99
archival assembly, 149–53
archivists, 3, 128–29, 134–35, 169, 205–6
Arkansas Teachers Association, 151
Association for the Study of Afro-American Life and History (ASALH), 10–15, 43, 54–55, 58, 92, 126, 154, 157, 176, 177
Association for the Study of Negro Life and History, 43, 54, 92, 126, 176
    and establishment of Negro History Week, 58, 154, 157

Association of Black Women Historians, 133
Atlanta University, 106
Attucks, Crispus, 59, 60–61, 74, 81, 166
Audubon Ballroom, 106

Baldwin, James, 46
Ballard, Allen, 21–22
Banneker, Benjamin, 74
Barrett, Janie Porter, 124
Bell's Chapel Elementary School, 164
Bennett, Lerone, Jr., 18–19, 20–21
Berry, Daina Ramey, 87
Bethel Literary and Historical Association, 53
Bethune, Mary McLeod, 37, 74, 134, 164
bicentennial (US), 10–11, 12
black agency, 24, 26, 47, 49, 119, 206, 215
Black Awakening in Capitalist America (Allen), 106
black consciousness, 7, 12, 85, 130, 181, 184, 214
Black Europe Summer School, 209–10, 211
Black Freedom Movement, 6, 45, 81, 109, 130, 132–33, 150, 193, 199
black historical consciousness, 60, 66–68
black histories of the everyday, 75
black history
   acknowledging the good in, 8–9
   attacks on, 39–40, 170, 190–91, 210–11
   authentic, 5–6
   banning of books about, 23
   commemoration of, 51, 55–57, 59–65, 66–67, 85–86, 90–91
   communal literacy of, 32, 213–14
   considered a contradiction in terms, 40–42
   construction of, 190
   creation of, 2, 44–45, 128
   criminalization of teaching of, 22–23
   as a critical history, 5–6, 8–9, 20–21, 190–91, 207–8
   as criticism of racial chattel slavery, 4
   erasure of, 67, 194–95
   of the everyday, 75–76
   futures of, 216–17
   "heroic tradition" of remembering, 46, 48
   individual connections to, 38–39
   loss and erasure of materials of, 147–49
   marginalization of, 39
   as more than American history, 4–5, 23–24
   mortuary politics, 81, 91
   as a mourning practice, 76–77
   observances of, 26
   as political, 27, 84–85, 190
   power of, 191, 195
   preservation of, 136–40, 148–49, 168–69
   prevalence of death in, 78–80, 82–83
   public celebrations of, 64
   remembering the dead, 71–72
   removal of from public sphere, 22
   as a resource, 183
   as a response to antiblackness, 8
   silencing of, 72, 139–40
   struggle for, 208–9
   students as participants in, 202–3
   suppression of, 42
   sustaining, 189–90
   tasks of, 5
   teaching of, 54–56, 95, 104, 121–23, 130–31, 153–60
   as a weapon, 66–67
   whitewashed, 16, 172, 186, 187–88

Black History Month
"America for All Americans" theme of first, 10–11
ASALH proclamation draft, 13
centennial, 197
as a commemorative practice, 72
corporate commercialization of, 15–20, 40, 199
creation of, 45–46
critics of, 18, 21, 23–24
early celebrations of, 13
establishment of, 2, 10, 33, 42, 191, 211
Ford's presidential message, 13–16
as formalized truth-telling, 130
future possibilities of, 206–7
as a means of public accountability, 40
Miss Butterfield's program, 30–38, 66, 192–93, 216
observances of, 199–200
tradition of black memory work and, 9, 76
worldwide celebrations of, 209
Black History Week, 33–34, 109
black intellectualism, 50, 55, 85, 131
Black Literary Society, 200–201, 212, 216
black lives, devaluation of, 138–39
black memory work and workers
bearing witness to the past, 8
commemoration of ordinary lives by, 73, 74–76, 212–13
cultivation of, 169–70
death and, 71–73
Du Bois's, 186
as forward looking, 8–9
as heroic, 24–25
language of, 128–29
motives of, 129–30
politics of, 27, 129–30, 169
positive project of, 67–68
power and, 66

preservation work of, 168–69
production of historical knowledge by, 45
as protest, 89
range of, 127–28
as response to antiblack silences in historical narratives, 49–50
as ritual, 65
social aim of, 7
vs. state memory, 129, 169
story of, 199
students as participants in, 159–60
teachers and, 3, 131, 178
technology and, 201–2
tradition of, 3–6, 9, 16, 24–25, 208
training of future, 201–3
truth telling, 38, 130
by women, 95, 132–33
black national anthem, 25, 31
blackness, 41
Black Panther Party for Self-Defense, 78, 107
Black Power movement, 12, 78, 124, 191
Black Reconstruction in America, 1860–1880 (Du Bois), 172, 178, 186–88
Black Renaissance, 32, 44, 78, 84, 97
black resistance, 6
The Black Scholar (periodical), 109
black student organizers, 13
Black Studies departments, 13, 198
Black Supplementary School Movement, 209, 211
Black Teacher Archive (BTA), 151–53, 159–60, 161, 167, 169, 184
black women
archivists, 3, 128–29
on board the *Hudibras*, 85–91
conventional notions of gender challenged by, 168

black women (*continued*)
  erasure of in historical record, 131–32
  leaders, 103
  memory work by, 95, 132–33
  schools and education for, 119–23, 132, 134–35
  sexual violence and, 78, 133
  stigmatization of physical features, 122–23
  Tubman's new standards of womanhood, 102–3
  women's groups, 123–24
black women's history, 131–33
black women's studies, 131
book bans, 23, 39, 42, 99–100, 137, 148
Booker T. Washington High School, 104, 105, 179–80, 181
Bordentown School, 158
Boston Massacre, 60–61
Bradley, Sarah Grace, 179, 183–84, 190, 193
Bradly, Marcel, 112
Bristol (enslaved boy), 87
Broadnax, Micha, 151, 169
Brooks, Daphne, 32
Brooks, Evelyn. *See* Higginbotham, Evelyn Brooks
Brown, Sterling A., 158
Brown, Vincent, 79–80, 143
Brown v. Board of Education, 12, 100, 152, 192, 196
Browser Books, 107
Bruce, John Edward, 85
The Bulletin (periodical), 154
Burleigh, A. W., 59
Burroughs, Nannie Helen, 119–21, 124–27, 129, 130–36, 137, 149, 158, 208–9, 212
Burton, Orisanmi, 76
Butterfield, Myron Ruth, 30–38, 66, 104, 110, 111, 113, 115, 160–61, 163, 192–94, 197, 216
Butterworth, William, 86–90

Calhoun, John C., 13–14
Campaign for the Study of Negro History and Literature, 56
capitalism
  black history celebration and, 15–20, 40, 199
  racial, 186
  racism and, 109–10
  scholarship, 198
  slavery and, 48–49
Carnegie Hall, 184
Casely-Hayford, Adelaide, 124
casket, Emmett Till's, 101–2, 103, 106
Cemetery for the Illustrious Negro Dead, 92–93, 96–98, 100, 166
censorship, 137
Central Congregational Church, 172
Central High School, 151, 214
chattel slavery, 4, 11, 47, 48–49
civic responsibility, 40
Civil Rights Movement, 11, 105, 188, 203
Claflin University, 141–42
Coard, Bernard, 209
Coca-Cola, 18
College Board, 39–40
colonialism, 4, 123
Colored Teachers Associations (CTA), 149–51, 178
Colored Teachers State Association of Texas, 157
Columbia University, 174
Combahee Ferry Raid, 102
commemoration
  abolition of slavery, 64–65, 210–11
  of black achievement, 73–74

Index

of black history, 51, 66–67, 85–86, 90–91
Black History Month as, 72
Cemetery for the Illustrious Negro Dead, 92–93, 96–98, 100, 166
of Crispus Attucks, 59–65, 166
of the dead, 72, 76–77, 79, 81, 98
of Du Bois, 184–88
museums and monuments, 100–103
Negro History and Literature Week, 56–57
observance of Negro History Week in schools, 44, 58–59, 70, 153–60, 166–67
of ordinary lives, 73, 74–76, 212–13
commercialization, 17–20
communal literacy, 32, 213–14
Communist Party, 186
community storytellers, 3
Compromise of 1877, 173–74
Compton Unified School District, 35
corporations
    commercialization of Black History Month, 15–20, 40, 199
    exploitation of black power politics by, 17
"The Creation" (Johnson), 25–26
Crispus Attucks Day, 60–62, 81, 166
Cromwell, John W., 54, 95–96
Crummell, Alexander, 85
culture wars, 39

Daughters of the American Revolution, 182
Davis, Angela, 211
Davis, Ossie, 112
death
    aboard slave ships, 88–89
    black memory work and, 71–73
    on board the *Hudibras*, 85–91
commemoration of, 72, 76–77, 79, 81, 98
denigration of as erasure, 79–80
funerals, 71–72, 77–78, 96, 110–16
memorialization, 72, 92
mortuary politics, 79–80, 81, 91
as motivation for black study, 106
prevalence of in black history, 78–80, 82–83
prevalence of in black lives, 76–77, 81–82
"Democracy and the Man Far Down" (Woodson), 56
department stores, 19–20
DeSantis, Ron, 39–40
desegregation, 12, 100, 152, 191–94
Dictionary of American Negro Biography (Logan, ed.), 134
District of Columbia School Board, 52
domestic work, 120
"Don't Buy Where You Can't Work" campaigns, 19
Douglass, Aaron, 96
Douglass, Frederick, 20, 48, 51, 52, 53, 74, 81, 92, 154, 203–4, 213. *See also* Frederick Douglass Day
Downey, Aruelia, 135
Dramatic Festival and Student Activity Day, 163–64, 167
"Dreams" (Hughes), 31, 112
Du Bois, W. E. B.
    black history workshops, 54
    Black Reconstruction in America, 1860–1880, 172, 178, 186–88
    on broader black history commemorations, 59–60
    Ghana exile, 184–85, 186
    historical recovery project, 175–76
    Hurston's correspondence with, 92, 97–98

Du Bois, W. E. B. (*continued*)
   King's speech commemorating, 184–88, 189
   Negro History Week lecture, 172–73, 176, 177, 180, 181
   praise for Negro History Week, 44
   The Souls of Black Folk, 115
   and struggle for black history, 208
   at *When Truth Gets a Hearing* performance, 125
Dunbar, Paul Laurence, 53
Dunbar High School, 54, 59
Dunbar Nelson, Alice, 125
Dunning, William Archibald, 174

East Putnam Consolidated School, 164, 167–68
Eatonville community, 97
Ebony magazine, 18
education
   access to, 54
   as a community value, 140–41
   criminalization of, 141
   free public, 174, 187
   liberatory, 6, 100, 146, 169, 207
   multicultural, 198
   occupational, 119–23
   political, 6–7, 105–6
   violent opposition to, 165–66
   See also schools; teachers
educators. *See* teachers
Emancipation Day, 63–65
Emancipation Proclamation, 64
embodied learning, 32
Emmett Generation, 104–6, 181
Emory University, 147
enslaved people
   archival silencing of, 143–44
   black historical tradition and, 4, 208
   on board the *Hudibras*, 85–91
   erasure of identities and histories of, 80, 86

   freedom narratives, 46–48, 85
   fugitives, 205
   political education, 6–7
   See also slavery
Essentials in American History (Hart), 53
ethnographic studies of black sound, 32
Europe, M. L., 59
European colonialism, 123
Evening Star (newspaper), 51, 55
Evers, Medgar, 11

Fairfax, Myra E., 154
Fayetteville State Teachers College, 155
Ferreira, Kysean, 204, 216
Field Day, 160–64, 166
filmmakers, 3
Fisk University, 96
Florida, African American History Standards in, 23
Ford, Gerald, 13–16, 191
Forest Lawn Cemetery, 110
formalism, 35
Forten, Charlotte, 204–5
Fort Valley State College, 155
Franklin, John Hope, 17–18, 130, 137–38
fraternities, 56–57
Frederick Douglass Day, 51–58, 81, 123
Frederick Douglass High School, 154
freedom movement. *See* Black Freedom Movement
freedom narratives, 46–48, 85
freedom workers, 24
Fuentes, Marisa, 143
The Fugitive Blacksmith (Pennington), 48, 144–46
fugitive slave narratives, 46–48, 85
funerals, 71–72, 77–78, 96, 110–16

gang violence, 111, 112
Garrison, William Lloyd, 53

Garvey, Marcus, 97, 211
Georgia Teachers and Education Association, 162
Giddings, Paula, 103
Givens, Jarvis Ray, II, 110–16
Givens, Jarvis Ray, Sr., 110
Glympy, Thavolia, 143
"God Bless the Child" (song), 37
Gospel Memorial Church of God in Christ, 115
Greenfeld, Eloise, 93, 94, 102

Haitian Revolution, 4, 63, 85
Hamer, Fannie Lou, 78
Hampton, Fred, 12
Hampton University, 203
Hannah Jones, Nikole, 22
Harley, Sharon, 133
Harris, LaShawn, 76
Harsh, Vivian, 129
Hart, Albert Bushnell, 53
Hartman, Saidiya, 76, 81, 89, 143–44
Harvard University, 40, 43–44, 53, 106, 205, 211
Hegel, Georg W. F., 40–41
The Herald (periodical), 162, 167
Hickory Hill School, 156
Higginbotham, Evelyn Brooks, 119, 131–36, 138
high schools, 53–54
Historically Black Colleges and Universities (HBCU), 154–55, 203
historical accounts, 2
history
  antiblack silences in, 49–50
  black people written out of, 61–62
  collective influence of, 46
  distorted interpretations of Reconstruction, 174
  Eurocentric, in schools, 42
  human agency and, 45–46

power and production of, 27, 137, 190, 206
silences of marginalized communities in, 198
weaponization of, 174
whitewashed conceptions of, 38, 81–82, 172
See also black history
History of the Negro Race in America from 1619 to 1880 (Williams), 50–51
Hoke, Christian, 212–13, 216
Holiday, Billie, 37
Holloway, Karla F. C., 76–77
Howard, Wesley, 59
Howard University, 56, 133, 134, 158, 203
How the West Indian Child Is Made Educationally Subnormal in the British School System (Coard), 209
Hudibras (slave ship), 85–91, 166, 209
Hughes, Langston, 31, 112
human agency, 45–46
Hurston, Zora Neale, 32, 65, 83, 91–93, 94–101, 112, 131, 163, 166
hymns, 32

"I Am the Black Child" (poem), 112
"In Search of Zora Neale Hurston" (Walker), 98
integration, 195–97
International Council of Women of the Darker Races, 123–24

Jackson State University, 70
Jacobs, Harriet, 48, 85
Jet magazine, 102, 104, 105
Jim Crow era, 21, 54, 78, 109, 151, 161–62, 172, 183
Johnson, Edward A., 73–74
Johnson, James Weldon, 25, 164

John W. Hoffman Junior High School, 176–77
Jones, Mary Ross, 70–71, 72–79, 82–83
Jones, Quincy, 99
The Journal of Blacks in Higher Education, 17–18, 21
The Journal of Negro History, 55, 95–96
joy, 9
Juneteenth, 64–65, 210

Kelley, Robin D. G., 76
Kent State University, 13
Keti Koti, 210–11, 212
King, Coretta Scott, 195–96
King, Martin, 194
King, Martin Luther, Jr.
 at Booker T. Washington High School, 105
 death of, 78, 189
 Du Bois commemoration speech, 172, 184–88, 189
 "I Have a Dream" speech, 184
 "mountaintop" speech, 30–31, 34–37, 112, 160, 192
 at "Music That Has Made America Great" school program, 195–96
 "The Negro and the Constitution" speech, 179–84, 216
 school desegregation and, 191–94
 Where Do We Go from Here, 194–95
King, Yolanda, 194
knowledge production, 45
knowledge sharing, 32
Ku Klux Klan, 177

Labat, Inez, 172
labor organizers, 19
Lamar Elementary School, 156–57
Langston University, 142
LaNier, Carlotta Walls, 214–15

Lanier High School, 20
Lectures on the Philosophy of History (Hegel), 41
Legacy Museum, 100–101
Lemon, Eva Grace, 193
Lewis Sarah, 147
liberatory education, 6, 100, 146, 169, 207
Library of Congress, 126, 135, 137
"Lift Every Voice and Sing" (Johnson), 25, 31, 112
Lincoln, Abraham, 20, 53
lining out, 32, 87
literacy, communal, 32, 213–14
literary societies, 2, 200–201, 212, 216
Little Rock Nine, 214
Locke, Alain, 84
Logan, Rayford W., 134
Lomack, James B., 59
"Lord, How Come Me Here?" (song), 115
Louisiana Colored Teachers' Association, 172
The Louisiana Weekly (periodical), 172
Lovett, Pamela, 200–207
lunch counter demonstrations, 19
lynching, 78, 81, 100–101, 103–4

Mac, Charlie, 113
Marable, Manning, 199, 215
March on Washington, 184
Martin, Trayvon, 103, 104
Mason, Pamela, 159
Mason, Vaughn C., 158–59
Before the Mayflower (Bennett), 21
Mays, Benjamin Elijah, 107, 108, 109
McDaniels, Pellom, III, 147
Meharry Medical College, 56
Mellon Mays Undergraduate Fellowship (MMUF), 108
memorialization, 72, 76–77, 92

The Michigan Daily (newspaper), 109
Middle Passage, 78–79, 85, 142
Million Man March, 108
Mississippi Teacher Association, 161
Moorland-Spingarn Research Center, 134–35
Morehouse College, 104, 106, 107, 155
Morgan, Jennifer, 143
mortuary politics, 79–80, 81, 91, 92, 101–3
The Moving Finger (periodical), 178
M Street School, 53, 123
multicultural education, 198
museum curators, 3
museums and monuments, 100–3
music, 32, 87, 195–96
musicians, 3

Namin (Savage), 97
National Association for the Advancement of Colored People (NAACP), 54, 78, 186
National Association of Colored Women's Clubs, 54
National Baptist Convention, 64–65
  Golden Jubilee, 127
  Women's Convention Auxiliary, 119
National Guardian (newspaper), 107
National Memorial for Peace and Justice, 100–101
National Museum of African American History and Culture, 101–3, 106, 203
National Park Service, 137
National Training School for Women and Girls, 119–23, 132, 134–35, 137, 158
negative assembly, 147
"The Negro and the Constitution" (King), 179–84, 216
The Negro Caravan (Brown), 158

"The Negro Digs Up His Past" (Schomburg), 83–84
Negro Health Week, 59
Negro History and Literature Week, 56–57
The Negro History Bulletin, 61
Negro History Week
  in the Black Teacher Archive, 152, 159–60
  department store observances, 19–20
  establishment of, 2, 33, 40, 43–44, 53–54
  expansion to Black History Month, 2, 10, 12, 17, 33, 191, 211
  fiftieth anniversary, 10
  first celebration of, 41, 43–44, 191
  as formalized truth-telling, 130
  founding of, 211–12
  grassroots expansion of, 43–44, 149–50
  National Training School observances, 121
  observation of in schools, 44, 58–59, 70, 153–60, 166–67, 179
The Negro in Our History (Woodson), 121
Negro Makers of History (Woodson), 158–59, 176–78
Negro Society for Historical Research, 85
Nell, William Cooper, 60–62, 166, 204
New Jersey Organization of Teachers of Colored Children, 158
"the New Negro," 78
The New Negro: An Interpretation (Locke), 84
New Orleans Teacher Association, 172
newspapers, 2
The New York Times Magazine, 22–23

Nimako, Kwame, 209–10
Nkrumah, Kwame, 184
"Nobody Knows the Trouble I've Seen" (song), 125
North Carolina College of Agriculture and Mechanic Arts, 174
"Not Color but Character" (Burroughs), 122–23

Oklahoma Colored Agricultural and Normal University, 142
Omega Psi Phi, 56–58
The Oracle (publication), 57
oral tradition, 2, 175
Out of Darkness Comes a New Day (Overton), 157
Overton, Minnie C., 157

Pan-African Congresses, 186
Parker, Traci, 19
the past
  bearing witness to, 8
  black perspectives about, 8–9
  knowledge about, 9
  See also black history; black memory work and workers; history
patriarchy, 198
Pendleton, Leila Amos, 54
Pennington, James W. C., 48–50, 85, 144–46
Perry, Imani, 9, 151, 152, 167
Perry, Thelma D., 11–12, 16
Philip Morris, 18
Pickney, Estelle, 59
Picott, J. Rupert, 10, 12, 13–14, 16
The Pittsburgh Courier (newspaper), 121
poets, 3
political organizers, 3
politics of respectability, 136
Pope, Oliver, 175, 178–79, 184, 187, 189, 193

power dynamics, production of history and, 27, 137, 190, 206
preachers, 3
preservation of black history, 138–40, 148–49, 168–69
print culture, 2, 143–44
propaganda, 187–88
public transportation boycotts, 19
publishing industry, 18

Quarles, Benjamin, 13, 16

Race Rebels (Kelley), 76
racialization, 4, 41
racial justice, 5
racial oppression, 198
racial prejudice, 41
racial violence, 177, 204
racism, capitalism and, 109–10
reading rooms, 2
Reagan, Ronald, 13
rebellions, 7–8
Reconstruction Amendments, 179, 182–83
Reconstruction period, 10, 172–78, 187–88
religion
  schools in churches, 71–72, 77–78
  "the shout," 65
Revolution, 11
Righteous Discontent (Higginbotham), 136
rituals, 2
Robinson, Vivian, 178
Rodney, Walter, 73
Royall House, 203

San Jose State University, 109
Savage, Augusta, 96–97
Schomburg, Arturo, 83–86, 129
A School History of the Negro Race in America from 1619 to 1890 (Johnson), 73–74

schools
  antiblackness in curricula, 158, 162, 192
  for black girls and women, 119–23, 132, 134–35
  black high schools, 105–6, 123
  black school burnings, 165
  in churches, 71–72, 77–78
  desegregation of, 12, 100, 152, 191–94
  integration, 195–97
  Negro History Week celebrations in, 44, 58–59, 70, 153–60, 166–67, 179
  overcrowding in, 70–71
  Reconstruction creation of free public, 174, 187
  segregated, 20, 25, 44, 49, 52, 106, 159
  See also education; teachers
schoolteachers. *See* teachers
Scott, Julius S., 143
scriptive things, 143
segregation, 20, 25, 44, 52, 59, 99, 106, 159
semiquincentennial, 22, 197
sexual violence, 78, 133
Sex Workers, Psychics, and Numbers Runners (Harris), 76
shawl, Tubman's, 101–3
"the shout," 65
Silencing the Past (Trouillot), 139
Simmons, Dave Henry, 167
"Sister, Can You Line It Out?" (Brooks), 32
The 1619 Project, 22–23
Slave Quarters, 203
slavery
  American exceptionalism and, 11
  archive of, 143–44
  black historical tradition and, 4
  capitalism and, 48–49
  chattel principle, 48–49
  commemorations of abolition of, 64–65, 210–11
  estate ledgers, 140, 142–43, 145–46
  freedom narratives, 46–48, 85
  Hudibras slave ship, 85–91
  Reconstruction Amendments and, 182–83
  transatlantic, 78–79, 84, 143–44
  white presentation of, 178
  See also enslaved people
Smallwood, Stephanie, 143
Smith, James McCune, 63–64, 66
songs, 32, 195–96
soul quality, 124
The Souls of Black Folk (Du Bois), 115
Spelman College, 105, 109
Spillers, Hortense, 143
state memory, 129, 169
Stewart, Maria, 204
St. Mary's Parish, Jamaica, 7
"Strange Fruit" (song), 115
St. Timothy's Episcopal Day School, 30–38
suffering, 83

Taylor, Arnold, 133
teachers
  archival sources on, 139–40
  black history taught by, 54–56, 95, 104, 121–23, 130–31, 153–60
  as black memory workers, 3, 131, 178
  Black Teacher Archive, 151–53, 159–60, 161, 167
  Colored Teachers Associations, 149–51, 164, 178
  daily lives of, 70–71, 164–65
  grassroots expansion of Negro History Week by, 43–44, 149–50
  resourcefulness of, 76
Terborg-Penn, Rosalyn, 133

Terrell, Mary Church, 51–54, 58, 60, 81, 123, 134
The Texas Standard (publication), 157
A Text Book of the Origins and History, &c. &c. of the Colored People (Pennington), 48
Their Eyes Were Watching God (Hurston), 99–100
Thomas, Neval H., 59
Till, Emmett, 101–2, 103–5, 108
Till-Mobley, Mamie, 104
Tip of the Spear (Burton), 76
Todman, Shirley, 93–95, 102, 103, 104
Toppin, Edgar Allan, 13, 16
Trades Hall, 134, 135
transatlantic slavery, 78–79, 84, 143–44
Trayvon Generation, 104, 105
Trouillot, Michel-Rolph, 139
Trump, Donald, 22, 39
Truth, Sojourner, 20, 74
Tubman, Harriet, 20, 93, 94, 101–3, 213
Turner, Nat, 92–96, 101, 112
Tuskegee University, 179–80

UC Berkeley, 104, 108
Universal Negro Improvement Association, 97
University of Chicago, 40, 211
University of Michigan, 109
University of Rochester, 134, 135

Valena C. Jones Normal and Practice School, 178
vernacular traditions, 35
Victoria, Queen, 102
violence
  antiblack, 41, 43, 72, 123
  black school burnings, 165
  gang, 111, 112
  lynching, 78, 81–82, 100–101, 103–4

opposition to black education, 165–66
against oppressed communities, 198
racial, 177, 204
recorded in slavery's print culture, 143–46
school desegregation and, 192–93, 197
sexual, 78, 133
Turner's death and dismemberment, 93–96
Virginia Education Bulletin (periodical), 156
Virginia State University, 203

Walker, Alice, 80–81, 83, 98–99, 131–32, 162–68, 216
Walker, David, 204
Walker, Joseph A., 59
Walker, Margaret, 25
Walker, Willie Lee, 165
Washington, Booker T., 59, 120, 179–80
Washington, Margaret Murray, 124
The Washington Tribune, 58–59
Wayward Lives, Beautiful Experiments (Hartman), 76
Welfare Department (Harlem), 106–7
Wesley, Charles H., 46, 59
Wesley, Dorothy Parker, 129
West Virginia State Teachers' Association, 154
Whaley, Soraya, 214–16
"What the Belgians Did to the Negro" (Burroughs), 123
Wheatley, Phillis, 74
When and Where I Enter (Giddings), 103
When Truth Gets a Hearing (Burroughs), 119–27
Where Do We Go from Here (King), 194–95

white backlash, 11
white paternalism, 97, 118
white supremacy, 47, 49, 72, 146, 192
Wilkinson, Garnet C., 57–58
Williams, George Washington, 2, 50, 95
Willis, Aretha, 193
Winfrey, Oprah, 99
"The Women's Movement in the Black Baptist Church, 1880–1920" (Brooks), 135
Woodson, Carter G.
   ASALH founding, 10, 14–15, 43, 92, 154
   birth, 10
   black history commemoration, 24, 68, 75, 81, 119
   collaboration with black teachers, 149–50
   in the Colored Teachers Association records, 164
   on Crispus Attucks Day, 58–59
   at Frederick Douglass High School, 154
   Negro History Week founding, 2, 10, 33, 40, 41–42, 43–44, 53–56, 58–59, 211–12
   The Negro in Our History, 121, 158
   Negro Makers of History, 158–59, 176–78
   Omega Psi Phi work, 56–58
   When Truth Gets a Hearing endorsement, 125–26
   on young people, 203
The Worker (newspaper), 123
World War II, 97
Wright, Richard, 101

X, Malcolm, 78, 106–7, 109–10, 112, 211

Youngblood, Edwin, 140–41, 144
Youngblood, Judy, 141
Youngblood, Sandy Rufus, 140–42, 144, 146–49
youth activists, 3

Zinn, Howard, 109
Zwarte Piet, 211, 212

ABOUT THE AUTHOR

JARVIS R. GIVENS is a professor of education and African and African American studies and the cofounding faculty director of the Black Teacher Archive at Harvard University. He is also the current Leverhulme Visiting Professor at University College London's Institute of the Americas. Givens is the author of three books, *Fugitive Pedagogy: Carter G. Woodson and the Art of Black Teaching*; *School Clothes: A Collective Memoir of Black Student Witness*; and *American Grammar: Race, Education, and the Building of a Nation*. Givens is originally from Compton, California, and lives in Boston, Massachusetts.